INTERNATIONAL FINANCIAL MANAGEMENT

INTERNATIONAL FINANCIAL MANAGEMENT

Bhavna Bahuguna

CENTRUM PRESS
NEW DELHI-110002 (INDIA)

CENTRUM PRESS
H.O.: 4360/4, Ansari Road, Daryaganj,
New Delhi-110002 (India)
Tel: 23278000, 23261597, 23255577, 23286875

B.O.: No. 1015, Ist Main Road, BSK IIIrd Stage,
IIIrd Phase, IIIrd Block, Bangalore-560085 (INDIA)
Tel: 080-41723429

Email: centrumpress@gmail.com
Visit us at: www.centrumpress.com

International Financial Management

First Edition, 2011

ISBN 978-93-80921-23-5

PRINTED IN INDIA

Printed at Mehra Offset Press, Delhi.

Contents

Preface

The international financial management is the financial system consisting of institutions and regulators that performance on the international level, as opposed to those that performance on a national or regional level. The main players are the global institutions, such as International Monetary Fund and Bank for International Settlements, national agencies and government departments, e.g., central banks and finance ministries, and private institutions acting on the global scale, e.g., banks and hedge funds.

This book should also be of considerable value to professional, non-financial, managers who wish to improve their managerial career prospects by gaining an understanding and appreciation of the essential ingredients of financial management.

Author

1

International Finance

International finance, an offshoot of economics, encompasses a detailed understanding of exchange rates and foreign investment and their impact on international trade. Analysis of international projects, overseas investments, cross border capital flows, trade deficits, currency swaps and global financial markets are some of its key areas of study. Individual investors usually focus on that part of international finance that deals with global futures and options and the forex market.

INTERNATIONAL FINANCE: PROMINENT INSTITUTES

There are various global bodies regulating different aspects of international finance.

These include:

- *IFC*: International Finance Corporation is a prominent entity supporting sustainable investments in the private sector of developing countries to stimulate their growth. It is the biggest source of multilateral loans and equity financing for projects undertaken by the private sector in developing countries. IFC plays a key role in providing technical assistance to businesses and governments of developing countries.
- *IMF*: International Monetary Fund monitors the balance of payments of its member countries. It is regarded as the lender of last resort for countries facing a financial crisis, such as deficits and currency crisis. The relief amount is relative to the size of the country's contribution in the global trading system

- *World Bank*: It funds the development of projects, mainly in developing countries, that are not financed by the private sector.
- *WTO*: World Trade Organization resolves multilateral and bilateral trade disputes in addition to the negotiation of different trade agreements among its various member nations.

INTERNATIONAL FINANCE: BENEFITS

Some of the benefits of international finance are:

- Access to capital markets across the world enables a country to borrow during tough times and lend during good times.
- It promotes domestic investment and growth through capital import.
- Worldwide cash flows can exert a corrective force against bad government policies.
- It prevents excessive domestic regulation through global financial institutions.
- International finance leads to healthy competition and, hence, a more effective banking system.
- It provides information on the vital areas of investments and leads to effective capital allocation.

International finance promotes the integration of economies, facilitating the easy flow of capital. The free transfer of funds would eventually result in more equality among countries that are a part of the global financial system.

INTERNATIONAL FINANCE MANAGER

A fantastic international opportunity has arisen for a candidate who has extensive international NGO experience. Working within a large international charity this role offers the ideal candidate the opportunity to travel to vulnerable areas of the globe for extensive periods of time.

Main Role and Responsibilities of the International Finance Manager include:

- To provide a high standard of financial accounting

in international emergency programmes, ensuring compliance to local statutory law and the charities accounting policies.

- Ensuring all accounting systems, policies, internal controls and procedures are quickly established for the collection of accurate, complete and timely financial data.
- To Manage the cash flow to ensure timely and secure transfer of funds to meet programme needs, liaising with local bankers as required
- Supporting budget holders to produce quality budgeting information
- Preparing management reports for budget holders to monitor budgets on a regular and timely basis
- To Prepare donor financial reports and proposal budgets. Ensure all donor requirements are complied with and that proposals and reports are submitted on time
- To Build and maintain relationships with the local representatives of donor organisations and finance staff of similar organisations. Skills required of the International Finance Manager include:
- Having in depth knowledge and understanding of financial accounting rules and regulations
- Proven competence in an international NGO emergency arena
- Be a part qualified CCAB accountant or equivalent.
- Good level in at least one other language, preferably French, Spanish, Portuguese or Arabic
- Proven experience in staff management, supervision and capacity building
- Willingness to travel extensively and at short notice and to work in extremely demanding circumstances in an uncertain security setting.
- Excellent written and oral communication skills

GLOBAL FINANCIAL SYSTEM

The global financial system is the financial system

consisting of institutions and regulators that performance on the international level, as opposed to those that performance on a national or regional level. The main players are the global institutions, such as International Monetary Fund and Bank for International Settlements, national agencies and government departments, e.g., central banks and finance ministries, and private institutions acting on the global scale, e.g., banks and hedge funds.

Deficiencies and reform of the GFS have been hotly discussed in recent years. The history of financial institutions must be differentiated from economic history and history of money. In Europe, it may have started with the first commodity exchange, the Bruges Bourse in 1309 and the first financiers and banks in the 1400–1600s in central and western Europe. The first global financiers the Fuggers in Germany; the first stock company in England; the first foreign exchange market; the first stock exchange. Milestones in the history of financial institutions are the Gold Standard, the founding of International Monetary Fund, World Bank at Bretton Woods, and the abolishment of fixed exchange rates in 1973.

PERSPECTIVES

There are three primary approaches to viewing and understanding the global financial system. The liberal view holds that the exchange of currencies should be determined not by state institutions but instead individual players at a market level. This view has been labelled as the Washington Consensus. This view is challenged by a social democratic front which advocates the tempering of market mechanisms, and instituting economic safeguards in an attempt to ensure financial stability and redistribution. Examples include slowing down the rate of financial transactions, or enforcing regulations on the behaviour of private firms. Outside of this contention of authority and the individual, neoMarxists are highly critical of the modern financial system in that it promotes inequality between state players, particularly holding the view that the political North abuse the financial system to exercise control of developing countries' economies.

2

International Financial Environment

MACROECONOMIC ENVIRONMENT

Over the last two decades investors in the surplus countries have become more selective about the kind of claims they wish to acquire in the deficit countries, resulting in a change in the nature of financial intermediation. The trend in capital market liberalization, the spread of innovative techniques and the development of derivative products have facilitated better matching of investors' preferences and debtors' needs. Yet, the developments of the mid-1980s, that culminated in the equity market crash of October 1987, delineated the significance of macroeconomic policies that create market confidence and promote intermediation through international capital markets. Lapses on this count can lead to adverse consequences for exchange and interest rates as well as abrupt and unwelcome shifts in financial flows. They can also weaken the market confidence and lead to situations like that seen in 1987.

International trade in goods and services recorded impressive increases in the 1980s. The volume of world trade increased by 50 per cent, while in value terms it increased by three-quarters. During the mid-1980s, the external imbalances among the major industrialized countries were large and reached $168 billion in 1986 and $183 billion in 1987. The current account deficits of the developing countries, which had declined from their high level of 1982, registered a tiny surplus in the overall current account balances in 1987 before moving into the red in 1988. These imbalances are important because they are considered to be an indicator of the required net movement of capital through the financial system. Coupled with progress in financial market liberalization, the imbalances were to a great extent responsible for capital flows during these years. The macroeconomic environment in which these flows took place was characterized by a good deal of financial uncertainty associated with an upswing in interest rates in 1987, renewed concern about inflation, and sizeable official market interventions that followed the Plaza Agreement of 22 September 1985. Interest rates, that had started falling during late 1982, began to firm up in 1987. At the beginning of the year, they were at their lowest levels since the late 1970s in the USA, Japan, Canada and Italy. However, in late 1987 they began to rise in most of the major industrial economies except Japan, a trend that was to continue during the following year.

The LIBOR on six-month dollar deposits increased from 6.4 per cent in the first half of 1987 to 9.4 per cent in December 1988. In Japan, in the aftermath of the Plaza Agreement, interest rates kept on declining until the discount rate reached its lowest ever level in 1989. Some commentators of the international financial scene argued that rising long-term interest rates in the industrial countries, especially in the USA, reflected the changing expectations regarding the stability of exchange rates among the major currencies. In fact, the depreciation of the dollar during this period was accompanied by an increase in the premium in dollar interest rates over interest rates on instruments denominated in the yen or deutsche mark. The continued depreciation of the dollar against other SDR currencies during this period was in accordance with the Plaza Agreement between the G5 countries.

A falling dollar led investors to avoid the somewhat illiquid securities of the Eurobond market in favour of the domestic bond markets. The Eurobond investors became reluctant to acquire dollar-denominated debt. The international securities markets also remained depressed during

1987, particularly during the third and fourth quarters. At the beginning of 1988, the dollar started to recover against the other SDR currencies and in the second quarter the exchange rate movement between the dollar, yen and deutsche mark became much less volatile. The subdued volatility partly reflected the public commitment made by the G5 countries to promote exchange rate stability.

There was a marked improvement in world trade and economic activity in 1988. The output growth in most industrial countries was strong and inflation remained moderate. The growth rate of real GNP in the industrial countries was 4.4 per cent which was the second highest in the 1980s. The stable macroeconomic conditions in 1988 and 1989 brought about a rebound in the capital markets from their previous somewhat depressed levels. The Eurobond market recovered faster than expected. The buoyant activity level reflected settled market conditions, market resilience and generally higher expectations of stability in the main economic variables. Some of the favourable developments in the international economy were a reduction in the fiscal deficits in major industrial economies during 1988 and 1989, a reduction in claims on developing countries, a high level of investment activity leading to strong economic expansion in most industrial countries and an environment of relatively stable prices and exchange rates. In the aftermath of the Plaza Agreement, a period of exchange rate stability began, although the Agreement was not wholly responsible for it.

Therefore, nominal interest rate differentials started having a greater influence on the financial flows. The apprehension that inflation might come back made the industrial economies take a tight monetary stand which was reflected in a widespread increase in short-term interest rates in 1988. As opposed to this, the longer-term interest rates by and large remained stable. Their yield curve flattened and even became inverted, partly reflecting the confidence in inflation control measures as well as anti-inflationary commitments of the governments. During this period the interest rate differentials gradually widened in favour of the dollar, in particular vis-à-vis the yen. But from the second quarter of 1989 the inflationary pressures began to recede in the USA, leading to a fall in the US interest rates and a reversal of interest rate differentials against other currencies. The recovery in the nominal value of the US dollar against the other major SDR currencies during the period 1988-9 had started after three years of decline.

Because of relatively stable exchange markets, official intervention was not necessary after 1988 and financing of the imbalances was more or less autonomous through the capital accounts. The stability of the international currency markets inspired private capital flows to respond to interest rate differentials more strongly than in 1987. Before this point in time, large-scale intervention by central banks was needed to do the same job.

At the end of the decade, intervention played a minor role in the major industrialized countries, with the notable exception of the UK. The return to autonomous financing was made possible by sharp increases in net direct investment and net financing through international bond markets. The former was partly associated with the high level of merger and acquisition activity.

Such outflows were particularly high in the case of Japan, with a good deal of these flows directed to the USA, which was the major deficit country. It saw a significant increase in inward capital flows with respect to direct investment as well as through bond markets. Both of these are private-sector-dominated channels. Similar large surges were also recorded in outflows from Germany and the UK.

INTERNATIONAL TRANSACTIONS

Despite the large number of advertisements from the U.S., the Usenet Marketplace is a global institution. All advertisers, even individuals, need to be aware of the international culture and reflect it in their ads. Also, they need to be prepared to deal with international issues if a potential buyer sends an offer from a foreign nation. Many successful transactions occur across country boundaries, but a few more topics need to be covered before shipping to other countries.

USE THE ESCROW METHOD

Unless a transaction involves items of very low value, use the escrow method for completing the sale. The advantages, in this case, are manyfold.

For one, paying an escrow service by credit card solves the problem of trying to deposit a check drawn on a foreign bank. The major credit card companies usually give better exchange rates than most banks because they can trade currency amongst their international operations. Meanwhile, most banks will charge a hefty fee, often US$20 to process a check drawn on a foreign bank. Meanwhile it can cost just as much for the buyer to acquire a cashier's check drawn on a bank in the seller's country.

These charges, and the impossibility of recovering your money or items in case of fraud, makes the effective cost of escrow minimal to negative. Some people successfully send cash through the mail for small items, but as this is not recommended in the U.S., it is even less recommended internationally. Finally, COD is not available across international boundaries.

CHOOSE A COURIER CAREFULLY [H

Before shipping a package internationally, ask the shipping company how it handles international packages. Sending packages through many major couriers may result in additional fees on the receiving end for delivery to certain countries. These charges may cover expenses in clearing customs, or they may represent a brokering fee to transfer the package to a courier that delivers in the buyer's country. France and Canada are two prime examples with certain couriers. Some major couriers operate in different countries, so packages sent by one courier may not incur a fee for a package shipped from the U.S. to Japan, while another will. You must ask, and it may take a few tries because many representatives may not be fully aware of the international situation.

TAXES AND LEGAL RESTRICTIONS

Most international sales are subject to import duties, if properly declared. Gifts and small transactions often pass by unnoticed by customs in many countries, but the buyer can expect to pay sales, value-added, or import taxes in large international transactions. Make sure you know what those fees will be in your country before you finalize an offer to buy, because these taxes sometimes exceed 100%. Duties can often negate the benefits of buying from a foreign country.

While the buyer worries about duties, the seller needs to know of any restrictions on business to the buyer's country. For example, it is illegal to send many kinds of advanced technology from the United States to certain countries, and likewise across other international borders. Advanced technology is more encompassing than just weaponry and militaria. Many common software packages and computers may face export restrictions punishable by jail time in the U.S.

INTERNATIONAL TRADE

International trade is exchange of capital, goods, and services across international borders or territories.. In most countries, it represents a significant share of gross domestic product. While international trade has been present throughout much of history, its economic, social, and political importance has been on the rise in recent centuries.

Industrialization, advanced transportation, globalization, multinational corporations, and outsourcing are all having a major impact on the international trade system. Increasing international trade is crucial to the continuance of globalization. Without international trade, nations would be limited to the goods and services produced within their own borders.

International trade is in principle not different from domestic trade as the motivation and the behaviour of parties involved in a trade do not change fundamentally regardless of whether trade is across a border or not. The main difference is that international trade is typically more costly than domestic trade. The reason is that a border typically imposes additional costs such as tariffs, time costs due to border delays and costs associated with country differences such as language, the legal system or culture.

Another difference between domestic and international trade is that factors of production such as capital and labour are typically more mobile within a country than across countries. Thus international trade is mostly restricted to trade in goods and services, and only to a lesser extent to trade in capital, labour or other factors of production. Then trade in goods and services can serve as a substitute for trade in factors of production. Instead of importing a factor of production, a country can import goods that make intensive use of the factor of production and are thus embodying the respective factor. An example is the import of labour-intensive goods by the United States from China. Instead of importing Chinese labour the United States is importing goods from China that were produced with Chinese labour. International trade is also a branch of economics, which, together with international finance, forms the larger branch of international economics.

MODELS

Several different models have been proposed to predict patterns of trade and to analyse the effects of trade policies such as tariffs.

Ricardian Model

The Ricardian model focuses on comparative advantage and is perhaps the most important concept in international trade theory. In a Ricardian model, countries specialize in producing what they produce best. Unlike other models, the Ricardian framework predicts that countries will fully specialize instead of producing a broad array of goods.

Also, the Ricardian model does not directly consider factor endowments, such as the relative amounts of labour and capital within a country. The main merit of Ricardian model is that it assumes technology differences between countries. Technology gap is easily included in the Ricardian and Ricardo-Sraffa model.

The Ricardian model makes the following assumptions:

- Labour is the only primary input to production.
- Constant Marginal Product of Labour
- Limited amount of labour in the economy
- Labour is perfectly mobile among sectors but not internationally.
- Perfect competition.

The Ricardian model measures in the short-run, therefore technology differs internationally. This supports the fact that countries follow their comparative advantage and allows for specialization. For the ```modern development``` of Ricardian model: Ricardian theory of international trade.

Heckscher-Ohlin Model

In the early 1900s an international trade theory called factor proportions theory emerged by two Swedish economists, Eli Heckscher and Bertil Ohlin. This theory is also called the Heckscher-Ohlin theory. The Heckscher-Ohlin theory stresses that countries should produce and export goods that require resources that are abundant and import goods that require resources in short supply. This theory differs from the theories of comparative advantage and absolute advantage since these theory focuses on the productivity of the production process for a particular good. On the contrary, the Heckscher-Ohlin theory states that a country should specialise production and export using the factors that are most abundant, and thus the cheapest. Not to produce, as earlier theories stated, the goods it produces most efficiently.

The Heckscher-Ohlin model was produced as an alternative to the Ricardian model of basic comparative advantage. Despite its greater complexity it did not prove much more accurate in its predictions. However from a theoretical point of view it did provide an elegant solution by incorporating the neoclassical price mechanism into international trade theory.

The theory argues that the pattern of international trade is determined by differences in factor endowments. It predicts that countries will export those goods that make intensive use of locally abundant factors and will import goods that make intensive use of factors that are locally scarce. Empirical problems with the H-O model, known as the Leontief paradox, were exposed in empirical tests by Wassily Leontief who found that the United States tended to export labour intensive goods despite having a capital abundance.

The H-O model makes the following core assumptions:

- Labour and capital flow freely between sectors
- The production of shoes is labour intensive and the production of computers is capital intensive
- The amount of labour and capital in two countries differ
- Free trade
- Technology is the same across countries
- Tastes are the same.

The problem with the H-O theory is that it excludes the trade of capital goods. In the H-O theory, labour and capital are fixed entities endowed to each country. In a modern economy, capital goods are traded internationally. Gains from trade of intermediate goods are considerable, as it was emphasized by Samuelson.

Reality and Applicability of the Heckscher-Ohlin Model

The Heckscher-Ohlin theory is preferred to the Ricardo theory by many economists, because it makes fewer simplifying assumptions. In 1953, Wassily Leontief published a study, where he tested the validity of the Heckscher-Ohlin theory. The study showed that the U.S was more abundant in capital compared to other countries, therefore the U.S would export capital- intensive goods and import labour-intensive goods. Leontief found out that the U.S's export was less capital intensive than import.

After the appearance of Leontief's paradox, many researchers tried to save the Heckscher-Ohlin theory, either by new methods of measurement, or either by new interpretations. Leamer emphasized that Leontief did not interpret HO theory properly and claimed that with a right interpretation paradox did not occur. Brecher and Choudri found that, if Leamer was right, the American workers consumption per head should be lower than the workers world average consumption.

Many other trials followed but most of them failed. Many of famous textbook writers, including Krugman and Obstfeld and Bowen, Hollander and Viane, are negative about the validity of H-O model. After examining the long history of empirical research, Bowen, Hollander and Viane concluded: "Recent tests of the factor abundance theory that directly examine the H-O-V equations also indicate the rejection of the theory."

Heckscher-Ohlin theory is not well adapted to the analyse South-North trade problems. The assumptions of HO are less realistic with respect to N-S than N-N trade. Income differences between North and South is the one that third world cares most. The factor price equalization has not shown much sign of realization. HO model assumes identical production functions between countries. This is highly unrealistic. Technological gap between developed and developing countries is the main concern of the poor countries.

Specific Factors Model

In this model, labour mobility between industries is possible while capital is immobile between industries in the short-run. Thus, this model can be interpreted as a 'short run' version of the Heckscher-Ohlin model. The specific factors name refers to the given that in the short-run, specific factors of production such as physical capital are not easily transferable between industries. The theory suggests that if there is an increase in the price of a good, the owners of the factor of production specific to that good will profit in real terms.

Additionally, owners of opposing specific factors of production are likely to have opposing agendas when lobbying for controls over immigration of labour. Conversely, both owners of capital and labour profit in real terms from an increase in the capital endowment. This model is ideal for particular industries. This model is ideal for understanding income distribution but awkward for discussing the pattern of trade.

New Trade Theory

New Trade theory tries to explain several facts about trade, which the two main models above have difficulty with. These include the fact that most trade is between countries with similar factor endowment and productivity levels, and the large amount of multinational production which exists. In one example of this framework, the economy exhibits monopolistic competition and increasing returns to scale.

There are three basic theories that global marketer has to comprehend:

1. Comparative Advantage Theory
2. Trade or product trade cycle theory
3. Business orientation theory

Gravity Model

The Gravity model of trade presents a more empirical analysis of trading patterns rather than the more theoretical models. The gravity model, in its basic form, predicts trade based on the distance between countries and the interaction of the countries' economic sizes. The model mimics the Newtonian law of gravity which also considers distance and physical size between two objects. The model has been proven to be empirically strong through econometric analysis. Other factors such as income level, diplomatic relationships between countries, and trade policies are also included in expanded versions of the model.

Ricardian Theory of International Trade

The Ricardian theory of comparative advantage became a basic constituent of neoclassical trade theory. Any undergraduate course in trade theory includes expansions of Ricardo's example of four numbers in for form of a two commodity, two country model. This model was expanded to many-country and many-commodity cases. Major general results were obtained by the beginning of 1960's by McKenzie and Jones, including his famous formula.

Contemporary Theories

Ricardo's idea was even expanded to the case of continuum of goods by Dornbusch, Fischer, and Samuelson This formulation is employed for example by Matsuyama and others.

Neo-Ricardian Trade Theory

Inspired by Piero Sraffa, a new strand of trade theory emerged and was named neo-Ricardian trade theory. The main contributors include Ian Steedman and Stanley Metcalfe. They have criticized neoclassical international trade theory, namely the Heckscher-Ohlin model on the basis that the notion of capital as primary factor has no method of measuring it before the determination of profit rate. This was a second round of the Cambridge capital controversy, this time in the field of international trade.

The merit of neo-Ricardian trade theory is that input goods are explicitly included to the analytical framework. This is in accordance with Sraffa's idea that any commodity is a product made by means of commodities. The limit of their theory is that the analysis is limited to small country cases.

Traded Intermediate Goods

Ricardian trade theory ordinarily assumes that the labour is the unique input. This is a great deficiency as trade theory, for the intermediate goods occupy the major part of the world international trade. Yeats found that 30% of world trade in manufacturing is intermediate inputs.

Bardhan and Jafee found that intermediate inputs occupy 37 to 38% in the imports to the US for years 1992 and 1997, whereas the percentage of intrafirm trade grew from 43% in 1992 to 52% in 1997.

McKenzie and Jones emphasized the necessity to expand the Ricardian theory to the cases of traded inputs. In a famous comment McKenzie pointed that "A moment's consideration will convince one that Lancashire would be unlikely to produce cotton cloth if the cotton had to be grown in England." Paul Samuelson coined a term Sraffa bonus to name the gains from trade of inputs.

Ricardo-Sraffa Trade Theory

John Chipman observed in his survey that McKenzie stumbled upon the questions of intermediate products and discovered that "introduction of trade in intermediate product necessitates a fundamental alteration in classical analysis." It took may years until recently Y. Shiozawa succeded to remove this deficiency.

The Ricardian trade theory was now constructed in a form to include intermediate input trade for the most general case of many countries and many goods. This new theory is called Ricardo-Sraffa trade theory. It is emphasized that the Ricardian trade theory now provides a general theory which includes trade of intermediates such as fuel, machine tools, machinery parts and processed materials. The traded intermediate goods are then used as inputs of productions in the importing country. Capital goods are nothing other than inputs to the productions. Thus, in the Ricardo-Sraffa trade theory, capital goods moves freely from country to country. Labour is the unique factor of production that remains immobile in the country of its origin.

In a blog post of April 28, 2007, Gregory Mankiw compared Ricardian theory and Heckscher-Ohlin theory and stood by the Ricardian side. Mankiw argued that Ricardian theory is more realistic than the Heckscher-Ohlin theory as the latter assumes that capital does not move from country to country. Mankiw's argument contains a logical slip, for the traditional Ricardian trade theory does not admit any inputs. Shiozawa's result saves Mankiw from his slip. The neoclassical Heckscher-Ohlin-Samuelson theory only assumes production factors and finished goods. It contains no concept of intermediate goods. Therefore, it is the Ricardo-Sraffa trade theory that provides theoretical bases for the topics such as outsourcing, fragmentation and intra-firm trade.

TOP TRADING NATIONS

Rank	Country	Exports + Imports	Date of Infomation
-	European Union	$3,197,000,000,000	2009
1	United States	$2,439,700,000,000	2009 est.
2	Germany	$2,209,000,000,000	2009 est.
3	People's Republic of China	$2,115,500,000,000	2009 est.
4	Japan	$1,006,900,000,000	2009 est.
5	France	$989,000,000,000	2009 est.
6	United Kingdom	$824,900,000,000	2009 est.
7	Netherlands	$756,500,000,000	2009 est.
8	Italy	$727,700,000,000	2009 est.
-	Hong Kong	$672,600,000,000	2009 est.
9	South Korea	$668,500,000,000	2009 est.
10	Belgium	$611,100,000,000	2009 est.
11	Canada	$603,700,000,000	2009 est.
12	Spain	$508,900,000,000	2009 est.
13	Russia	$492,400,000,000	2009 est.
14	Mexico	$458,200,000,000	2009 est.
15	Singapore	$454,800,000,000	2009 est.
16	India	$387,300,000,000	2009 est.
17	Taiwan	$371,400,000,000	2009 est.
18	Switzerland	$367,300,000,000	2009 est.
19	Australia	$322,400,000,000	2009 est.
20	United Arab Emirates	$315,000,000,000	2009 est.

REGULATION OF INTERNATIONAL TRADE

Traditionally trade was regulated through bilateral treaties between two nations. For centuries under the belief in mercantilism most nations had high tariffs and many restrictions on international trade. In the 19th century, especially in the United Kingdom, a belief in free trade became paramount. This belief became the dominant thinking among western nations since then. In the years since the Second World War, controversial multilateral treaties like the General Agreement on Tariffs and Trade and World Trade Organization have attempted to promote free trade while creating a globally regulated trade structure. These trade agreements have often resulted in discontent and protest with claims of unfair trade that is not beneficial to developing countries.

Free trade is usually most strongly supported by the most economically powerful nations, though they often engage in selective protectionism for those industries which are strategically important such as the protective tariffs applied to agriculture by the United States and Europe. The Netherlands and the United Kingdom were both strong advocates of free trade when they were economically dominant, today the United States, the United Kingdom, Australia and Japan are its greatest proponents. However, many other countries are increasingly becoming advocates of free trade as they become more economically powerful themselves. As tariff levels fall there is also an increasing willingness to negotiate non tariff measures, including foreign direct investment, procurement and trade facilitation. The latter looks at the transaction cost associated with meeting trade and customs procedures.

Traditionally agricultural interests are usually in favour of free trade while manufacturing sectors often support protectionism. This has changed somewhat in recent years, however. In fact, agricultural lobbies, particularly in the United States, Europe and Japan, are chiefly responsible for particular rules in the major international trade treaties which allow for more protectionist measures in agriculture than for most other goods and services.

During recessions there is often strong domestic pressure to increase tariffs to protect domestic industries. This occurred around the world during the Great Depression. Many economists have attempted to portray tariffs as the underlining reason behind the collapse in world trade that many believe seriously deepened the depression.

The regulation of international trade is done through the World Trade Organization at the global level, and through several other regional arrangements such as MERCOSUR in South America, the North American Free Trade Agreement between the United States, Canada and Mexico, and the European Union between 27 independent states. The 2005 Buenos Aires talks on the planned establishment of the Free Trade Area of the Americas failed largely because of opposition from the populations of Latin American nations. Similar agreements such as the Multilateral Agreement on Investment have also failed in recent years.

RISK IN INTERNATIONAL TRADE

Companies doing business across international borders face many of the same risks as would normally be evident in strictly domestic transactions.

For example:

- Buyer insolvency;
- Non-acceptance;
- Credit risk;
- Regulatory risk;
- Intervention;
- Political risk; and
- War and other uncontrollable events.

In addition, international trade also faces the risk of unfavorable exchange rate movements.

INTERNATIONAL CAPITAL FLOW

International capital flows have increased dramatically since the 1980s. During the 1990s gross capital flows between industrial countries rose by 300 per cent, while trade flows increased by 63 per cent and real GDP by a comparatively modest 26 per cent. Much of the increase in capital flows is due to trade in equity and debt markets, with the result that the international pattern of asset ownership looks very different today than it did a decade ago. These developments are often attributed to the increased integration of world financial markets. Easier access to foreign financial markets, so the story goes, has led to the changing pattern of asset ownership as investors have sought to realise the benefits from international diversification.

It is much less clear how the growth in the size and volatility of capital flows fits into this story. If the benefits of diversification were well-known, the integration of debt and equity markets should have been accompanied by a short period of large capital flows as investors re-allocated their portfolios towards foreign debt and equity. After this adjustment period is over, there seems little reason to suspect that international portfolio flows will be either large or volatile. With this perspective, the prolonged increase in the size and volatility of capital flows we observe suggests that the adjustment to greater financial integration is taking a very long time, or that integration has little to do with the recent behaviour of capital flows.

We present a model that allows us to examine how greater integration in world financial markets affects the structure of asset ownership and the behaviour of international capital flows.

We use the model to address three main questions:

1. How is the size and volatility of international capital flows affected by greater financial integration in world debt and equity markets?
2. What factors drive international portfolio flows, and does their influence change with the degree of integration?
3. How does the degree of financial integration affect the behaviour of equity prices and returns?

To the best of our knowledge, these questions have yet to be addressed in the literature. The model we present captures the effects of financial integration in the simplest possible way. We consider a symmetric two-country model with production for traded and nontraded goods. Firms in both the traded and nontraded sectors issue equity on domestic stock markets. We examine the impact of financial integration in this world by considering three configurations: Financial Autarky, Partial

Integration, and Full Financial Integration. Under fa, households only have access to the domestic stock market and so can only hold their wealth in the form of the equity of domestic firms producing traded and nontraded goods.

The equilibrium in this economy serves as a benchmark for gauging the effects of financial integration. Under pi, we open a world bond market. Now households can allocate their wealth between domestic equity and international bonds. This configuration roughly corresponds the state of world financial markets before the mid-1980's where bonds are the main medium for international financial transactions. The third configuration, fi, corresponds to the current state of world financial markets. Under fi, households have access to international bonds, equity issued by domestic firms, and equity issued by foreign firms producing traded goods.

Two aspects of our model deserve special note. First, in all three market configurations we consider, international risk-sharing among households is less than perfect. In other words, we only consider interna- tional capital flows in equilibria where markets are incomplete. As we move from the fa to pi and then to fi configurations of the model, the degree of risk-sharing increases, but households never have access to a rich enough array of financial assets to make markets complete. We view this as an important feature of the model. There is ample evidence that incomplete risk-sharing persists even with the high degree of financial integration we see today. This observation precludes us from characterizing our fi configuration as an equilibrium with complete markets.

The second important feature of the model concerns information. The equilibria we study are derived under the assumption that all households and firms have access to the same information regarding the current state of the world economy. While this common-knowledge assumption is standard in international macro models, it does have important implications for the role played by international capital flows. Specifically, capital flows in our model do not result from differences of opinion concerning the future returns or risks associated with different assets. As such, capital flows do not convey any information to firms and households that is unavailable from other sources.

We do not view this common-knowledge framework as necessarily the best one for analyzing capital flows. Nevertheless we adopt it here to establish a theoretical benchmark for how greater financial integration affects capital flows when information about risks and returns is commonknowledge. By contrast, Evans and Lyons present a model where information about the state of the economy is dispersed internationally, and as a result capital flows convey information that is not available elsewhere. That does not undertake the task of analyzing the effects of increased financial integration.

Our analysis is related to three major strands of research. The first strand studies the effects of financial liberalization on capital flows and returns. Examples of theoretical research with this focus include Obstfeld, Bacchetta and van Wincoop, and Martin and Rey, while empirical assessments can be found in Bekaert, Harvey and Lumsdaine, Henry, Bekaert and Harvey, Albuquerque, Loayza and Serven and many others. The second strand of research focuses on the joint determination of capital flows and equity returns. Representative in this area include Bohn and Tesar, Froot and Teo, Stulz, and Froot, O'Connell and Seasholes.

Hau and Rey extend the analysis of equity return-capital flow interaction to include the real exchange rate. The third strand of the literature studies the macroeconomic implications of financial integration. Baxter and Crucini and Heathcote and Perri compare the equilibrium of models with restricted asset trade against an equilibrium with complete markets. The comparative approach adopted is closest to the methodology we adopt, but our model does not equate financial integration with complete markets. An alternative view of integration is that it reduces the frictions that inhibit asset trade. Examples of this approach include Buch and Pierdzioch, Sutherland, and Senay.

Although the model we develop has a relatively simple structure, several technical problems need to be solved in order to find the equilibrium associated with any of our market configurations. The first of these problems concerns portfolio choice.

We interpret increased financial integration as giving households a wider array of assets in which to hold their wealth. How households choose to allocate their wealth among these assets is key to understanding how financial integration affects international capital flows, so there is no way to side-step portfolio allocation decisions. We model the portfolio problem as part of the intertemporal optimization problem of the households allowing for the fact that returns do not follow i.i.d. processes in equilibrium.

The second problem relates to market incompleteness. Since markets are incomplete in all the configurations we study, we cannot find the equilibrium allocations by solving an appropriate planning problem. Instead, the equilibrium allocations must be established by directly checking the market clearing conditions implied by the decisions of households and firms.

This uses a new solution methodology, developed in Evans and Hnatkovska, to compute equilibrium allocations and prices in this decentralized setting. The methodology also incorporates the complications of portfolio choice in an intertemporal setting. The third problem concerns non-stationarity.

In the equilibria we study, temporary productivity shocks have permanent effects on a number of state-variables. This general feature of models with incomplete markets arises because the shocks permanently affect the distribution of wealth.

Recognizing this aspect of our model, the solution method provides us with equilibrium dynamics for the economy in a large neighbourhood of a specified initial wealth distribution. A comparison of the equilibria associated with our three market configurations provides us with several striking results. First, in the pi configuration where all international asset trading takes place via the bond market, international capital flows are large and very volatile.

Second, when households gain access to foreign equity markets, the size and volatility of international bond flows falls dramatically. Third, the size and volatility of bond flows remains above the size and volatility of equity portfolio flows under fi.

The standard deviation of quarterly bond flows measured relative to GDP is approximately 1.6 per cent, while the corresponding value for equity is 0.88 per cent, figures that exceed the estimates from the data. Thus, our analysis overturns the conventional view that actual capital flows are excessively volatile.

Our fourth main finding concerns the factors driving capital flows. In our model, variations in the equity risk premia account for almost all of the international portfolio flows in bonds and equities.

Changes in the risk premia arise endogenously as productivity shocks affect the distribution of wealth, with the result that households are continually adjusting their portfolios. Although these portfolio adjustments are small, their implications for international capital flows are large relative to GDP.

Our model also makes a number of predictions concerning the behaviour of asset prices and returns. In particular, we find that as integration rises the volatility of returns falls and global risk factors become more important in the determination of expected returns. We also show that international equity price differentials can be used as reliable measures of financial integration.

THE GLOBALIZATION OF FINANCIAL MARKETS

The large increase in international capital flows represents one of the most striking developments in the world economy over the past thirty years.

In recent years, the rise in international capital flows has been particularly dramatic. IMF data indicates that gross capital flows between industrialized countries expanded 300 per cent between 1991 and 20002. Much of this increase was attributable to the rise in foreign direct investment and portfolio equity flows, which both rose by roughly 600 per cent. By contrast, gross bond flows increased by a comparatively modest 130 per cent. The expansion in all these flows vastly exceeds the growth in the real economy or the growth in international trade. During 1991-2000 period, real GDP in industrialized countries increased by 26 per cent, and international trade rose by 63 percent3. So while the growth in international trade is often cited as indicating greater interdependence between national economies, the growth in international capital flows suggests that the integration of world financial markets has proceeded even more rapidly.

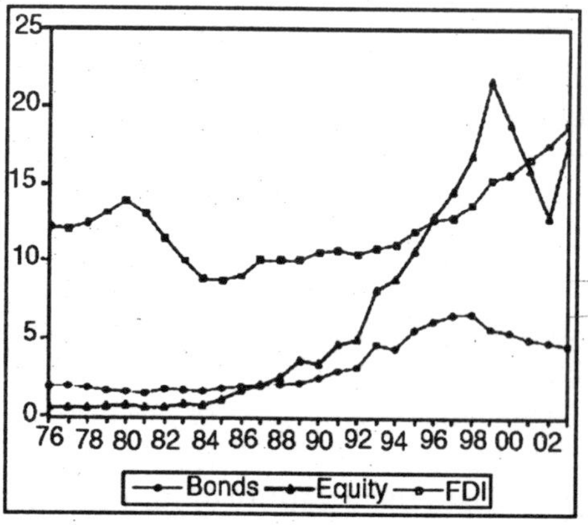

Fig. U.S.-owned Assest Abroad,%GDP

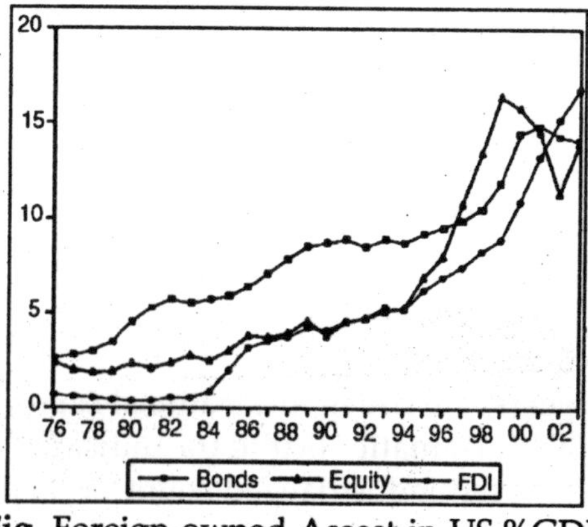

Fig. Foreign-owned Assest in US,%GDP

Greater financial integration is manifested in both asset holdings and capital flows. Figures show how the scale and composition of foreign asset holdings have changed between 1976 and 2003.

US ownership of foreign equity, bonds and capital is plotted in Figure, while foreign ownership of US corporate bonds, equity, and capital are shown in Figure. All the series are shown as a fraction of US GDP.

Before the mid-1980s, capital accounted for the majority of foreign assets held by US residents, followed by bonds. US ownership of foreign equity was below 1% of GDP.

The size and composition of these asset holdings began to change in the mid-1980s when the fraction of foreign equity surpassed bonds.

Thereafter, US ownership of foreign equity increased rapidly peeking at roughly 22 per cent of GDP in 1999. US ownership of foreign capital and bonds also increased during this period but to a lesser extent.

In short, foreign equities have become a much more important component of US financial wealth in the last decade or so. Foreign ownership of US assets has also risen significantly. As Figure shows, foreign ownership of corporate bonds, equity and capital have steadily increased as a fraction of US GDP over the past thirty years.

By 2003, foreign ownership of debt, equity and capital totalled 45 per cent of US GDP. The pattern of asset ownership depicted in Figures is consistent with increased international portfolio diversification by both US and non-US residents.

More precisely, the plots show changes in ownership similar to those that would be necessary to reap the benefits of diversification.

This is most evident in the pattern of equity holdings. Foreign ownership of equities has been at historically high levels over the past five years.

The change in asset ownership has been accompanied by a marked change in international capital flows. Figures plot the quarterly capital flows associated with transactions in US assets and liabilities as a fraction of GDP.

Negative outflows represent US net purchases of foreign assets, while positive inflows represent foreign net purchases of US assets.

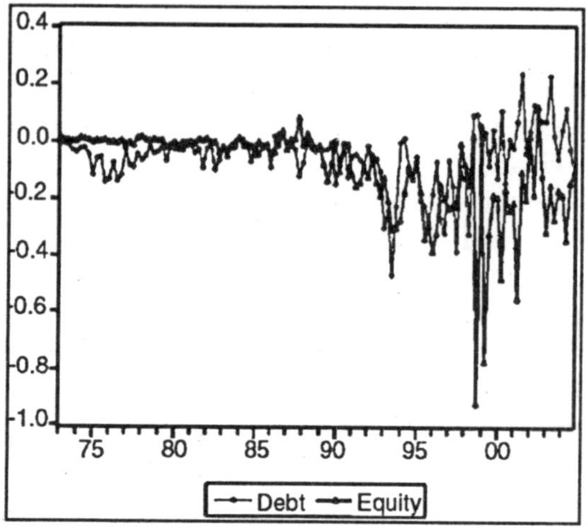

Fig. US Portfolio Investment, Outflow,% GDP

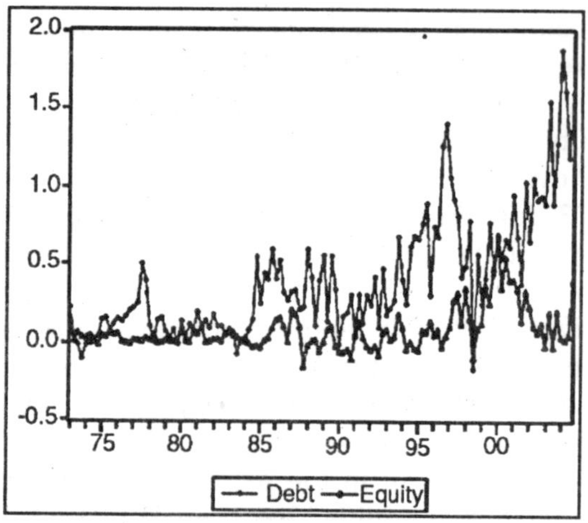

Fig. US Portfolio Investment, Inflow,% GDP

Two features of these plots stand out. First, capital flows were a small fraction of GDP before the mid-1980s. On average, annual gross capital flows accounted for only 1 per cent of US GDP until the mid 1980s, but by 2003 amounted to almost 6 per cent of GDP. Second, the volatility of capital inflows and outflows increased markedly in the 1990s. This is most clearly seen in Figures where we plot the standard deviation of the capital flows over a rolling window of 58 quarters. The increased volatility of equity outflows is particularly noticeable: between 1987 and 2004 volatility increased eleven-fold as a fraction of GDP.

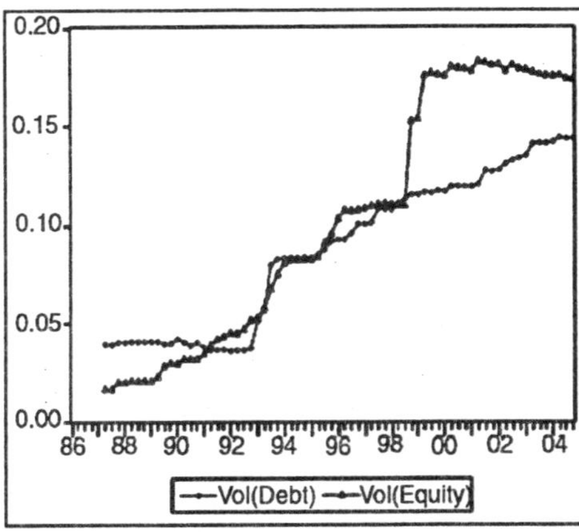

Fig. Volatility of Portfolio Investment, Outflows,%GDP

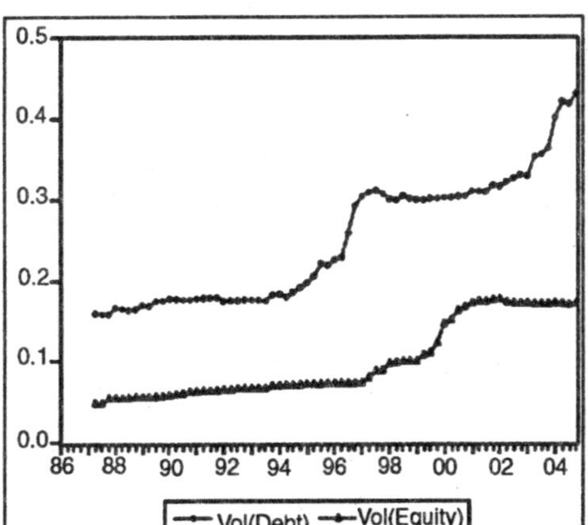

Fig. Volatility of Portfolio Investment, Inflows,%GDP

Increased financial integration has also coincided with changes in the behaviour of equity returns. Figures depict the volatility of equity returns in U.S. and U.K. Both volatilities are calculated as a standard deviation over the 58 quarters rolling window. As the plots clearly indicate, there has been a general downward trend in the volatility of equity returns in both countries over the past twenty years.

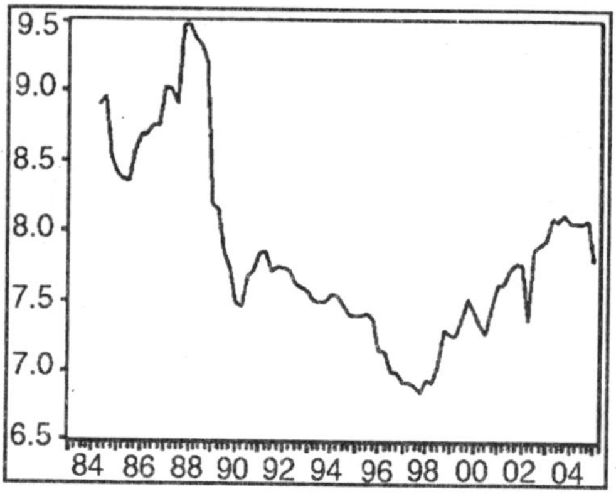

Fig. Volatility of U.S. Equity Return,%

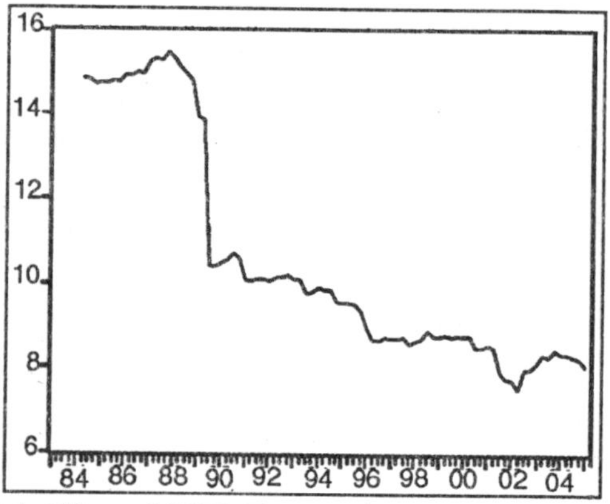

Fig. Volatility of U.K. Equity Return,%

As suggested, focus on the three outstanding features of the data in our analysis:

- The increase in the size of portfolio flows,
- The rise in the volatility of portfolio flows, and
- The decline in the volatility of equity returns.

In particular, as suggested, investigate whether all three features arise as natural consequences of greater integration in world financial markets.

THE MODEL

We consider a world economy consisting of two identical countries, called home and foreign. Each country is populated by a continuum of identical households who supply their labour inelastically to domestic firms in the traded and nontraded goods sectors. Firms in both sectors are perfectly competitive, and issue equity that is traded on the domestic stock market. Our model is designed to study how the degree of financial integration affects international capital flows and returns. For this purpose, we focus on three equilibria.

First we consider the benchmark case of financial autarky. In this environment, households allocate their portfolios between equity in domestic firms producing traded and nontraded goods. Second, we consider a world with partial integration where households allocate their portfolios between domestic equity and an international bond. Finally, we allow for financial integration of equity markets. Here households can hold shares issued by foreign traded-good firms as well as domestic equities and the international bond. This is not to say that markets are complete. In all three cases {i.e., fa, pi, fi}, the array of assets available to households is insufficient to provide complete risk-sharing.

We first describe the production of traded and nontraded goods. Next we present the consumption, saving and portfolio choice problems facing households. Finally, we characterize the market clearing conditions that apply under different degrees of financial market integration.

EQUILIBRIUM

An equilibrium in our world comprises a set of asset prices and relative goods prices that clear markets given the state of productivity, the optimal investment decisions of firms producing tradable goods, and the optimal consumption, savings and portfolios decisions of households. Since markets are incomplete under all three levels of financial integration we consider, an equilibrium can only be found by solving the firm and households' problems for a conjectured set of equilibrium price processes, and then checking that resulting decisions are indeed consistent with market clearing. We first characterize the solutions to the optimization problems facing households and firms. We then describe a procedure for finding the equilibrium price processes.

INFLATION

In economics, inflation is a rise in the general level of prices of goods and services in an economy over a period of time. When the price level rises, each unit of currency buys fewer goods and services; consequently, annual inflation is also an erosion in the purchasing power of money – a loss of real value in the internal medium of exchange and unit of account in the economy. A chief measure of price inflation is the inflation rate, the annualized percentage change in a general price index over time.

Inflation's effects on an economy are manifold and can be simultaneously positive and negative. Negative effects of inflation include a decrease in the real value of money and other monetary items over time; uncertainty about future inflation may discourage investment and saving, or may lead to reductions in investment of productive capital and increase savings in non-producing assets. e.g. selling stocks and buying gold. This can reduce overall economic productivity rates, as the capital required to retool companies becomes more elusive or expensive. High inflation may lead to shortages of goods if consumers begin hoarding out of concern that prices will increase in the future. Positive effects include a mitigation of economic recessions, and debt relief by reducing the real level of debt.

High rates of inflation and hyperinflation can be caused by an excessive growth of the money supply. Views on which factors determine low to moderate rates of inflation are more varied. Low or moderate inflation may be attributed to fluctuations in real demand for goods and services, or changes in available supplies such as during scarcities, as well as to growth in the money supply. However, the consensus view is that a long sustained period of inflation is caused by money supply growing faster than the rate of economic growth.

Today, most mainstream economists favour a low steady rate of inflation. Low inflation may reduce the severity of economic recessions by enabling the labour market to adjust more quickly in a downturn, and reduce the risk that a liquidity trap prevents monetary policy from stabilizing the economy. The task of keeping the rate of inflation low and stable is usually given to monetary authorities. Generally, these monetary authorities are the central banks that control the size of the money supply through the setting of interest rates, through open market operations, and through the setting of banking reserve requirements.

The term "inflation" originally referred to increases in the amount of money in circulation. Today, the term monetary inflation is generally used to distinguish such an occurrence from a general rise in prices, sometimes called price inflation. The occurrence of an increase of the quantity of money and the overall money supply has occurred in many different societies throughout history, changing with different forms of money used.

For instance, when gold was used as currency, the government could collect gold coins, melt them down, mix them with other metals such as silver, copper or lead, and reissue them at the same nominal value. By diluting the gold with other metals, the government could issue more coins without also needing to increase the amount of gold used to make them. When the cost of each coin is lowered in this way, the government profits from an increase in seigniorage. This practice would increase the money supply but at the same time the relative value of each coin would be lowered. As the relative value of the coins becomes less, consumers would need to give more coins in exchange for the same goods and services as before. These goods and services would experience a price increase as the value of each coin is reduced.

From second half of the 15th century to the first half of the 17th, Western Europe experienced a major inflationary cycle referred to as "price revolution", with prices on average rising perhaps sixfold over 150 years. It was thought that this was caused by the increase in wealth of Habsburg Spain, with a large influx of gold and silver from the New World. The spent silver, suddenly spread throughout a previously cash starved Europe, caused widespread inflation. Demographic factors also contributed to upward pressure on prices, with European population growth after depopulation caused by the Black Death pandemic.

By the nineteenth century, economists categorized three separate factors that cause a rise or fall in the price of goods: a change in the value or resource costs of the good, a change in the price of money which then was usually a fluctuation in the commodity price of the metallic content in the currency, and currency depreciation resulting from an increased supply of currency relative to the quantity of redeemable metal backing the currency. Following the proliferation of private bank note currency printed during the American Civil War, the term"inflation" started to appear as a direct reference to the currency depreciation that occurred as the quantity of redeemable bank notes outstripped the quantity of metal available for their redemption. The term inflation then referred to the devaluation of the currency, and not to a rise in the price of goods.

This relationship between the over-supply of bank notes and a resulting depreciation in their value was noted by earlier classical economists such as David Hume and David Ricardo, who would go on to examine and debate to what effect a currency devaluation has on the price of goods.

The term"inflation" usually refers to a measured rise in a broad price index that represents the overall level of prices in goods and services in the economy. The Consumer Price Index, the Personal Consumption Expenditures Price Index and the GDP deflator are some examples of broad price indices. The term inflation may also be used to describe the rising level of prices in a narrow set of assets, goods or services within the economy, such as commodities, financial assets. The Reuters-CRB Index, the Producer Price Index, and Employment Cost Index are examples of narrow price indices used to measure price inflation in particular sectors of the economy. Asset price inflation is a rise in the price of assets, as opposed to goods and services. Core inflation is a measure of price fluctuations in a sub-set of the broad price index which excludes food and energy prices. The Federal Reserve Board uses the core inflation rate to measure overall inflation, eliminating food and energy prices to mitigate against short term price fluctuations that could distort estimates of future long term inflation trends in the general economy.

Other related economic concepts include: deflation - a fall in the general price level; disinflation - a decrease in the rate of inflation; hyperinflation - an out-of-control inflationary spiral; stagflation - a combination of inflation, slow economic growth and high unemployment; and reflation - an attempt to raise the general level of prices to counteract deflationary pressures.

MEASURES

Inflation is usually estimated by calculating the inflation rate of a price index, usually the Consumer Price Index. The Consumer Price Index measures prices of a selection of goods and services purchased by a"typical consumer". The inflation rate is the percentage rate of change of a price index over time.

For instance, in January 2007, the U.S. Consumer Price Index was 202.416, and in January 2008 it was 211.080. The formula for calculating the annual percentage rate inflation in the CPI over the course of 2007 is

The resulting inflation rate for the CPI in this one year period is 4.28%, meaning the general level of prices for typical U.S. consumers rose by approximately four per cent in 2007.

Other widely used price indices for calculating price inflation include the following:

- Producer price indices which measures average changes in prices received by domestic producers for their output. This differs from the CPI in that price subsidization, profits, and taxes may cause the amount received by the producer to differ from what the consumer paid. There is also typically a delay between an increase in the PPI and any eventual increase in the CPI. Producer price index measures the pressure being put on producers by the costs of their raw materials. This could be"passed on" to consumers, or it could be absorbed by profits, or offset by increasing productivity. In India and the United States, an earlier version of the PPI was called the Wholesale Price Index.

- Commodity price indices, which measure the price of a selection of commodities. In the present commodity price indices are weighted by the relative importance of the components to the "all in" cost of an employee.
- *Core price indices*: because food and oil prices can change quickly due to changes in supply and demand conditions in the food and oil markets, it can be difficult to detect the long run trend in price levels when those prices are included. Therefore most statistical agencies also report a measure of 'core inflation', which removes the most volatile components from a broad price index like the CPI. Because core inflation is less affected by short run supply and demand conditions in specific markets, central banks rely on it to better measure the inflationary impact of current monetary policy.

Other common measures of inflation are:

- GDP deflator is a measure of the price of all the goods and services included in Gross Domestic Product. The US Commerce Department publishes a deflator series for US. GDP, defined as its nominal GDP measure divided by its real GDP measure.
- Regional inflation The Bureau of Labour Statistics breaks down CPI-U calculations down to different regions of the US.
- Historical inflation Before collecting consistent econometric data became standard for governments, and for the purpose of comparing absolute, rather than relative standards of living, various economists have calculated imputed inflation figures. Most inflation data before the early 20th century is imputed

based on the known costs of goods, rather than compiled at the time. It is also used to adjust for the differences in real standard of living for the presence of technology.

- Asset price inflation is an undue increase in the prices of real or financial assets, such as stock and real estate. While there is no widely accepted index of this type, some central bankers have suggested that it would be better to aim at stabilizing a wider general price level inflation measure that includes some asset prices, instead of stabilizing CPI or core inflation only. The reason is that by raising interest rates when stock prices or real estate prices rise, and lowering them when these asset prices fall, central banks might be more successful in avoiding bubbles and crashes in asset prices.

Issues in Measuring

Measuring inflation in an economy requires objective means of differentiating changes in nominal prices on a common set of goods and services, and distinguishing them from those price shifts resulting from changes in value such as volume, quality, or performance. For example, if the price of a 10 oz. can of corn changes from $0.90 to $1.00 over the course of a year, with no change in quality, then this price difference represents inflation. This single price change would not, however, represent general inflation in an overall economy.

To measure overall inflation, the price change of a large "basket" of representative goods and services is measured. This is the purpose of a price index, which is the combined price of a "basket" of many goods and services. The combined price is the sum of the weighted average prices of items in the "basket". A weighted price is calculated by multiplying the unit price of an item to the number of those items the average consumer purchases. Weighted pricing is a necessary means to measuring the impact of individual unit price changes on the economy's overall inflation. The Consumer Price Index, for example, uses data collected by surveying households to determine what proportion of the typical consumer's overall spending is spent on specific goods and services, and weights the average prices of those items accordingly. Those weighted average prices are combined to calculate the overall price. To better relate price changes over time, indexes typically choose a "base year" price and assign it a value of 100. Index prices in subsequent years are then expressed in relation to the base year price.

Inflation measures are often modified over time, either for the relative weight of goods in the basket, or in the way in which goods and services from the present are compared with goods and services from the past. Over time adjustments are made to the type of goods and services selected in order to reflect changes in the sorts of goods and services purchased by 'typical consumers'. New products may be introduced, older products disappear, the quality of existing products may change, and consumer preferences can shift. Both the sorts of goods and services which are included in the "basket" and the weighted price used in inflation measures will be changed over time in order to keep pace with the changing marketplace.

Inflation numbers are often seasonally adjusted in order to differentiate expected cyclical cost shifts. For example, home heating costs are expected to rise in colder months, and seasonal adjustments are often used when measuring for inflation to compensate for cyclical spikes in energy or fuel demand. Inflation numbers may be averaged or otherwise subjected to statistical techniques in order to remove statistical noise and volatility of individual prices.

When looking at inflation economic institutions may focus only on certain kinds of prices, or special indices, such as the core inflation index which is used by central banks to formulate monetary policy. Most inflation indices are calculated from weighted averages of selected price changes. This necessarily introduces distortion, and can lead to legitimate disputes about what the true inflation rate is. This problem can be overcome by including all available price changes in the calculation, and then choosing the median value.

EFFECTS

General

An increase in the general level of prices implies a decrease in the purchasing power of the currency. That is, when the general level of prices rises, each monetary unit buys fewer goods and services. The effect of inflation is not distributed evenly in the economy, and as a consequence there are hidden costs to some and benefits to others from this decrease in the purchasing power of money. For example, with inflation, lenders or depositors who are paid a fixed rate of interest on loans or deposits will lose purchasing power from their interest earnings, while their borrowers benefit. Individuals or institutions with cash assets will experience a decline in the purchasing power of their holdings. Increases in payments to workers and pensioners often lag behind inflation, especially for those with fixed payments.

Increases in the price level erodes the real value of money and other items with an underlying monetary nature. However, inflation has no effect on the real value of non-monetary items.

Negative

High or unpredictable inflation rates are regarded as harmful to an overall economy. They add inefficiencies in the market, and make it difficult for companies to budget or plan long-term. Inflation can performance as a drag on productivity as companies are forced to shift resources away from products and services in order to focus on profit and losses from currency inflation. Uncertainty about the future purchasing power of money discourages investment and saving. And inflation can impose hidden tax increases, as inflated earnings push taxpayers into higher income tax rates unless the tax brackets are indexed to inflation.

With high inflation, purchasing power is redistributed from those on fixed nominal incomes, such as some pensioners whose pensions are not indexed to the price level, towards those with variable incomes whose earnings may better keep pace with the inflation. This redistribution of purchasing power will also occur between international trading partners. Where fixed exchange rates are imposed, higher inflation in one economy than another will cause the first economy's exports to become more expensive and affect the balance of trade. There can also be negative impacts to trade from an increased instability in currency exchange prices caused by unpredictable inflation.

Cost-push Inflation

High inflation can prompt employees to demand rapid wage increases, to keep up with consumer prices. Rising wages in turn can help fuel inflation. In the case of collective bargaining, wage growth will be set as a function of inflationary expectations, which will be higher when inflation is high. This can cause a wage spiral. In a sense, inflation begets further inflationary expectations, which beget further inflation.

Hoarding

People buy consumer durables as stores of wealth in the absence of viable alternatives as a means of getting rid of excess cash before it is devalued, creating shortages of the hoarded objects.

Hyperinflation

If inflation gets totally out of control, it can grossly interfere with the normal workings of the economy, hurting its ability to supply goods. Hyperinflation can lead to the abandonment of the use of the country's currency, leading to the inefficiencies of barter.

Allocative Efficiency

A change in the supply or demand for a good will normally cause its relative price to change, signalling to buyers and sellers that they should re-allocate resources in response to the new market conditions. But when prices are constantly changing due to inflation, price changes due to genuine relative price signals are difficult to distinguish from price changes due to general inflation, so agents are slow to respond to them. The result is a loss of allocative efficiency.

Shoe Leather Cost

High inflation increases the opportunity cost of holding cash balances and can induce people to hold a greater portion of their assets in interest paying accounts. However, since cash is still needed in order to carry out transactions this means that more "trips to the bank" are necessary in order to make withdrawals, proverbially wearing out the "shoe leather" with each trip.

Menu Costs

With high inflation, firms must change their prices often in order to keep up with economy-wide changes. But often changing prices is itself a costly activity whether explicitly, as with the need to print new menus, or implicitly.

Business Cycles

The Austrian Business Cycle Theory, inflation sets off the business cycle. Austrian economists hold this to be the most damaging effect of inflation. Austrian theory, artificially low interest rates and the associated increase in the money supply lead to reckless, speculative borrowing, resulting in clusters of malinvestments, which eventually have to be liquidated as they become unsustainable.

Positive

Labour-market Adjustments

Keynesians believe that nominal wages are slow to adjust downwards. This can lead to prolonged disequilibrium and high unemployment in the labour market. Since inflation would lower the real wage if nominal wages are kept constant, Keynesians argue that some inflation is good for the economy, as it would allow labour markets to reach equilibrium faster.

Debt Relief

Debtors who have debts with a fixed nominal rate of

interest will see a reduction in the "real" interest rate as the inflation rate rises. The "real" interest on a loan is the nominal rate minus the inflation rate.

For example if you take a loan where the stated interest rate is 6% and the inflation rate is at 3%, the real interest rate that you are paying for the loan is 3%. It would also hold true that if you had a loan at a fixed interest rate of 6% and the inflation rate jumped to 20% you would have a real interest rate of -14%.

Banks and other lenders adjust for this inflation risk either by including an inflation premium in the costs of lending the money by creating a higher initial stated interest rate or by setting the interest at a variable rate.

Room to Maneuver

The primary tools for controlling the money supply are the ability to set the discount rate, the rate at which banks can borrow from the central bank, and open market operations which are the central bank's interventions into the bonds market with the aim of affecting the nominal interest rate. If an economy finds itself in a recession with already low, or even zero, nominal interest rates, then the bank cannot cut these rates further in order to stimulate the economy - this situation is known as a liquidity trap.

A moderate level of inflation tends to ensure that nominal interest rates stay sufficiently above zero so that if the need arises the bank can cut the nominal interest rate.

Tobin Effect

The Nobel prize winning economist James Tobin at one point argued that a moderate level of inflation can increase investment in an economy leading to faster growth or at least a higher steady state level of income.

This is due to the fact that inflation lowers the real return on monetary assets relative to real assets, such as physical capital. To avoid this effect of inflation, investors would switch from holding their assets as money to investing in real capital projects.

CAUSES

Historically, a great deal of economic literature was concerned with the question of what causes inflation and what effect it has. There were different schools of thought as to the causes of inflation. Most can be divided into two broad areas: quality theories of inflation and quantity theories of inflation. The quality theory of inflation rests on the expectation of a seller accepting currency to be able to exchange that currency at a later time for goods that are desirable as a buyer. The quantity theory of inflation rests on the quantity equation of money, that relates the money supply, its velocity, and the nominal value of exchanges. Adam Smith and David Hume proposed a quantity theory of inflation for money, and a quality theory of inflation for production.

Currently, the quantity theory of money is widely accepted as an accurate model of inflation in the long run. Consequently, there is now broad agreement among economists that in the long run, the inflation rate is essentially dependent on the growth rate of money supply. However, in the short and medium term inflation may be affected by supply and demand pressures in the economy, and influenced by the relative elasticity of wages, prices and interest rates.

The question of whether the short-term effects last long enough to be important is the central topic of debate between monetarist and Keynesian economists.

In monetarism prices and wages adjust quickly enough to make other factors merely marginal behaviour on a general trend-line. In the Keynesian view, prices and wages adjust at different rates, and these differences have enough effects on real output to be "long term" in the view of people in an economy.

Keynesian View

Keynesian economic theory proposes that changes in money supply do not directly affect prices, and that visible inflation is the result of pressures in the economy expressing themselves in prices. The supply of money is a major, but not the only, cause of inflation.

There are three major types of inflation, as part of what Robert J. Gordon calls the "triangle model":

- Demand-pull inflation is caused by increases in aggregate demand due to increased private and government spending, etc. Demand inflation is constructive to a faster rate of economic growth since the excess demand and favourable market conditions will stimulate investment and expansion.
- Cost-push inflation, also called "supply shock inflation," is caused by a drop in aggregate supply. This may be due to natural disasters, or increased prices of inputs. For example, a sudden decrease in the supply of oil, leading to increased oil prices, can cause cost-push inflation. Producers for whom oil is a part of their costs could then pass this on to consumers in the form of increased prices.
- Built-in inflation is induced by adaptive expectations, and is often linked to the "price/wage spiral". It involves workers trying to keep their wages up with prices and firms passing these higher labour costs on to their customers as higher prices, leading to a 'vicious circle'. Built-in inflation reflects events in the past, and so might be seen as hangover inflation.

Demand-pull theory states that the rate of inflation accelerates whenever aggregate demand is increased beyond the ability of the economy to produce. Hence, any factor that increases aggregate demand can cause inflation. However, in the long run, aggregate demand can be held above productive capacity only by increasing the quantity of money in circulation faster than the real growth rate of the economy. Another cause can be a rapid decline in the demand for money, as happened in Europe during the Black Death, or in the Japanese occupied territories just before the defeat of Japan in 1945.

The effect of money on inflation is most obvious when governments finance spending in a crisis, such as a civil war, by printing money excessively. This sometimes leads to hyperinflation, a condition where prices can double in a month or less. Money supply is also thought to play a major role in determining moderate levels of inflation, although there are differences of opinion on how important it is. For example, Monetarist economists believe that the link is very strong; Keynesian economists, by contrast, typically emphasize the role of aggregate demand in the economy rather than the money supply in determining inflation. That is, for Keynesians, the money supply is only one determinant of aggregate demand.

Some Keynesian economists also disagree with the notion that central banks fully control the money supply, arguing that central banks have little control, since the money supply adapts to the demand for bank credit issued by commercial banks. This is known as the theory of endogenous money, and has been advocated strongly by post-Keynesians as far back as the 1960s. It has today become a central focus of Taylor rule advocates. This position is not universally accepted – banks create money by making loans, but the aggregate volume of these loans diminishes as real interest rates increase. Thus, central banks can influence the money supply by making money cheaper or more expensive, thus increasing or decreasing its production.

A fundamental concept in inflation analysis is the relationship between inflation and unemployment, called the Phillips curve. This model suggests that there is a trade-off between price stability and employment. Therefore, some level of inflation could be considered desirable in order to minimize unemployment. The Phillips curve model described the U.S. experience well in the 1960s but failed to describe the combination of rising inflation and economic stagnation experienced in the 1970s.

Thus, modern macroeconomics describes inflation using a Phillips curve that shifts because of such matters as supply shocks and inflation becoming built into the normal workings of the economy. The former refers to such events as the oil shocks of the 1970s, while the latter refers to the price/wage spiral and inflationary expectations implying that the economy "normally" suffers from inflation. Thus, the Phillips curve represents only the demand-pull component of the triangle model.

Another concept of note is the potential output, a level of GDP, where the economy is at its optimal level of production given institutional and natural constraints. If GDP exceeds its potential, the theory says that inflation will accelerate as suppliers increase their prices and built-in inflation worsens. If GDP falls below its potential level, inflation will decelerate as suppliers attempt to fill excess capacity, cutting prices and undermining built-in inflation.

However, one problem with this theory for policy-making purposes is that the exact level of potential output is generally unknown and tends to change over time. Inflation also seems to performance in an asymmetric way, rising more quickly than it falls. Worse, it can change because of policy: for example, high unemployment under British Prime Minister Margaret Thatcher might have led to a rise in the NAIRU because many of the unemployed found themselves as structurally unemployed, unable to find jobs that fit their skills. A rise in structural unemployment implies that a smaller percentage of the labour force can find jobs at the NAIRU, where the economy avoids crossing the threshold into the realm of accelerating inflation.

Monetarist View

Monetarists believe the most significant factor influencing inflation or deflation is the management of money supply through the easing or tightening of credit. They consider fiscal policy, or government spending and taxation, as ineffective in controlling inflation. The famous monetarist economist Milton Friedman, "Inflation is always and everywhere a monetary phenomenon."

Monetarists assert that the empirical study of monetary history shows that inflation has always been a monetary phenomenon. The quantity theory of money, simply stated, says that any change the amount of money in a system will change the price level. This theory begins with the equation of exchange:

$$M.V = P.Q$$

Where:

M is the quantity of money.

V is the velocity of money in final expenditures;

P is the general price level;

Q is an index of the real value of final expenditures;

In this formula, the general price level is affected by the level of economic activity (Q), the quantity of money (M) and the velocity of money (V). The formula is an identity because the velocity of money (V) is defined to be the ratio of final expenditure (P.Q) to the quantity of money (M).

Monetarists assume that the velocity of money is constant, and the real value of output is determined in the long run by the productive capacity of the economy. Under these assumptions, the primary driver of the change in the general price level is changes in the quantity of money. With constant velocity, the money supply determines the value of nominal output in the short run. In practice, velocity is not constant, and can only be measured indirectly and so the formula does not necessarily imply a stable relationship between money supply and nominal output. However, in the long run, changes in money supply and level of economic activity usually dwarf changes in velocity. If velocity is relatively constant, the long run rate of increase in prices is equal to the difference between the long run growth rate of money supply and the long run growth rate of real output.

Unemployment

A connection between inflation and unemployment has been drawn since the emergence of large scale unemployment in the 19th century, and connections continue to be drawn this today. In Marxian economics, the unemployed serve as a reserve army of labour, which restrain wage inflation. In the 20th century, similar concepts in Keynesian economics include the NAIRU and the Phillips curve.

Rational Expectations Theory

Rational expectations theory holds that economic actors

look rationally into the future when trying to maximize their well-being, and do not respond solely to immediate opportunity costs and pressures. In this view, while generally grounded in monetarism, future expectations and strategies are important for inflation as well.

A core assertion of rational expectations theory is that actors will seek to "head off" central-bank decisions by acting in ways that fulfill predictions of higher inflation. This means that central banks must establish their credibility in fighting inflation, or have economic actors make bets that the economy will expand, believing that the central bank will expand the money supply rather than allow a recession.

Austrian Theory

The Austrian School asserts that inflation is an increase in the money supply, rising prices are merely consequences and this semantic difference is important in defining inflation. Austrian economists believe there is no material difference between the concepts of monetary inflation and general price inflation. Austrian economists measure monetary inflation by calculating the growth of new units of money that are available for immediate use in exchange, that have been created over time. This interpretation of inflation implies that inflation is always a distinct action taken by the central government or its central bank, which permits or allows an increase in the money supply. In addition to state-induced monetary expansion, the Austrian School also maintains that the effects of increasing the money supply are magnified by credit expansion, as a result of the fractional-reserve banking system employed in most economic and financial systems in the world.

Austrians argue that the state uses inflation as one of the three means by which it can fund its activities, the other two being taxation and borrowing. Various forms of military spending is often cited as a reason for resorting to inflation and borrowing, as this can be a short term way of acquiring marketable resources and is often favoured by desperate, indebted governments.

In other cases, Austrians argue that the government actually creates economic recessions and depressions, by creating artificial booms that distort the structure of production. The central bank may try to avoid or defer the widespread bankruptcies and insolvencies which cause economic recessions or depressions by artificially trying to "stimulate" the economy through "encouraging" money supply growth and further borrowing via artificially low interest rates. Many Austrian economists support the abolition of the central banks and the fractional-reserve banking system, and advocate returning to a 100 per cent gold standard, or less frequently, free banking. They argue this would constrain unsustainable and volatile fractional-reserve banking practices, ensuring that money supply growth would never spiral out of control.

Real Bills Doctrine

Within the context of a fixed specie basis for money, one important controversy was between the quantity theory of money and the real bills doctrine. Within this context, quantity theory applies to the level of fractional reserve accounting allowed against specie, generally gold, held by a bank. Currency and banking schools of economics argue the RBD, that banks should also be able to issue currency against bills of trading, which is "real bills" that they buy from merchants. This theory was important in the 19th century in debates between "Banking" and "Currency" schools of monetary soundness, and in the formation of the Federal Reserve.

In the wake of the collapse of the international gold standard post 1913, and the move towards deficit financing of government, RBD has remained a minor topic, primarily of interest in limited contexts, such as currency boards. It is generally held in ill repute today, with Frederic Mishkin, a governor of the Federal Reserve going so far as to say it had been "completely discredited."

Even so, it has theoretical support from a few economists, particularly those that see restrictions on a particular class of credit as incompatible with libertarian principles of laissez-faire, even though almost all libertarian economists are opposed to the RBD.

The debate between currency, or quantity theory, and banking schools in Britain during the 19th century prefigures current questions about the credibility of money in the present. In the 19th century the banking school had greater influence in policy in the United States and Great Britain, while the currency school had more influence "on the continent", that is in non-British countries, particularly in the Latin Monetary Union and the earlier Scandinavia monetary union.

Anti-classical or Backing Theory

Another issue associated with classical political economy is the anti-classical hypothesis of money, or "backing theory". The backing theory argues that the value of money is determined by the assets and liabilities of the issuing agency. Unlike the Quantity Theory of classical political economy, the backing theory argues that issuing authorities can issue money without causing inflation so long as the money issuer has sufficient assets to cover redemptions. There are very few backing theorists, making quantity theory the dominant theory explaining inflation.

CONTROLLING INFLATION

A variety of methods have been used in attempts to control inflation.

Monetary Policy

Today the primary tool for controlling inflation is monetary policy. Most central banks are tasked with keeping the federal funds lending rate at a low level, normally to a target rate around 2% to 3% per annum, and within a targeted low inflation range, somewhere from about 2% to 6% per annum. A low positive inflation is usually targeted, as deflationary conditions are seen as dangerous for the health of the economy.

There are a number of methods that have been suggested to control inflation. Central banks such as the U.S. Federal

Reserve can affect inflation to a significant extent through setting interest rates and through other operations. High interest rates and slow growth of the money supply are the traditional ways through which central banks fight or prevent inflation, though they have different approaches. For instance, some follow a symmetrical inflation target while others only control inflation when it rises above a target, whether express or implied.

Monetarists emphasize keeping the growth rate of money steady, and using monetary policy to control inflation. Keynesians emphasize reducing aggregate demand during economic expansions and increasing demand during recessions to keep inflation stable. Control of aggregate demand can be achieved using both monetary policy and fiscal policy.

Fixed Exchange Rates

Under a fixed exchange rate currency regime, a country's currency is tied in value to another single currency or to a basket of other currencies. A fixed exchange rate is usually used to stabilize the value of a currency, vis-a-vis the currency it is pegged to. It can also be used as a means to control inflation. However, as the value of the reference currency rises and falls, so does the currency pegged to it. This essentially means that the inflation rate in the fixed exchange rate country is determined by the inflation rate of the country the currency is pegged to. In addition, a fixed exchange rate prevents a government from using domestic monetary policy in order to achieve macroeconomic stability.

Under the Bretton Woods agreement, most countries around the world had currencies that were fixed to the US dollar. This limited inflation in those countries, but also exposed them to the danger of speculative attacks. After the Bretton Woods agreement broke down in the early 1970s, countries gradually turned to floating exchange rates. However, in the later part of the 20th century, some countries reverted to a fixed exchange rate as part of an attempt to control inflation. This policy of using a fixed exchange rate to control inflation was used in many countries in South America in the later part of the 20th century.

Gold Standard

The gold standard is a monetary system in which a region's common media of exchange are paper notes that are normally freely convertible into pre-set, fixed quantities of gold. The standard specifies how the gold backing would be implemented, including the amount of specie per currency unit. The currency itself has no innate value, but is accepted by traders because it can be redeemed for the equivalent specie. A U.S. silver certificate, for example, could be redeemed for an actual piece of silver.

The gold standard was partially abandoned via the international adoption of the Bretton Woods System. Under this system all other major currencies were tied at fixed rates to the dollar, which itself was tied to gold at the rate of $35 per ounce. The Bretton Woods system broke down in 1971, causing most countries to switch to fiat money – money backed only by the laws of the country. Austrian economists strongly favour a return to a 100 per cent gold standard.

Under a gold standard, the long term rate of inflation would be determined by the growth rate of the supply of gold relative to total output. Critics argue that this will cause arbitrary fluctuations in the inflation rate, and that monetary policy would essentially be determined by gold mining, which some believe contributed to the Great Depression.

Wage and Price Controls

Another method attempted in the past have been wage and price controls. Wage and price controls have been successful in wartime environments in combination with rationing. However, their use in other contexts is far more mixed. Notable failures of their use include the 1972 imposition of wage and price controls by Richard Nixon. More successful examples include the Prices and Incomes Accord in Australia and the Wassenaar Agreement in the Netherlands.

In general wage and price controls are regarded as a

temporary and exceptional measure, only effective when coupled with policies designed to reduce the underlying causes of inflation during the wage and price control regime, for example, winning the war being fought. They often have perverse effects, due to the distorted signals they send to the market.

Artificially low prices often cause rationing and shortages and discourage future investment, resulting in yet further shortages. The usual economic analysis is that any product or service that is under-priced is overconsumed. For example, if the official price of bread is too low, there will be too little bread at official prices, and too little investment in bread making by the market to satisfy future needs, thereby exacerbating the problem in the long term.

Temporary controls may complement a recession as a way to fight inflation: the controls make the recession more efficient as a way to fight inflation, while the recession prevents the kinds of distortions that controls cause when demand is high. However, in general the advice of economists is not to impose price controls but to liberalize prices by assuming that the economy will adjust and abandon unprofitable economic activity. The lower activity will place fewer demands on whatever commodities were driving inflation, whether labour or resources, and inflation will fall with total economic output. This often produces a severe recession, as productive capacity is reallocated and is thus often very unpopular with the people whose livelihoods are destroyed.

Cost-of-living Allowance

The real purchasing-power of fixed payments is eroded by inflation unless they are inflation-adjusted to keep their real values constant. In many countries, employment contracts, pension benefits, and government entitlements are tied to a cost-of-living index, typically to the consumer price index. A cost-of-living allowance adjusts salaries based on changes in a cost-of-living index. Salaries are typically adjusted annually. They may also be tied to a cost-of-living index that varies by geographic location if the employee moves.

Annual escalation clauses in employment contracts can specify retroactive or future percentage increases in worker pay which are not tied to any index. These negotiated increases in pay are colloquially referred to as cost-of-living adjustments or cost-of-living increases because of their similarity to increases tied to externally determined indexes.

Many economists and compensation analysts consider the idea of predetermined future"cost of living increases" to be misleading for two reasons:

1. For most recent periods in the industrialized world, average wages have increased faster than most calculated cost-of-living indexes, reflecting the influence of rising productivity and worker bargaining power rather than simply living costs, and
2. Most cost-of-living indexes are not forward-looking, but instead compare current or historical data.

INTERNATIONAL EXCHANGE CONTROLS

International exchange controls are various forms of controls imposed by a government on the purchase/sale of foreign currencies by residents or on the purchase/sale of local currency by nonresidents.

Common foreign exchange controls include:

- Banning the use of foreign currency within the country
- Banning locals from possessing foreign currency
- Restricting currency exchange to government-approved exchangers
- Fixed exchange rates
- Restrictions on the amount of currency that may be imported or exported

Countries with foreign exchange controls are also known as After the provision in the International Monetary Fund agreement allowing exchange controls for transitional economies. Such controls used to be common in most countries, particularly poorer ones, until the 1990s when free trade and globalization started a trend towards economic liberalization. Today, countries which still impose exchange controls are the exception rather than the rule.

CURRENCY DEVALUATION

Currency devaluation takes place when one country's currency is reduced in value in comparison to other currencies. After currency devaluation, more of the devalued currency is required in order to purchase the same amount of other currencies. A fictional example: If last year, one U.S. dollar purchased 10 Mexican pesos, then this year, one U.S. dollar can only purchase five Mexican pesos, the U.S. dollar has undergone a currency devaluation.

ORIGINS

Currency devaluation can take two forms. It can either be the natural result of market forces, or it can be the result of government intervention. In the first scenario, the global market changes its opinion about the stability, value or future of a currency and decides that it is willing to pay less. In the second scenario, a nation's government fixes the relative price of their currency below its present level and prohibits currency exchange at any other rate.

BENEFITS

Currency devaluation can help to achieve a more desirable balance of trade. For nations experiencing a trade deficit, a currency devaluation will reduce the price of their products abroad and increase the price of foreign products in domestic markets. Increased demand for products in other countries due to lower prices can also mean more jobs and lower unemployment rates at home.

DRAWBACKS

Currency devaluation also has negative consequences. Individuals holding a recently devalued currency have lost international buying power. Their ability to purchase goods or services from other countries has diminished. Additionally, if a government artificially devalues its currency, it may be forced to purchase its own currency with foreign reserves, depleting its own assets and ability to pay public debt. This occurred in Russia after its 1998 currency crisis.

ARGENTINA

In 2001, the Argentine peso was pegged to the U.S. dollar. One peso was equal to one dollar. However, the government grew increasingly unable to pay its public debt and in the beginning of 2002, the government devalued the peso. While the initial effects were chaotic, leading to rampant unemployment and poverty, they have improved. Unemployment and poverty have diminished, and exports as a percentage of gross domestic product have skyrocketed.

UNITED STATES

Between 2002 and 2009, the U.S. dollar has been devalued, although the change has taken place more slowly than in Argentina, and from market forces rather than government edict. In 2002, one euro cost about $0.86. In August 2009, the price reached $1.41. This resulted in a decrease in Americans traveling in Europe and buying European products and an increase in Europeans traveling to the U.S. and buying U.S. products. The same effects on the U.S. dollar took place in the United Kingdom with the British pound, Japan with the yen, and Canada with Canadian dollars.

COUNTRY RISK ANALYSIS

Country risk analysis attempts to identify imbalances that increase the risk of a shortfall in the expected return of a cross-border investment. The general process used to create risk measures and discusses some of the weaknesses of this process. It then examines the degree of association of six measures and analyses the ability of these measures to predict returns for a manufacturing investment. The concludes that company analysts may improve the performance of risk measures available from commercial services by adjusting risk measurement to fit the company's specific type of foreign direct investment.

All business transactions involve some degree of risk. When business transactions occur across international borders, they carry additional risks not present in domestic transactions. These additional risks, called country risks, typically include risks arising from a variety of national differences in economic structures, policies, socio-political institutions, geography, and currencies. Country risk analysis attempts to identify the potential for these risks to decrease the expected return of a cross-border investment.

"Risk" implies that an analyst can identify a well-defined event drawn from a large sample of observations. A large sample contains enough observations to develop a statistical function amenable to probability analysis. An event that lacks these requirements moves towards uncertainty on the continuum between pure risk and pure uncertainty. For example, the probability of death from an auto accident classifies as a risk; the probability of death from a nuclear meltdown falls into uncertainty, given a lack of nuclear meltdown observations. Many of the individual events investigated by country risk analysis fall closer to uncertainties than well-defined statistical risks. This forces analysts to construct risk measures from theoretical or judgmental, rather than probabilistic, foundations.

Uncertainty makes CRA more similar to a soft art than a hard science. Analysts deal with the soft nature of CRA in different ways, which can result in widely varying views of the risk level of a country. For this reason, users of risk measures developed from commercial country-risk services must understand analysts' construction methods if they wish to analyse a company investment risk appropriately. Company analysts should be able to improve upon outside measures by adapting risk systems to their specific company investments.

THEORY VS. PRACTICE

Country risk analysis rests on the fundamental premise that growing imbalances in economic, social, or political factors increase the risk of a shortfall in the expected return on an investment. Imbalances in a specific risk factor map to one or more risk categories. Mapping all the factors at the appropriate level of influence creates an overall assessment of investment risk. The mapping structure differs for each type of investment, so an imbalance in a given factor produces different risks for different investments.

This fundamental premise provides a simple theoretical underpinning to CRA. Unfortunately, no comprehensive country risk theory exists to guide the mapping process. In practice, most country-risk services create risk measures using an eclectic mix of economic or sociopolitical indicators based on selection criteria arising from their analysts' experiences and judgment.

The services usually combine a variety of factors representing actual and potential imbalances into a comprehensive risk assessment that applies to a broad investment category. Most CRA literature emphasizes a number of common points, then slips into a detailed discussion of ways the respective authors enumerate risk for various investments. The best authors emphasize the necessity to adapt their analyses for a specific investment decision given the judgmental nature of their methods.

COUNTRY RISK CATEGORIES AND MEASUREMENTS

Analysts have tended to separate country risk into the six main categories of risk. Many of these categories overlap each other, given the interrelationship of the domestic economy with the political system and with the international community.

Even though many risk analysts may not agree completely with this list, these six concepts tend to show up in risk ratings from most services:

1. Economic Risk
2. Transfer Risk
3. Exchange Rate Risk
4. Location or Neighbourhood Risk
5. Sovereign Risk
6. Political Risk

Economic Risk is the significant change in the economic structure or growth rate that produces a major change in the expected return of an investment. Risk arises from the potential for detrimental changes in fundamental economic policy goals or a significant change in a country's comparative advantage. Economic risk often overlaps with political risk in some measurement systems since both deal with policy.

Economic risk measures include traditional measures of fiscal and monetary policy, such as the size and composition of government expenditures, tax policy, the government's debt situation, and monetary policy and financial maturity. For longer-term investments, measures focus on long-run growth factors, the degree of openness of the economy, and institutional factors that might affect wealth creation.

Transfer Risk is the risk arising from a decision by a foreign government to restrict capital movements. Restrictions could make it difficult to repatriate profits, dividends, or capital. Because a government can change capital-movement rules at any time, transfer risk applies to all types of investments. It usually is analysed as a function of a country's ability to earn foreign currency, with the implication that difficulty earning foreign currency increases the probability that some form of capital controls can emerge. Quantifying the risk remains difficult because the decision to restrict capital may be a purely political response to another problem. For example, Malaysia's decision to impose capital controls and fix the exchange rate in the midst of the Asian currency crisis was a political solution to an exchange-rate problem. Quantitative measures typically used to assess transfer risk provided little guidance to predict Malaysia's actions.

Transfer risk measures typically include the ratio of debt service payments to exports or to exports plus net foreign direct investment, the amount and structure of foreign debt relative to income, foreign currency reserves divided by various import categories, and measures related to the current account status. Trends in these quantitative measures reveal potential imbalances that could lead a country to restrict certain types of capital flows. For example, a growing current account deficit as a per cent of GDP implies an ever-greater need for foreign exchange to cover that deficit. The risk of a transfer problem increases if no offsetting changes develop in the capital account.

Exchange Risk is an unexpected adverse movement in the exchange rate. Exchange risk includes an unexpected change in currency regime such as a change from a fixed to a floating exchange rate. Economic theory guides exchange rate risk analysis over longer periods of time. Short-term pressures, while influenced by economic fundamentals, tend to be driven by currency trading momentum best assessed by currency traders. In the short run, risk for many currencies can be eliminated at an acceptable cost through various hedging mechanisms and futures arrangements. Currency hedging becomes impractical over the life of the plant or similar direct investment, so exchange risk rises unless natural hedges can be developed.

Many of the quantitative measures used to identify transfer risk also identify exchange rate risk since a sharp depreciation of the currency can reduce some of the imbalances that lead to increased transfer risk. A country's exchange rate policy may help isolate exchange risk. Managed floats, where the government attempts to control the currency in a narrow trading range, tend to possess higher risk than fixed or currency board systems. Floating exchange rate systems generally sustain the lowest risk of producing an unexpected adverse exchange movement. The degree of over- or under-valuation of a currency also can help isolate exchange rate risk.

Location or Neighbourhood Risk includes spillover effects caused by problems in a region, in a country's trading partner, or in countries with similar perceived characteristics. While similar country characteristics may suggest susceptibility to contagion, this category provides analysts with one of the more difficult risk assessment problems.

Geographic position provides the simplest measure of location risk. Trading partners, international trading alliances, size, borders, and distance from economically or politically important countries or regions can also help define location risk.

Sovereign Risk concerns whether a government will be unwilling or unable to meet its loan obligations, or is likely to renege on loans it guarantees. Sovereign risk can relate to transfer risk in that a government may run out of foreign exchange due to unfavorable developments in its balance of payments. It also relates to political risk in that a government may decide not to honour its commitments for political reasons. The CRA literature designates sovereign risk as a separate category because a private lender faces a unique risk in dealing with a sovereign government. Should the government decide not to meet its obligations, the private lender realistically cannot sue the foreign government without its permission.

Sovereign-risk measures of a government's ability to pay are similar to transfer-risk measures. Measures of willingness to pay require an assessment of the history of a government's repayment performance, an analysis of the potential costs to the borrowing government of debt repudiation, and a study of the potential for debt rescheduling by consortiums of private lenders or international institutions. The international setting may further complicate sovereign risk. In a recent example, IMF guarantees to Brazil in late 1998 were designed to stop the spread of an international financial crisis. Had Brazil's imbalances developed before the Asian and Russian financial crises, Brazil probably would not have received the same level of support, and sovereign risk would have been higher.

Political Risk concerns risk of a change in political institutions stemming from a change in government control, social fabric, or other noneconomic factor. This category covers the potential for internal and external conflicts, expropriation risk and traditional political analysis. Risk assessment requires analysis of many factors, including the relationships of various groups in a country, the decision-making process in the government, and the history of the country. Insurance exists for some political risks, obtainable from a number of government agencies and international organizations.

Few quantitative measures exist to help assess political risk. Measurement approaches range from various classification methods, to surveys or analyses by political experts. Most services tend to use country experts who grade or rank multiple socio-political factors and produce a written analysis to accompany their grades or scales. Company analysts may also develop political risk estimates for their business through discussions with local country agents or visits to other companies operating similar businesses in the country. In many risk systems, analysts reduce political risk to some type of index or relative measure. Unfortunately, little theoretical guidance exists to help quantify political risk, so many "systems" prove difficult to replicate over time as various socio-political events ascend or decline in importance in the view of the individual analyst.

3

Investment

FOREIGN DIRECT INVESTMENT

Foreign direct investment refers to long term participation by country A into country B. It usually involves participation in management, joint-venture, transfer of technology and expertise. There are two types of FDI: inward foreign direct investment and outward foreign direct investment, resulting in a net FDI inflow. Foreign direct investment is a measure of foreign ownership of productive assets, such as factories, mines and land. Increasing foreign investment can be used as one measure of growing economic globalization. Figure shows net inflows of foreign direct investment as a percentage of gross domestic product. The largest flows of foreign investment occur between the industrialized countries. But flows to non-industrialized countries are increasing sharply.

US International Direct Investment Flows:

Period	FDI Outflow	FDI Inflows	Net
1960-69	$ 42.18 bn	$ 5.13 bn	+ $ 37.04 bn
1970-79	$ 122.72 bn	$ 40.79 bn	+ $ 81.93 bn
1980-89	$ 206.27 bn	$ 329.23 bn	- $ 122.96 bn
1990-99	$ 950.47 bn	$ 907.34 bn	+ $ 43.13 bn
2000-07	$ 1,629.05 bn	$ 1,421.31 bn	+ $ 207.74 bn
Total	$ 2,950.69 bn	$ 2,703.81 bn	+ $ 246.88 bn

TYPES

A foreign direct investor may be classified in any sector of the economy and could be any one of the following:

- An individual;
- A group of related individuals;
- An incorporated or unincorporated entity;
- A public company or private company;
- A group of related enterprises;
- A government body;
- An estate, trust or other societal organisation; or
- Any combination of the above.

METHODS

The foreign direct investor may acquire 10% or more of the voting power of an enterprise in an economy through any of the following methods:

- By incorporating a wholly owned subsidiary or company
- By acquiring shares in an associated enterprise
- Through a merger or an acquisition of an unrelated enterprise
- Participating in an equity joint venture with another investor or enterprise

Foreign direct investment incentives may take the following forms:

- Low corporate tax and income tax rates
- Lax holidays
- Other types of tax concessions
- Preferential tariffs
- Special economic zones
- EPZ - Export Processing Zones
- Bonded Warehouses
- Maquiladoras
- Investment financial subsidies
- Soft loan or loan guarantees
- Free land or land subsidies
- Relocation and expatriation subsidies
- Job training and employment subsidies
- Infrastructure subsidies
- RandD support
- Derogation from regulations

DEBATES ABOUT THE BENEFITS OF FDI FOR LOW-INCOME COUNTRIES

Some countries have put restrictions on FDI in certain sectors. India, with its restriction on FDI in the retail sector is an example. In a country like India, the "walmartization" of the country could have significant negative effects on the overall economy by reducing the number of people employed in the retail sector and depressing the income of people involved in the agriculture sector.

FOREIGN INSTITUTIONAL INVESTMENT

The term foreign institutional investment denotes all those investors or investment companies that are not located within the territory of the country in which they are investing. These are actually the outsiders in the financial markets of the particular company. Foreign institutional investment is a common term in the financial sector of India.

The type of institutions that are involved in the foreign institutional investment are as follows:

- Mutual Funds
- Hedge Funds
- Pension Funds
- Insurance Companies

The economies like India, which are growing very rapidly, are becoming hot favourite investment destinations for the foreign institutional investors. These markets have the potential to grow in the near future. This is the prime reason behind the growing interests of the foreign investors. The promise of rapid growth of the investable fund is tempting the investors and so they are coming in huge numbers to these countries. The money, which is coming through the foreign institutional investment is referred as 'hot money' because the money can be taken out from the market at anytime by these investors.

The foreign investment market was not so developed in the past. But once the globalization took the whole world in its grip, the diversified global market became united. Because of this the investment sector became very strong and at the same time allowed the foreigners to enter the national financial market.

At the same time the developing countries understood the value of foreign investment and allowed the foreign direct investment and foreign institutional investment in their financial markets. Although the foreign direct investments are long term investments but the foreign institutional investments are unpredictable. The Securities and Exchange Board of India looks after the foriegn institutional investments in India. SEBI has imposed several rules and regulations on these investments.

Some important facts about the foreign institutional investment:

- The number of registered foreign institutional investors on June 2007 has reached 1042 from 813 in 2006
- US $6 billion has been invested in equities by these investors
- The total amount of these investments in the Indian financial market till June 2007 has been estimated at US $53.06 billion
- The foreign institutional investors are preferring the construction sector, banking sector and the IT companies for the investments
- Most active foreign institutional investors in India are HSBC, Merrill Lynch, Citigroup, CLSA

FOREIGN COLLABORATION

Keeping these objectives in view, Joint Working Group on coal had been set up with France, Germany, Russia, Canada, Australia and China. Department of Coal is also the nodal Department for the Joint Commission with Poland. The priority areas, inter-alia, include acquisition of modern underground mining technology, introduction of high productive opencast mining technology, working undergr-ound in difficult geological conditions, fire control and mine safety. Training of Indian personnel as well as assimilation of the technology are an important consideration. With the liberalization of the economy, greater thrust is being given to get the foreign investments/assistance on the basis of cost competitiveness.

The latest policy pursued by CIL is to encourage technology up gradation through Global Tender. Bilateral co-operation, although limited, continues to play an important role for search of new technologies and process improvement. Global tender approach has been used towards introduction of high productivity Continuous Miners at SECL and WCL. Bilateral co-operation mode has been adopted for the introduction of PSLW mining at 3 mines in SECL.

COOPERATION WITH CANADA

The meeting of Indo-Canada Working Group on Coal was held in Canada during 24th -30th June, 2003. Indian delegation led by the then JSandFA and CMD, ECL discussed over Rajmahal Expansion Project of ECL during the meeting.

COOPERATION WITH FRANCE

France has developed expertise in thick seam underground mining with the introduction of advance technologies like Blasting Galleries and Longwall Sub-level Caving. It has assisted India in introduction of blasting gallery method at East Katras and Chora. France has also assisted in the introduction of sub-level caving technology at East Katras mine of Bharat Coking Coal Limited. France had also cooperated in the introduction of high face long wall mining technology in Kottadih Project of ECL. GDK-10 and GDK-8 incline projects in SCL were taken up for introducing blasting gallery technology in collaboration with France. These two projects have already been completed. SCCL has signed another contract for introducing Blasting Gallery method at VK-7 project.

In order to strengthen the cooperation between two countries and broaden the scope of cooperation especially in coal industry, a Joint Working Group on coal was constituted, which used to meet annually to address the various problems covering bilateral cooperation. In view of the declining cooperation with France in the field of coal, it has been decided to merge this Working Group with the proposed Working Group on Energy. Three meetings of Working Group on Energy have so far been held and the last meeting of the Working Group on Energy was held on 14th November, 2002 in New Delhi.

The 4th joint meeting of Indo-French Working Group was held from 7th to 9th April, 2004 at Paris in France. The delegation was led by Secretary in which Department of coal was represented by Joint Secretary.

The following issues were taken up in the joint meeting of working group:

- Power
- Petroleum, Gas and Liquified Natural Gas
- Security of big Hydel Power dams.
- Renewable energy: rural electrification, geothermal energy.
- Energy efficiency: clean development mechanism.
- Process of fly ash.

COOPERATION WITH U.K.

In January, 1997 an Indo-British Coal Forum was established to foster greater cooperation between the two countries in coal sector. The Forum provides a platform for mutual consultations and cooperation between the coal industries of both the countries under the auspices of the Govt. of the India and U.K.. The activities which are envisaged under the MOU include sharing of latest know-how technology, organization of meetings for exchange of information, identification of suitable projects as well as methods of funding, introduction of compatible technology for more efficient management in Indian Coal Industry and skill development etc. Ten meetings have been held till now in pursuance of these objectives. Tenth meeting of IBCF was held on 6-7th November, 2003 at New Delhi. As a follow-up of decisions taken in the meeting held on 6-7th November, 2003, an Inward Mission from Indian side visited UK in April, 2004. Apart from underground mining technologies, issues on stabilization of seams on fire, restoration and reclamation were discussed by the Mission. The report of the Inward Mining Mission is under finalization.

COOPERATION WITH POLAND

Prior to January 14, 2004, Ministry of Coal was acting as the nodal Ministry for Indo-Polish Joint Commission on Economic, Trade, Scientific and Technical Cooperation. The last meeting of the Joint Commission was held in January, 1996.

The Commission has 4 sub-committee on:

1. Coal Mining and power
2. Trade
3. Industry and
4. Science and Technology.

The Projects which were taken up earlier in the coal sector with Poland have since been completed. The Polish Coal Industry has offered their expertise in underground mining, Washery construction, Thermal Power Generation, mine safety and rescue. For furthering Indo-Polish Cooperation in the coal sector, it was decided by both sides to form a Working Group for coal sector. Two meetings of the Indo-Polish Working Group on Coal have so far been held and last meeting was held on 3-4th September, 2002 in New Delhi, India.

Ministry of External Affairs vide their D.O.No.184/FS/2004 dated January 14, 2004 has designated Ministry of Commerce and Industry as nodal agency for Indo-Polish Joint Commission for Economic, Trade, Scientific and Technical Cooperation from Indian side. A Review Meeting prior to the 15th Session of the Joint Commission was held in Warsaw, Poland from 21st-23rd April, 2004. The Department of Coal was represented by Director as Chairman of the Sub-Group on Coal, Mines and Power. Report in this regard is awaited.

COOPERATION WITH RUSSIA

The 4th meeting of Russian Indian Working Group on Metallurgy and Mines of the Indian-Russian Intergovernmental Commission for Trade, Economic, Scientific, Technical and Cultural Co-operation was held on 22nd and 23rd

October, 2008 at New Delhi. The Indian delegation was headed by Dr. Dalip Singh, Joint Secretary, in the Ministry of Steel of the Indian Government. The Russian delegation was headed by Mr. A.V. Pinchuk, Deputy Head of the Department of Basic Industries, Ministry of Industry and Trade of the Russian Federation.

In the field of Coal Industry it was informed that:

- The Russian side is interest in participating in tendering for design and construction of the existing coal mining enterprises in India. Indian side intimated that CIL's policy is to procure equipment, materials and spare parts through tendering process/ Global tendering. Amarpali and Magadh OC project of CCL will be developed through outsourcing. Russia was requested to participate in the tendering process. Representative of Russian companies in India will be in touch with CIL about the tenders that are likely to be floated.
- Indian side requested Russian side to expedite response from Zarubezhugól Company in respect of Indian investment in the coal sector of the Russian economy.
- Indian side informed that the issue of MoUs between CMPDIL and Giproshakaht, VNIMI and Skochinsky on various issues are under review/examination by CMPDIL.
- It was noted that Indian side will make official request for training of Indian specialists at the Russian Coal Mining enterprises with specific areas in which training is required.
- It was noted the need to take on board more projects and proposals in the context of the ambitious goals set for Indo-Russian trade and commerce and resolved to take further action towards achieving the same.

The Russian side will look into these new areas of technological co-operation. The 5th meeting of the Working Group will be held in Moscow in 2009.

COOPERATION WITH KAZAKHSTAN

A proposal has been received from embassy of the Republic of Kazakhstan regarding various projects for Industrial and Innovation development of Kazakhstan. There is a project relating to extraction and realization of coal.

COOPETATION WITH MOZAMBIQUE

Memorandum of Understanding for co-operation for development of coal mining in Mozambique exists between Govt. of India and Govt. of Mozambique.

2nd meeting of Indo-Mozambique Joint Working Group was held in New Delhi on 30th March, 2009. In the meeting CIL made 2 presentations. The first one elaborated the core competence of CIL in the field of exploration, mine planning and mining, CIL's offer in the areas of Rehabilitation and Resettlement, Corporate Social Responsibility, Community Development etc. in Mozambique. The second presentation explained, in details, the progress in bilateral cooperation between two countries since the first JWG meeting held in Maputo in May, 2006. The presentation also covered many aspects of cooperation including training to be offered to concerned people of Mozambique.

The Mozambique delegation under the leadership of Mr. Obete Francisco Matine also visited Nigahi OCP and CHP, Bina CPP of NCL, NCL hospital, CETI Singrauli and Community Development Sites, Tree plantation etc. from 1st April to 3rd April, 2009.

Initiatives have been undertaken by CIL through Ministry of Coal to acquire coal concessions in Mozambique. CIL has emerged as the successful bidder in the global tender process run by Govt. of Mozambique, for allocation of prospecting licenses for coal concessions in Mozambique. CIL has been awarded prospecting license for two coal concessions in Mozambique. CIL will shortly undertake the activities of exploration and formation of a company in Mozambique.

Further, to promote Indian interest in Mozambique, Govt. of India is considering approval of sovereign fund for development to Apex Planning Organization and Apex

Training Organization to look after scientific mine planning in coal projects in Mozambique as well as train people in different aspects of coal mining.

COOPERATION WITH GERMANY

The Indo-German Working Group on coal has been meeting regularly and alternatively in Germany and in India. The 17th meeting of the Indo-German Working Group on Coal, constituted under the auspices of the German-Indian Joint Commission for Industrial Economic Cooperation, was held in Kolkata on 7th November, 2008.

After detailed discussions, following areas were identified to strengthen the working group cooperation efforts:

- Developing technology, essential for deep shaft sinking for extraction of deep seated coal.
- Technology for hard group management in coal mines.
- Establishing techniques to assess and extract Coal Bed Methane/Coal Mine Methane.
- Underground Coal Gasification for coal resources at greater depth/isolated deposits.
- 3D seismic survey with borehole imaging system.
- Ventilation Air Methane —mitigation and utilization of Indian Mining scenario.
- In Seam seismic survey for underground coal mining operation.
- Joint Venture for mining abroad with technological cooperation from Germany.
- Cooperation in capacity building specially in underground mines.
- High pressure water jet technology for extinguishing mine fire and excavation.
- Exchange of expertise in coal mine safety, technology and equipment through training, seminar, workshop etc.

It was agreed that the next meeting of the Working Group will be held in April, 2010 at Munich, Germany.

COOPERATION WITH AUSTRALIA

The 5th Australia-India Joint Working Group on Energy and Minerals was held on 12-3 July, 2007 at Canberra, Australia. Australia outlined the importance of coal as an export commodity and a major source of low cost power generation.

Both delegations highlighted the outcomes of the Australia-India Coal and Mining Forum held in February, 2006 in India and the collaborative activity which has occurred since.

Australia presented the findings of the Minerals Council of Australia and Federation of Indian Mineral Industries joint report on trade, investment and regulatory issues impeding two-way trade and investment including:

- Indian companies report no significant barriers or constraints to trade and investment into Australia apart from shortages of skilled labour and some minerals inputs;
- Significant impediments remain for trade and investment in India, particularly high WTO bindings for tariffs on many products, onerous requirements on foreign companies with existing or former joint ventures in the Indian market.
- Delays and unpredictable costs due to the actions of sub-national governments and high costs associated with inefficient customs clearance systems.

Australia and India agreed to support further work to develop industry collaboration on mining technology services and equipment and export opportunities – under the framework of the Australia-India Resources Strategy and/or as part of a broader Asia Pacific Partnership strategy in relation to sustainable use of fossil fuels.

Action Plan

An MoU on "Action Plan for Indo-Australian collaboration on the Coal Sector" was signed on 5th November, 2008 between Ministry of Coal and Department of Resources, Energy and Tourism. The main objectives of the Action Plan are to enhance opportunities in two way trade and investments; increase bilateral cooperation and collaboration in the coal sector, including mining services; identify and address barriers to trade ad investment opportunities.

The key areas that this Action Plan will focus upon are:

- Mining Technology Services
- Underground Coal Mining
- Underground Coal Gasification
- Coal to Liquid Technologies
- Coal Bed Methane Technologies
- Coal Washeries
- Abandoned Coal Mine Rehabilitation
- Sustainable Mining Practices
- Skilling, Training and Capacity Building

The activities envisaged under this Action Plan in the year 2008-09 are:

- Encouragement of two-way visits and promotion of information exchanges by Ministers, senior officials, industry delegations, scientists and researchers working on the coal sector.
- Continued Bi-lateral collaboration on existing projects under the Asia Pacific Partnership on clean development and climate, coal mining task force.
- Follow-up conference to the bi-lateral Coal and Mining Conference held in February, 2006 and encouragement of attendance at other premier coal related conference in India and Australia.

The 6th Meeting of the India-Australia Joint Working Group on Energy and Minerals was held on 17th March, 2009 in New Delhi.

The Joint Working Group meeting discussed:

- Recent trade and Investment developments
- The implications of the global financial crisis on the resources and energy sectors
- Recent energy and mineral policy developments

The Joint Working Group agreed to activities in 2009-11 under the Action Plan signed between Australia and India in November, 2008.

COOPERATION WITH CHINA

The 9th meeting of the Indo-China Joint Working Group on Coal held during 9th – 11th February 2004 in India. Chinese delegation was led by Mr. Zhao Tiechui, Deputy Administrator of State of Administration of Work Safety State Administration of Coal Mines Safety, PR China and Indian delegation led by Dr. P.K.Mishra, Secretary and the following bilateral issues/ projects were discussed in the meeting.

- BCCL -Moonidih project-Seam RXVI Top.
- Jhanjra project of ECL.
- Performance of existing Longwall faces at SECL.
- Co-manufacturing of spares in India.
- Spare parts catalogue and price list.
- Short Longwall equipment for Balrampur project of SECL.
- The strengthening of the power support of three Longwall projects at SECL.
- Foreclosure of Deferred Guarantee Payment issued by SBI to CMEI&E towards 3 sets of Longwall equipment of SECL.
- Hard Roof management techniques of Churcha west mine of SECL.
- Development of opencast mine in China with co-operation from Indian side.
- Re-training and Rehabilitation of mine workers.
- Resin capsule manufacturing.
- Madhuban project.
- Co-manufacturing of spare parts.
- Short supply of spares.
- Joint review on status of Longwalls supplied by CME.
- Extraction of pillars developed by Board and pillar by Longwall equipment.
- Longwall mining in deep seated reserves.
- Extraction of deep seated and coastal lignite deposits by hydro excavation technology.
- Latest reconditioning technique to improve the life of reconditioned belt from 50% to 80% of new one.

- Method of Fly Ash Utilization from lignite based thermal Power stations.
- Extraction and utilization of Lignite Bed Methane.
- Method of Marcasite segregation from RCM Lignite.

A 14 member Chinese delegation led by Mr. Hou Shenjian, Vice President of China National Administration of Coal Geology visited Ministry of Coal on 27th October, 2005. Secretary met the delegation and briefly interacted with members, followed by formal presentation on coal sector in India by Shri S. Chaudhury, Chairman-cum-Managing Director, CMPDIL.

After presentation covering areas like coal exploration, demand and supply, emerging importance of coal as primary fuel source etc. both sides interacted and exchanged information relating to coal production, technology, prospecting, exploration etc. Useful information was exchanged in general and inputs obtained would be useful in future interaction/exchange. First Secretary Mr. Cao Jianru of Chinese Embassy was also present during the visit of the delegation to the Ministry.

The 10th meeting of the Indo-China Joint Working Group on Coal was held during 10th – 11th November 2005 in Shanghai, PR China. Indian delegation was led by Shri P.C. Parakh, Secretary and Chinese delegation was led by Mr. Zhao Tiechui, Administrator of State of Administration of Work Safety State Administration of Coal Mines Safety, PR China.

The following areas were discussed in the meeting:

- Exchange of coal mining technology, equipments and coal mine safety.
- Cooperation in Coal Bed Methane, Underground Coal gasification and Coal liquefaction.
- Cooperation in capacity building.
- Promotion of investment opportunities.
- Retraining and rehabilitation of mining workers.

COOPERATION WITH USA

Indo-US Coal Advisory Group was constituted vide letter no. 14020/1/99-CPD dated 21st June, 2001. The first meeting of this Indo-US CAG was held at Kolkata between April 2nd to 5th, 2002 where it was, interalia, decided that potential specific sites and other relevant background information could be provided by the Indian side for computing software for mine planning and operation management, a proposal on mine waste/reject utilisation could also be considered, along with support on a joint US-India demonstration project on selective mining and improved coal sampling processes as per standard US experiences.

The second meeting of the Indo-US CAG was held at Washington DC between April 2nd to 7th, 2003 and the following areas of bilateral co-operation were agreed upon:

- Waste coal utilisation where a preliminary feasibility report for a specific project dealing with mine waste and/or washery rejects would be prepared by the Indian side, with US side proving an example to facilitate the process and later running test samples from India for utilisation potential.
- Mine planning and operation management where the US side would try to identify high level mine planning and designed and operation planning software for use in Indian mines so that existing software in India example MINEX and SURPAC were upgraded.
- Selective mining involving multi agency initiative to obtain support for implementing a selective mining demonstration project in India.

Subsequently, an MOU was also signed between the Ministry of Coal and the Department of Energy of the US on Energy Consultations and Information Exchange.

The areas of consultation and information exchange includes:

- Coal Science with emphasis on projection, combustion, coal structure and related chemical and thermo physical properties.
- Process modelling for advanced fossil related technology.
- Impact on boilers by the use of variable ash content control including high ash content.

- Coal cleaning, grinding and preparation for utilisation.
- Status of fuel combustion projects including cleanup and environmental effects.

COOPERATION WITH SOUTH AFRICA

A Working Group was constituted on 3rd March, 2003 Chaired by the Secretary, Ministry of Coal, Govt. of India with Director General Republic of South Africa as Co-Chairman.

The following areas were identified for co operation by the visiting South Africa delegation in August, 2002.

- Mechanisation in Bord and Pillar System of Mining.
- Beneficiation of Coal
- Technology for conversion from coal to oil.

Govt. of South Africa has been requested for an early convenient date and place for the meeting of the Working Group of Coal between the two countries. Response is awaited.

SHORT INVESTMENT

In finance, short selling is the practice of selling assets, usually securities, that have been borrowed from a third party with the intention of buying identical assets back at a later date to return to the lender. The short seller hopes to profit from a decline in the price of the assets between the sale and the repurchase, as the seller will pay less to buy the assets than the seller received on selling them. Conversely, the short seller will incur a loss if the price of the assets rises. Other costs of shorting may include a fee for borrowing the assets and payment of any dividends paid on the borrowed assets. Shorting and going short also refer to entering into any derivative or other contract under which the investor profits from a fall in the value of an asset.

Going short can be contrasted with the more conventional practice of"going long", whereby an investor profits from any increase in the price of the asset.

CONCEPT

To profit from a decrease in the price of a security, a short seller can borrow the security and sell it, expecting that it will be cheaper to repurchase in the future. When the seller decides that the time is right, the seller buys equivalent securities and returns them to the lender. The process relies on the fact that the securities are fungible; the term"borrowing" is used in the sense of borrowing $10, where the same or different $10 note can be returned to the lender assuming the value of the note is the same that it was at the time of the contract's execution.

A short seller typically borrows through a broker, who is usually holding the securities for another investor who owns the securities; the broker itself seldom purchases the securities to lend to the short seller. The lender does not lose the right to sell the securities while they have been lent, as the broker will usually hold a large pool of such securities for a number of investors which, as such securities are fungible, can instead be transferred to any buyer. In most market conditions there is a ready supply of securities to be borrowed, held by pension funds, mutual funds and other investors.

The performance of buying back the securities that were sold short is called"covering the short" or"covering the position". A short position can be covered at any time before the securities are due to be returned. Once the position is covered, the short seller will not be affected by any subsequent rises or falls in the price of the securities, as he already holds the securities required to repay the lender.

The terms shorting and going short are also used as blanket terms for tactics that allow an investor to gain from the decline in price of a security. Such tactics are generally based on a derivative contract, such as an option, a future or a similar synthetic position.

For example, a put option consists of the right to sell an asset at a given strike price; the owner of the option therefore benefits when the market price of the asset falls below that price, as he can buy the asset at the lower price and sell it under the option at the strike price. Similarly, a short position in a futures contract means the holder of the position has an obligation to sell the underlying asset later at a given price; if the price falls below the given price, the person with the short position can buy the asset at the lower price and sell it under the future at the higher price.

Worked Example

If shares in C&Company currently trade at $10 per share, a short seller can borrow 100 shares of C&Company and immediately sell those shares for a total of $1,000. If the price of the shares falls to $8 per share, the short seller can buy 100 shares back for $800, return the shares to lender and keep the $200 profit. The lender accepts the return of the same number of shares as it originally lent, despite the fact that the market value of the shares has decreased. However, if the price of the shares in C&Company instead rises to $25 per share following the short sale, and the short seller is required to return the shares, the short seller would have to buy back 100 shares at $2,500 and would incur a loss of $1,500.

Comparison with Long Positions

Short selling is the opposite of "going long". A short seller takes a negative, or "bearish" stance, believing that the price of a security will fall. Investors who employ short selling often use it to allow them to profit on trading in securities which they believe are overvalued, just as traditional long investors attempt to profit on securities which are undervalued by buying them.

Because a short position is the opposite of a long position, many features of the position are reversed in comparison. In particular, the profit is limited to the value of the security, but the loss is unlimited. In practice, as the price of a security rises the short seller will receive a margin call from the broker, demanding that the short seller either cover his short position or provide additional cash in order to meet the margin requirement for the security, which effectively places a limit on the amount that can be lost.

MECHANISM

Short selling stock consists of the following:

- The investor instructs the broker to sell the shares

and the proceeds are credited to his broker's account at the firm upon which the firm can earn interest. Generally, the short seller does not earn interest on the short proceeds.

- Upon completion of the sale, the investor has 3 days to borrow the shares. If required by law, the investor first ensures that cash or equity is on deposit with his brokerage firm as collateral for the initial short margin requirement. Some short sellers, mainly firms and hedge funds, participate in the practice of naked short selling, where the shorted shares are not borrowed or delivered.
- The investor may close the position by buying back the shares. If the price has dropped, he makes a profit. If the stock advanced, he takes a loss.
- Finally, the investor may return the shares to the lender or stay short indefinitely.
- At any time, the lender may call for the return of his shares e.g. because he wants to sell them. The borrower must buy shares on the market and return them to the lender. When the broker completes this transaction automatically, it is called a 'buy-in'.

Shorting Stock in the U.S.

In the U.S., in order to sell stocks short, the seller must arrange for a broker-dealer to confirm that it is able to make delivery of the shorted securities. This is referred to as a "locate." Brokers have a variety of means to borrow stocks in order to facilitate locates and make good delivery of the shorted security.

The vast majority of stocks borrowed by U.S. brokers come from loans made by the leading custody banks and fund management companies. Institutions often lend out their shares in order to earn a little extra money on their investments. These institutional loans are usually arranged by the custodian who holds the securities for the institution. In an institutional stock loan, the borrower puts up cash collateral, typically 102% of the value of the stock. The cash collateral is then invested by the lender, who often rebates part of the interest to the borrower. The interest that is kept by the lender is the compensation to the lender for the stock loan.

Brokerage firms can also borrow stocks from the accounts of their own customers. Typical margin account agreements give brokerage firms the right to borrow customer shares without notifying the customer. In general, brokerage accounts are only allowed to lend shares from accounts for which customers have "debit balances", meaning they have borrowed from the account. SEC Rule 15c3-3 imposes such severe restrictions on the lending of shares from cash accounts or excess margin shares from margin accounts that most brokerage firms do not bother except in rare circumstances.

Most brokers will allow retail customers to borrow shares to short a stock only if one of their own customers has purchased the stock on margin. Brokers will go through the "locate" process outside their own firm to obtain borrowed shares from other brokers only for their large institutional customers.

Stock exchanges such as the NYSE or the NASDAQ typically report the "short interest" of a stock, which gives the number of shares that have been legally sold short as a per cent of the total float.

Alternatively, these can also be expressed as the short interest ratio, which is the number of shares legally sold short as a multiple of the average daily volume. These can be useful tools to spot trends in stock price movements but in order to be reliable, investors must also ascertain the number of shares brought into existence by naked shorters. Investors are cautioned to remember that for every share that has been shorted, a 'shadow owner' exists who also is part of the universe of owners of that stock, i.e. Despite not having any voting rights, he has not relinquished his interest and some rights in that stock.

Securities Lending

When a security is sold, the seller is contractually obligated to deliver it to the buyer. If a seller sells a security short without owning it first, the seller needs to borrow the security from a third party to fulfill its obligation. Otherwise, the seller will "fail to deliver," the transaction will not settle, and the seller may be subject to a claim from its counterparty. Certain large holders of securities, such as a custodian or investment management firm, often lend out these securities to gain extra income, a process known as securities lending. The lender receives a fee for this service. Similarly, retail investors can sometimes make an extra fee when their broker wants to borrow their securities. This is only possible when the investor has full title of the security, so it cannot be used as collateral for margin buying.

Sources of Short Interest Data

Time delayed short interest data is available in a number of countries, including the US, the UK, Hong Kong, and Spain. Some market participants believe that stock lending data provides a good proxy for short interest levels. The amount of stocks being shorted on a global basis has increased in recent years for various structural reasons.

Short Selling Terms

Days to Cover is a numerical term that describes the relationship between the amount of shares in a given equity that have been legally short sold and the number of days of typical trading that it would require to 'cover' all legal short positions outstanding. For example, if there are ten million shares of XYZ Inc. that are currently legally short sold and the average daily volume of XYZ shares traded each day is one million, it would require ten days of trading for all legal short positions to be covered.

Short Interest is a numerical term that relates the number of shares in a given equity that have been legally shorted divided by the total shares outstanding for the company, usually expressed as a per cent. For example, if there are ten million shares of XYZ Inc. that are currently legally short sold and the total, number of shares issued by the company is one hundred million; the Short Interest is 10%. If however, shares are being created through naked short selling, "fails" data must be accessed to assess accurately the true level of short interest.

Major lenders:

- Merrill Lynch
- State Street Corporation
- JP Morgan Chase
- Northern Trust
- Fortis
- Citibank
- Bank of New York Mellon Corporation
- UBS AG

Naked

A naked short sale occurs when a security is sold short without borrowing the security within a set time, 3 days in the US. This means that the buyer of such a short is buying the short-seller's promise to deliver a share, rather than buying the share itself. The short-seller's promise is known as a hypothecated share.

When the holder of the underlying stock receives a dividend, the holder of the hypothecated share would receive an equal dividend from the short seller.

Naked shorting has been made illegal except where allowed under limited circumstances by market makers. It is detected by the Depository Trust and Clearing Corporation as a "failure to deliver" or simply "fail." While many fails are settled in a short time, some have been allowed to linger in the system.

In the US, arranging to borrow a security before a short sale is called a locate. In 2005, to prevent widespread failure to deliver securities, the U.S. Securities and Exchange Commission put in place Regulation SHO, intended to prevent investors from selling some stocks short before doing a locate. Requirements that are more stringent were put in place in September 2008, ostensibly to prevent the practice from exacerbating market declines. The rules were made permanent in 2009. Some have defended the practice of naked short selling against these restrictions.

FEES

When a broker facilitates the delivery of a client's short sale, the client is charged a fee for this service, usually a standard commission similar to that of purchasing a similar security.

If the short position begins to move against the holder of the short position, money will be removed from the holder's cash balance and moved to his or her margin balance. If short shares continue to rise in price, and the holder does not have sufficient funds in the cash account to cover the position, the holder will begin to borrow on margin for this purpose, thereby accruing margin interest charges. These are computed and charged just as for any other margin debit.

When a security's ex-dividend date passes, the dividend is deducted from the shortholder's account and paid to the person from whom the stock was borrowed.

For some brokers, the short seller may not earn interest on the proceeds of the short sale or use it to reduce outstanding margin debt. These brokers may not pass this benefit on to the retail client unless the client is very large. This means an individual short-selling $1000 of stock will lose the interest to be earned on the $1000 cash balance in his or her account.

DIVIDENDS AND VOTING RIGHTS

Where shares have been shorted and the company which issues the shares distributes a dividend, the question arises as to who receives the dividend. The new buyer of the shares, who is the "holder of record" and holds the shares outright, will receive the dividend from the company. However, the lender, who may hold its shares in a margin account with a prime broker and is unlikely to be aware that these particular shares are being lent out for shorting, also expects to receive a dividend.

The short seller will therefore pay to the lender an amount equal to the dividend in order to compensate, though as this payment does not come from the company it is not technically a dividend as such. The short seller is therefore said to be "short the dividend".

A similar issue comes up with the voting rights attached to the shorted shares. Unlike a dividend, voting rights cannot legally be synthesized and so the buyer of the shorted share, as the holder of record, controls the voting rights. The owner of a margin account from which the shares were lent will have agreed in advance to relinquish voting rights to shares during the period of any short sale. As noted earlier, victims of Naked Shorting attacks sometimes report that the number of votes cast is greater than the number of shares issued by the company.

MARKETS

Futures and Options Contracts

When trading futures contracts, being 'short' means having the legal obligation to deliver something at the expiration of the contract, although the holder of the short position may alternately buy back the contract prior to expiration instead of making delivery. Short futures transactions are often used by producers of a commodity to fix the future price of goods they have not yet produced. Shorting a futures contract is sometimes also used by those holding the underlying asset as a temporary hedge against price declines. Shorting futures may also be used for speculative trades, in which case the investor is looking to profit from any decline in the price of the futures contract prior to expiration.

An investor can also purchase a put option, giving that investor the right to sell the underlying asset at a fixed price. In the event of a market decline, the option holder may exercise these put options, obliging the counterparty to buy the underlying asset at the agreed upon price, which would then be higher than the current quoted spot price of the asset.

Currency

Selling short on the currency markets is different from selling short on the stock markets. Currencies are traded in pairs, each currency being priced in terms of another. In this way, selling short on the currency markets is identical to going long on stocks. Novice traders or stock traders can be confused by the failure to recognize and understand this point: a contract is always long in terms of one medium and short another.

When the exchange rate has changed, the trader buys the first currency again; this time he gets more of it, and pays back the loan. Since he got more money than he had borrowed initially, he makes money. Of course, the reverse can also occur.

An example of this is as follows: Let us say a trader wants to trade with the US dollar and the Indian rupee currencies. Assume that the current market rate is USD $1 to Rs.50 and the trader borrows Rs.100. With this, he buys USD $2. If the next day, the conversion rate becomes USD $1 to Rs.51, then the trader sells his USD $2 and gets Rs.102. He returns Rs.100 and keeps the Rs.2 profit.

One may also take a short position in a currency using futures or options; the preceding method is used to bet on the spot price, which is more directly analogous to selling a stock short.

RISK

It is important to note that buying shares has a very different risk profile from selling short. In the former case, losses are limited but gains are unlimited. In short selling, this is reversed, meaning the possible gains are limited and the seller can lose more than the original value of the share, with, in theory, no upper limit. For this reason, short selling is usually used as part of a hedge rather than as an investment in its own right.

Many short sellers place a "stop order" with their stockbroker after selling a stock short. This is an order to the brokerage to cover the position if the price of the stock should rise to a certain level, in order to limit the loss and avoid the problem of unlimited liability. In some cases, if the stock's price skyrockets, the stockbroker may decide to cover the short seller's position immediately and without his consent, in order to guarantee that the short seller will be able to make good on his debt of shares.

The risk of large potential losses through short selling inspired financier Daniel Drew to warn:

"He who sells what isn't his'n, Must buy it back or go to pris'n"

Short selling is sometimes referred to as a "negative income investment strategy" because there is no potential for dividend income or interest income. One's return is strictly from capital gains.

Short sellers must be aware of the potential for a short squeeze. When the price of a stock rises significantly, some people who are shorting the stock will cover their positions to limit their losses; others may be forced to close their position to meet a margin call; others may be forced to cover, subject to the terms under which they borrowed the stock, if the person who lent the stock wishes to sell and take a profit. Since covering their positions involves buying shares, the short squeeze causes an ever further rise in the stock's price, which in turn may trigger additional covering. Because of this, most short sellers restrict their activities to heavily traded stocks, and they keep an eye on the "short interest" levels of their short investments. Short interest is defined as the total number of shares that have been legally sold short, but not covered.

A short squeeze can be deliberately induced. This can happen when large investors notice significant short positions, and buy many shares, with the intent of selling the position at a profit to the short sellers who will be panicked by the initial uptick or who are forced to cover their short positions in order to avoid margin calls.

Another disadvantage is that if a stock becomes "hard to borrow", which is defined by the SEC and based on lack of availability, a broker will charge a hard to borrow fee daily, for any day the SEC declares a share is hard to borrow. This occurs without any notification to short sellers. Additionally, a broker may be required to cover a short seller's position at any time. The short seller receives a warning from the broker that they are "failing to deliver" stock, which will then lead to the buy-in.

Short sellers have to deliver the securities to their broker eventually. At that point, they will need money to buy them, so there is a credit risk for the broker. To reduce this, the short seller has to keep a margin with the broker.

Short sellers tend to temper overvaluation by selling into exuberance. Likewise, short sellers are said to provide price support by buying when negative sentiment is exacerbated after a significant price decline. Short selling can have negative implications if it causes a premature or unjustified share price collapse when the fear of cancellation due to bankruptcy becomes contagious.

STRATEGIES

Speculation

A seller intentionally takes on directional risk in the belief that the value of the shorted asset will fall.

Hedging

Hedging often represents a means of minimizing the risk from a more complex set of transactions.

Examples of this are:

- A farmer who has just planted his wheat wants to lock in the price at which he can sell after the harvest. He would take a short position in wheat futures.
- A market maker in corporate bonds is constantly trading bonds when clients want to buy or sell. This can create substantial bond positions. The largest risk is that interest rates overall move. The trader can hedge this risk by selling government bonds short against his long positions in corporate bonds. In this way, the risk that remains is credit risk of the corporate bonds.
- An options trader may short shares in order to remain delta neutral so that he is not exposed to risk from price movements in the stocks that underlie his options

Arbitrage

A short seller may be trying to benefit from market inefficiencies arising from the mispricing of certain products.

Examples of this are:

- An arbitrageur who buys long futures contracts on a US Treasury security, and sells short the underlying US Treasury security.

Against the Box

One variant of selling short involves a long position. "Selling short against the box" consists of holding a long position on which the shares have already risen, whereupon one then enters a short sell order for an equal amount of shares. The term box alludes to the days when a safe deposit box was used to store shares. The purpose of this technique is to lock in profits on the long position without having to sell that position. Once the short position has been entered, it serves to balance the long position taken earlier. Thus, from that point in time, the profit is locked in, regardless of further fluctuations in the underlying share price. For example, one can ensure a profit in this way, while delaying sale until the subsequent tax year.

U.S. investors considering entering into a "short against the box" transaction should be aware of the tax consequences of this transaction. Unless certain conditions are met, the IRS deems a "short against the box" position to be a "constructive sale" of the long position, which is a taxable event. These conditions include a requirement that the short position be closed out within 30 days of the end of the year and that the investor must hold their long position, without entering into any hedging strategies, for a minimum of 60 days after the short position has been closed.

THE REGULATORY RESPONSE

In the US, Regulation SHO was the SEC's first update to short selling restrictions since 1938. It established "locate" and "close-out" requirements for broker-dealers, in an effort to curb naked short selling. Compliance with the regulation began on January 3, 2005. In the US, initial public offering s cannot be sold short for a month after they start trading. This mechanism is in place to ensure a degree of price stability during a company's initial trading period. However, some brokerages that specialize in penny stocks have used the lack of short selling during this month to pump and dump thinly traded IPOs. Canada and other countries do allow selling IPOs short.

In the UK, the Financial Services Authority had a moratorium on short selling 29 leading financial stocks, effective from 2300 GMT, 19 September 2008 until 16 January 2009. After the ban was lifted, John McFall, chairman of the Treasury Select Committee, House of Commons, made clear in public statements and a letter to the FSA that he believed it ought to be extended. In the US, a similar response was made by the Securities and Exchange Commission with a ban on short selling on 799 financial stocks from 19 September 2008 until 2 October 2008. Greater penalties for naked shorting, by mandating delivery of stocks at clearing time, were also introduced. Some state governors have been urging state pension bodies to refrain from lending stock for shorting purposes.

Soon thereafter, between 19 and 21 September 2008, Australia temporarily banned short selling,, and later placed an indefinite ban on naked short selling. The ban on short selling was further extended for another 28 days on 21 October 2008.Germany, Ireland, Switzerland and Canada banned short selling leading financial stocks, and France, the Netherlands and Belgium banned naked short selling leading financial stocks.

By contrast, Chinese regulators have responded by allowing short selling, along with a package of other market reforms.

An assessment of the effect of a ban on short-selling that was enacted in many countries in the fall of 2008 showed that it had only "little impact" on the movements of stocks, with stock prices moving in the same way as they would have moved anyhow, but the ban reduced volume and liquidity. By December, countries in Europe were considering to remove the ban, while the ban in the US was already lifted in October 2008. The SEC proposed new restrictions on short selling in April 2009.

VIEWS OF SHORT SELLING

Advocates of short selling say that the practice is an 'essential' part of the price discovery mechanism. Financial researchers at Duke University said in a study that short interest is an indicator of poor future stock performance and that short sellers exploit market mistakes about firms' fundamentals.

Such noted investors as Seth Klarman and Warren Buffett have said that short sellers help the market. Klarman argued that short sellers are a useful counterweight to the widespread bullishness on Wall Street, while Buffett believes that short sellers are useful in uncovering fraudulent accounting and other problems at companies.

Shortseller James Chanos received widespread publicity when he was an early critic of the accounting practices of Enron Corp.

Chanos responds to critics of short-selling by pointing to the critical role they played in identifying problems at Enron, Boston Market and other "financial disasters" over the years. Commentator Jim Cramer has expressed concern about short selling and started a petition calling for the reintroduction of the uptick rule.

Individual short sellers have been subject to criticism and even litigation. Short seller Manuel P. Asensio engaged in a lengthy legal battle with the pharmaceutical manufacturer Hemispherx Biopharma. Short seller Anthony Elgindy was subjected to regulatory sanctions before he was sentenced to prison in 2005 for racketeering conspiracy, securities fraud, wire fraud and extortion. His conviction and sentence was later upheld by an appeals court in New York.

LONG TERM INVESTMENT

Planning for your future and retirement relies on planning the right kinds of long term investments. There are many different types of long term financing investments, and everyone needs to have some sort of investments for their future. Planning your retirement and long term investments go hand in hand.

IMPORTANCE OF LONG TERM INVESTMENTS

Let's face it. You will not be able to work forever. No matter how healthy you are, there will come a time when you will not be able to work, due to health problems or simply aging. What will you do for an income when the time comes to retire? This is why planning your long term investments carefully is so important.

Maybe you think you will be able to rely on Medicare and social security to take care of you during your retirement. Well, if that is your plan, it is time to look at the news. Social security is in trouble.

Politicians are trying to repair the problem, but chances are in another twenty years, or even less, there will be little to nothing left for you in the social security budget.

Finally, you never know what the future is going to hold. Will you stay healthy? Or, will you have some serious medical expenses that you will need to have finances for. Long term investments give you the security to know that in dire circumstances, money is there.

LONG TERM INVESTMENT STRATEGIES

So, you realise that you need to start looking into long term investments.

But where do you start? How do you know which investments are the best long term investments? Should you use a broker, or do it on your own. Here are some of the most tried and true long term investment strategies.

START BY SETTING GOALS

As with any other type of investing, proper long term investments start by setting proper goals. How much do you want to have when you retire?

What age do you want to retire? How much should you invest monthly to reach that goal? Are you willing to do your own investing, or do you want someone to show you the ropes. Write these goals down to help guide you as you choose your investments.

CHOOSE THE RIGHT FIRM

If you decide to seek help looking for your investments, choosing the right firm is important. Make sure you choose a firm that will follow your investment goals. They should work with you to find the best investments, not against you. You should feel like you are in control, even with their help.

4

Multilateral Financial Institution

WORLD BANK AND INTERNATIONAL MONETARY FUND

WORLD BANK

World Bank is a term used to describe an international financial institution that provides leveraged loans to developing countries for capital programmes. The World Bank has a stated goal of reducing poverty.

The World Bank differs from the World Bank Group, in that the World Bank comprises only two institutions: the International Bank for Reconstruction and Development and the International Development Association, whereas the latter incorporates these two in addition to three more: International Finance Corporation, Multilateral Investment Guarantee Agency, and International Centre for Settlement of Investment Disputes.

The World Bank is one of five institutions created at the Bretton Woods Conference in 1944. The International Monetary Fund, a related institution, is the second. Delegates from many countries attended the Bretton Woods Conference. The most powerful countries in attendance were the United States and United Kingdom which dominated negotiations.

Although both are based in Washington, D.C., the World Bank is by custom headed by an American, while the IMF is led by a European.

From its conception until 1967 the bank undertook a relatively low level of lending. Fiscal conservatism and careful screening of loan applications was common. Bank staff attempted to balance the priorities of providing loans for reconstruction and development with the need to instill confidence in the bank.

Bank president John McCloy selected France to be the first recipient of World Bank aid; two other applications from Poland and Chile were rejected. The loan was for $987 million, half the amount requested and came with strict conditions. Staff from the World Bank monitored the use of the funds, ensuring that the French government would present a balanced budget and give priority of debt repayment to the World Bank over other governments. The United States State Department told the French government that communist elements within the Cabinet needed to be removed. The French Government complied with this diktat and removed the Communist coalition government. Within hours the loan to France was approved.

The Marshall Plan of 1947 caused lending by the bank to change as many European countries received aid that competed with World Bank loans. Emphasis was shifted to non-European countries and until 1968, loans were earmarked for projects that would enable a borrower country to repay loans.

From 1968 to 1980 the bank concentrated on meeting the basic needs of people in the developing world. The size and number of loans to borrowers was greatly increased as loan targets expanded from infrastructure into social services and other sectors.

These changes can be attributed to Robert McNamara who was appointed to the presidency in 1968 by Lyndon B. Johnson. McNamara imported a technocratic managerial style to the Bank that he had used as United States Secretary of Defence and President of the Ford Motor Company. McNamara shifted bank policy towards measures such as building schools and hospitals, improving literacy and agricultural reform. McNamara created a new system of gathering information from potential borrower nations that enabled the bank to process loan applications much faster. To finance more loans,

McNamara told bank treasurer Eugene Rotberg to seek out new sources of capital outside of the northern banks that had been the primary sources of bank funding. Rotberg used the global bond market to increase the capital available to the bank. One consequence of the period of poverty alleviation lending was the rapid rise of third world debt. From 1976 to 1980 developing world debt rose at an average annual rate of 20%.

In 1980 A.W. Clausen replaced McNamara after being nominated by US President Jimmy Carter. Clausen replaced a large number of bank staffers from the McNamara era and instituted a new ideological focus in the bank. The replacement of Chief Economist Hollis B. Chenery by Anne Krueger in 1982 marked a notable policy shift at the bank. Krueger was known for her criticism of development funding as well as third world governments as rent-seeking states.

Lending to service third world debt marked the period of 1980–1989. Structural adjustment policies aimed at streamlining the economies of developing nations were also a large part of World Bank policy during this period. UNICEF reported in the late 1980s that the structural adjustment programmes of the World Bank were responsible for the "reduced health, nutritional and educational levels for tens of millions of children in Asia, Latin America, and Africa".

From 1989 World Bank policy changed in response to criticism from many groups. Environmental groups and NGOs were incorporated in the lending of the bank in order to mitigate the effects of the past that prompted such harsh criticism. Bank projects "include" green concerns.The World Bank's current focus is on the achievement of the Millennium Development Goals, lending primarily to "middle-income countries" at interest rates which reflect a small mark-up over its own borrowings from capital markets; while the IDA provides low or no interest loans and grants to low income countries with little or no access to international credit markets. The IBRD is a market-based nonprofit organization, using its high credit rating to make up for the relatively low interest rate on its loans, while the IDA is funded primarily by periodic "replenishments" voted to the institution by its more affluent member countries. The Bank's mission is to aid developing countries and their inhabitants to achieve development and the reduction of poverty, including achievement of the MDGs, by helping countries develop an environment for investment, jobs and sustainable growth, thus promoting economic growth through investment and enabling the poor to share the fruits of economic growth.

The World Bank sees the five key factors necessary for economic growth and the creation of an enabling business environment as:

1. *Build capacity*: Strengthening governments and educating government officials.
2. *Infrastructure creation*: implementation of legal and judicial systems for the encouragement of business, the protection of individual and property rights and the honouring of contracts.
3. *Development of Financial Systems*: the establishment of strong systems capable of supporting endeavors from micro credit to the financing of larger corporate ventures.
4. *Combating corruption*: Support for countries' efforts at eradicating corruption.
5. *Research, Consultancy and Training*: the World Bank provides platform for research on development issues, consultancy and conduct training programmes open for those who are interested from academia, students, government and non-governmental organization officers etc.

The Bank obtains funding for its operations primarily through the IBRD's sale of AAA-rated bonds in the world's financial markets. The IBRD's income is generated from its lending activities, with its borrowings leveraging its own paid-in capital, plus the investment of its "float". The IDA obtains the majority of its funds from forty donor countries who replenish the bank's funds every three years, and from loan repayments, which then become available for re-lending.

Many achievements have brought the MDG targets for 2015 within reach in some cases. For the goals to be realized, six criteria must be met: stronger and more inclusive growth in Africa and fragile states, more effort in health and education, integration of the development and environment agendas, more and better aid, movement on trade negotiations, and stronger and more focused support from multilateral institutions like the World Bank.

- *Eradicate Extreme Poverty and Hunger*: From 1990 through 2004, the proportion of people living in extreme poverty fell from almost a third to less than a fifth. Although results vary widely within regions and countries, the trend indicates that the world as a whole can meet the goal of halving the percentage of people living in poverty. Africa's poverty, however, is expected to rise, and most of the 36 countries where 90% of the world's undernourished children live are in Africa. Less than a quarter of countries are on track for achieving the goal of halving under-nutrition.
- *Achieve Universal Primary Education*: The number of children in school in developing countries increased from 80% in 1991 to 88% in 2005. Still, about 72 million children of primary school age, 57% of them girls, were not being educated as of 2005.
- *Promote Gender Equality and Empower Women*: The tide is turning slowly for women in the labour market, yet far more women than men- worldwide more than 60% - are contributing but unpaid family workers. The World Bank Group Gender Action Plan was created to advance women's economic empowerment and promote shared growth.
- *Reduce Child Mortality*: There is some improvement in survival rates globally; accelerated improvements are needed most urgently in South Asia and Sub-Saharan Africa. An estimated 10 million-plus children under five died in 2005; most of their deaths were from preventable causes.
- *Improve Maternal Health*: Almost all of the half million women who die during pregnancy or childbirth

every year live in Sub-Saharan Africa and Asia. There are numerous causes of maternal death that require a variety of health care interventions to be made widely accessible.

- *Combat HIV/AIDS, Malaria, and Other Diseases*: Annual numbers of new HIV infections and AIDS deaths have fallen, but the number of people living with HIV continues to grow. In the eight worst-hit southern African countries, prevalence is above 15 per cent. Treatment has increased globally, but still meets only 30 per cent of needs. AIDS remains the leading cause of death in Sub-Saharan Africa. There are 300 to 500 million cases of malaria each year, leading to more than 1 million deaths. Nearly all the cases and more than 95 per cent of the deaths occur in Sub-Saharan Africa.
- *Ensure Environmental Sustainability*: Deforestation remains a critical problem, particularly in regions of biological diversity, which continues to decline. Greenhouse gas emissions are increasing faster than energy technology advancement.
- *Develop a Global Partnership for Development*: Donor countries have renewed their commitment. Donors have to fulfill their pledges to match the current rate of core programme development. Emphasis is being placed on the Bank Group's collaboration with multilateral and local partners to quicken progress towards the MDGs' realization.

Poverty Reduction Strategies

For the poorest developing countries in the world, the bank's assistance plans are based on poverty reduction strategies; by combining a cross-section of local groups with an extensive analysis of the country's financial and economic situation the World Bank develops a strategy pertaining uniquely to the country in question. The government then identifies the country's priorities and targets for the reduction of poverty, and the World Bank aligns its aid efforts correspondingly. Forty-five countries pledged US$25.1 billion in "aid for the world's poorest countries", aid that goes to the World Bank International Development Association which distributes the gifts to eighty poorer countries. While wealthier nations sometimes fund their own aid projects, including those for diseases, and although IDA is the recipient of criticism, Robert B. Zoellick, the president of the World Bank, said when the gifts were announced on December 15, 2007, that IDA money "is the core funding that the poorest developing countries rely on".

Clean Technology Fund Management

The World Bank has been assigned temporary management responsibility of the Clean Technology Fund, focused on making renewable energy cost-competitive with coal-fired power as quickly as possible, but this may not continue after UN's Copenhagen climate change conference in December, 2009, because of the Bank's continued investment in coal-fired power plants.

Clean Air Initiative

Clean Air Initiative is a World Bank initiative to advance innovative ways to improve air quality in cities through partnerships in selected regions of the world by sharing knowledge and experiences. It includes electric vehicles.

Country Assistance Strategies

As a guideline to the World Bank's operations in any particular country, a Country Assistance Strategy is produced, in cooperation with the local government and any interested stakeholders and may rely on analytical work performed by the Bank or other parties.

Effectiveness

The World Bank has long been criticized by non-governmental organizations, such as the indigenous rights group Survival International, and academics, including its former Chief Economist Joseph Stiglitz who is equally critical of the International Monetary Fund, the US Treasury Department, US and other developed country trade negotiators. Critics argue that the so-called free market reform policies which the Bank advocates are often harmful to economic development if implemented badly, too quickly, in the wrong sequence or in weak, uncompetitive economies.

In Masters of Illusion: The World Bank and the Poverty of Nations, Catherine Caufield argued that the assumptions and structure of the World Bank harms southern nations. Caufield criticized its formulaic recipes of "development". To the World Bank, different nations and regions are indistinguishable and ready to receive the "uniform remedy of development". She argued that to attain even modest success, Western practices are adopted and traditional economic structures and values abandoned. A second assumption is that poor countries cannot modernize without money and advice from abroad.

A number of intellectuals in developing countries have argued that the World Bank is deeply implicated in contemporary modes of donor and NGO imperialism, and that its intellectual contributions function to blame the poor for their condition.

One of the strongest criticisms of the World Bank has been the way in which it is governed. While the World Bank represents 186 countries, it is run by a small number of economically powerful countries. These countries choose the leadership and senior management of the World Bank, and so their interests dominate the bank.

The World Bank has dual roles that are contradictory: that of a political organization and that of a practical organization. As a political organization, the World Bank must meet the demands of donor and borrowing governments, private capital markets, and other international organizations. As an action-oriented organization, it must be neutral, specializing in development aid, technical assistance, and loans. The World Bank's obligations to donor countries and private capital markets have caused it to adopt policies which dictate that poverty is best alleviated by the implementation of "market" policies. In the 1990s, the World Bank and the IMF forged the Washington Consensus, policies which included deregulation and liberalization of markets, privatization and the downscaling of government. Though the Washington Consensus was conceived as a policy that would best promote development, it was criticized for ignoring equity, employment and how reforms like privatization were carried out. Many now agree that the Washington Consensus placed too much emphasis on the growth of GDP, and not enough on the permanence of growth or on whether growth contributed to better living standards.

Some analysis shows that the World Bank has increased poverty and been detrimental to the environment, public health and cultural diversity. Some critics also claim that the World Bank has consistently pushed a neoliberal agenda, imposing policies on developing countries which have been damaging, destructive and anti-developmental.

It has also been suggested that the World Bank is an instrument for the promotion of US or Western interests in certain regions of the world. Even South American nations have established the Bank of the South in order to reduce US influence in the region. Criticism of the bank, that the President is always a citizen of the United States, nominated by the President of the United States. There have been accusations that the decision-making structure is undemocratic as the US has a veto on some constitutional decisions with just over 16% of the shares in the bank; Decisions can only be passed with votes from countries whose shares total more than 85% of the bank's shares. A further criticism concerns internal management and the manner in which the World Bank is said to lack accountability.

Criticism of the World Bank often takes the form of protesting as seen in recent events such as the World Bank Oslo 2002 Protests, the October Rebellion, and the Battle of Seattle. Such demonstrations have occurred all over the world, even amongst the Brazilian Kayapo people.

In 2008, a World Bank report which found that biofuels had driven food prices up 75% was not published. Officials confided that they believed it was suppressed to avoid embarrassing the then-President of the United States, George W. Bush.

The World Bank has also been criticized for not publishing reports related to the Palestinian economic situation in the West Bank and Gaza. Economists in the region have often written damning reports of the Israeli occupation and its effects on the economy, but these reports remain internal and are not published.

Although controversial and far from proven, there is criticism that World Bank and IMF are used as a means to fulfill business or political needs of the main IMF donors, that were previously historically obtained by more direct activity - war, economic blockade, espionage.

The World Bank has been criticised for the manner in which it engages in "the production, accumulation, circulation and functioning" of knowledge. The Bank's production of knowledge has become integral to the funding and justification of large capital projects. The Bank relies on "a growing network of translocal scientists, technocrats, NGOs, and empowered citizens to help generate data and construct discursive strategies". Its capacity to produce authoritative knowledge is a response to intense scrutiny of Bank projects resulting from the successes of growing anti-Bank and alternative-development movements. "Development has relied exclusively on one knowledge system, namely, the modern Western one. The dominance of this knowledge system has dictated the marginalization and disqualification of non-Western knowledge systems". It has been remarked that in these alternative knowledge systems, researchers and activists might find alternative rationales to guide interventionist action away from Western ways of thinking. Knowledge production has become an asset to the Bank, and "it is generated and used in highly strategic ways" to provide justifications for development.

The effect of structural adjustment policies on poor countries has been one of the most significant criticisms of the World Bank. The 1979 energy crisis plunged many countries into economic crises. The World Bank responded with structural adjustment loans which distributed aid to struggling countries while enforcing policy changes in order to reduce inflation and fiscal imbalance. Some of these policies included encouraging production, investment and labour-intensive manufacturing, changing real exchange rates and altering the distribution of government resources. Structural adjustment policies were most effective in countries with an institutional framework that allowed these policies to be implemented easily. For some countries, particularly in Sub-Saharan Africa, economic growth regressed and inflation worsened. The alleviation of poverty was not a goal of structural adjustment loans, and the circumstances of the poor often worsened, due to a reduction in social spending and an increase in the price of food, as subsidies were lifted.

By the late 1980s, international organizations began to admit that structural adjustment policies were worsening life for the world's poor. The World Bank changed structural adjustment loans, allowing for social spending to be maintained, and encouraging a slower change to policies such as transfer of subsidies and price rises. In 1999, the World Bank and the IMF introduced the Poverty Reduction Strategy Paper approach to replace structural adjustment loans. The Poverty Reduction Strategy Paper approach has been interpreted as an extension of structural adjustment policies as it continues to reinforce and legitimize global inequities. Neither approach has addressed the inherent flaws within the global economy that contribute to economic and social inequities within developing countries. By reinforcing the relationship between lending and client states, many believe that the World Bank has usurped indebted countries' power to determine their own economic policy.

Sociologist Michael Goldman has argued that "Industry analysts predict that private water will soon be a capitalized market as precious, and as war-provoking, as oil". Goldman says "These days, an indebted country cannot borrow capital from the World Bank or IMF without a domestic water privatization policy as a precondition". The Bank is utilizing "the 'Washington Consensus' model of "development" to promote water privatization. Following this model, the World Bank is forcing many countries to commodify their water resources, rather than using their expertise in the public sector to acknowledge water as a universal human right and an essential public service". The push for water privatization development plays upon "the shocking tragedy that much of the world lacks affordable clean water". This is creates "new opportunities in development, though it may have little to do with ultimately quenching" the needs of impoverished countries. "The problem of water scarcity for the world's poor has been analysed by the World Bank as one in which the public sector has failed to deliver, and has therefore prevented development from "taking off", and the economy from modernizing. If the state cannot deliver something as basic as water and sanitation, the argument goes, it is a strong indication of a general failure of public-sector capacity". However, "with the sale or lease of a public good comes more than simply a privatized service; alongside it comes a wide set of postcolonial institutional forces that intervene in state-citizen relations and North-South dynamics". One notable example is the privatation of water forced upon Bolivians by the World Bank which led to multiple protests including the 2000 Cochabamba protests.Despite claiming goals of "good governance and anti-corruption3 the World Bank requires sovereign immunity from countries it deals with. Sovereign immunity waives a holder from all legal liability for their actions. It is proposed that this immunity from responsibility is a "shield which wants resort to, for escaping accountability and security by the people." As the United States has veto power, it can prevent the World Bank from taking action against its interests.

The World Bank's ongoing work to develop a strategy on climate change and environmental threats has been criticized for:

- Lacking of a proper overall vision and purpose,
- Having a limited focus on its own role in global and regional governance, and
- Having limited recognition of specific regional issues,

e.g. issues of rights to food and land, and sustainable land use. Critics have also commented that only 1% of the World Bank's lending goes to the environmental sector, narrowly defined.

Environmentalists are urging the Bank to stop worldwide support for the development of coal plants and other large emitters of greenhouse gas and operations that are proven to pollute or damage the environment. For instance, protesters in South Africa and abroad have criticized the 2010 decision of the World Bank's approval for a $3.75 billion loan to build the world's 4th largest coal-fired power plant in South Africa. The plant will greatly increase the demand for coal mining and corresponding harmful environmental effects of coal.

INTERNATIONAL MONETARY FUND

The International Monetary Fund is the international organization that oversees the global financial system by following the macroeconomic policies of its member countries, in particular those with an impact on exchange rate and the balance of payments. It is an organization formed with a stated objective of stabilizing international exchange rates and facilitating development through the enforcement of liberalising economic policies on other countries as a condition for loans, restructuring or aid. It also offers highly leveraged loans, mainly to poorer countries. Its headquarters are in Washington, D.C., United States.

Organization and Purpose

The International Monetary Fund was created in July 1944, originally with 45 members, with a goal to stabilize exchange rates and assist the reconstruction of the world's international payment system. Countries contributed to a pool which could be borrowed from, on a temporary basis, by countries with payment imbalances. The IMF was important when it was first created because it helped the world stabilize the economic system. The IMF works to improve the economies of its member countries.

The IMF describes itself as"an organization of 186

countries, working to foster global monetary cooperation, secure financial stability, facilitate international trade, promote high employment and sustainable economic growth, and reduce poverty". With the exception of Taiwan, North Korea, Cuba, Andorra, Monaco, Liechtenstein, Tuvalu and Nauru, all UN member states participate directly in the IMF. Member states are represented on a 24-member Executive Board and all members appoint a Governor to the IMF's Board of Governors.

The International Monetary Fund was conceived in July 1944 during the United Nations Monetary and Financial Conference. The representatives of 45 governments met in the Mount Washington Hotel in the area of Bretton Woods, New Hampshire, United States, with the delegates to the conference agreeing on a framework for international economic cooperation. The IMF was formally organized on December 27, 1945, when the first 29 countries signed its substances of Agreement. The statutory purposes of the IMF today are the same as when they were formulated in 1943.

The IMF's influence in the global economy steadily increased as it accumulated more members. The number of IMF member countries has more than quadrupled from the 44 states involved in its establishment, reflecting in particular the attainment of political independence by many developing countries and more recently the collapse of the Soviet bloc. The expansion of the IMF's membership, together with the changes in the world economy, have required the IMF to adapt in a variety of ways to continue serving its purposes effectively.

In 2008, faced with a shortfall in revenue, the International Monetary Fund's executive board agreed to sell part of the IMF's gold reserves. On April 27, 2008, IMF Managing Director Dominique Strauss-Kahn welcomed the board's decision of April 7, 2008 to propose a new framework for the fund, designed to close a projected $400 million budget deficit over the next few years. The budget proposal includes sharp spending cuts of $100 million until 2011 that will include up to 380 staff dismissals. At the 2009 G-20 London summit, it was decided that the IMF would require additional financial resources to meet prospective needs of its member countries during the ongoing-global financial crisis. As part of that decision, the G-20 leaders pledged to increase the IMF's supplemental cash tenfold to $500 billion, and to allocate to member countries another $250 billion via Special Drawing Rights.As of May 2010 Hungary, Romania and Ukraine are the largest borrowers of the fund.

Data Dissemination Systems

In 1995, the International Monetary Fund began work on data dissemination standards with the view of guiding IMF member countries to disseminate their economic and financial data to the public. The International Monetary and Financial Committee endorsed the guidelines for the dissemination standards and they were split into two tiers: The General Data Dissemination System and the Special Data Dissemination Standard. The International Monetary Fund executive board approved the SDDS and GDDS in 1996 and 1997 respectively and subsequent amendments were published in a revised"Guide to the General Data Dissemination System". The system is aimed primarily at statisticians and aims to improve many aspects of statistical systems in a country. It is also part of the World Bank Millennium Development Goals and Poverty Reduction Strategic Papers.

The IMF established a system and standard to guide members in the dissemination to the public of their economic and financial data. Currently there are two such systems: General Data Dissemination System and its superset Special Data Dissemination System, for those member countries having or seeking access to international capital markets.

The primary objective of the GDDS is to encourage IMF member countries to build a framework to improve data quality and increase statistical capacity building. This will involve the preparation of metadata describing current statistical collection practices and setting improvement plans. Upon building a framework, a country can evaluate statistical needs, set priorities in improving the timeliness, transparency, reliability and accessibility of financial and economic data.

ASIAN DEVELOPMENT BANK

ADB or the Asian Development Bank is an international financial institute operating since 1966. ADB provides financial assistance to its member nations for poverty reduction and improvement in the quality of life. To finance its projects, ADB issues bonds and also leverages the contributions made by participant countries.

The organization was started with the following objectives:

- The social and economic development of the Asian and Pacific countries.
- To boost cooperative and simultaneous regional growth among member countries.

As of early 2007, ADB had 67 members, with 48 regional and 19 non-Asian members. Since Japan has been the largest shareholder, the bank has always been governed by a Japanese President. ADB is headquartered at Metro Manila, Philippines.

HOW ADB WORKS

The main functions of ADB are:

- Technical assistance provided to members, so that they can plan and execute development strategies and projects.
- Assistance to DMCs to coordinate policies designed for development.
- Equity investments and loans to member nations.
- Encouragement to member nations to invest private and public capital for development.

ACHIEVEMENTS OF THE ASIAN DEVELOPMENT BANK

Asian and Pacific countries have shown considerable transformation in terms of modernization. Till the end of 2007, 1,106 projects funded by ADB were evaluated. Out of these, 65% were rated as successful and 27% partly successful.

Some of the highlights of the Asian Development Bank are:

- Funding projects led by the Utah State University to bring labour skills to Thailand.
- ROC Ping Hu Offshore Oil and Gas

Development:

- Technical assistance grant of US$2 million to Bangladesh to overcome the challenges linked to climate change.
- Trans-Afghanistan Gas Pipeline Feasibility Assessment.
- Greater Mekong Subregional Programme.
- Loan of $1.2 billion to bail Pakistan out of an impending economic crisis.
- Contributions towards the development of solar energy in India.
- Strategic Private Sector Partnerships for Urban Poverty Reduction in the Philippines.
- Earthquake and Tsunami Emergency Support Project in Indonesia.

ASIAN DEVELOPMENT BANK: CHALLENGES

Poverty is still one of the main challenges faced by ADB. The 2009 global recession has severely impacted ADB's poverty alleviation goals.

The following situations pose major challenges for ADB:

- Safe water is still not available to 60% of the people in the member countries.
- Improved sanitation facilities have still not reached 70% of the people.
- Out of every 100 children, 40 die before they reach the age of 15. Infant mortality rate is very high.
- Half of the undernourished population of the world lives in Asia.
- Rising inflation has adversely impacted growth rates in Asia.

IMPORT AND EXPORT FINANCING

Import and export financing exists to enable business to take place overseas. Import and export financing provides importers who have orders from customers in the United

States, or foreign customers backed by a letter of credit, with the necessary financial backing to provide their overseas supplier with a letter of credit to guarantee payment of goods.

There are many reasons for a business to engage in this sort of financing. One big reason is that the financing can be arranged to cover 100% of the transaction. This provides the importer with sufficient financial strength to sell larger orders than they would be able to on their own financial strength. Depending on the strength of the buyer, this may be done on open account with the domestic buyer, allowing the buyer to increase their purchasing power.

The whole process works because the importer will supply you with basic information on the import company and their customers. You then evaluate the credit worthiness of the customers. For each of the approved customers, the importer will supply us with copies of purchase orders that are to be filled. As suggested, then arrange a letter of credit to be issued to the suppliers' bank with the supplier as the beneficiary.

ROLE OF COMMERCIAL BANKS

This briefly traces the historical and contemporary imperatives to provide financial services to the rural poor in India and the institutional responses to the same.

EVOLUTION OF THE FINANCIAL LANDSCAPE

In post-independence India, in order to facilitate improvements in agricultural production and attain food self-sufficiency, the stance of policy was to ensure sufficient and timely credit at "reasonable" rates of interest to as large a segment of the rural population as possible.

The strategy to achieve this was threefold: expansion of the institutional base, directed lending to disadvantaged borrowers, and credit provision at concessional rates of interest.

The latter was justified in terms of the perceived mismatch between the longer term returns of farm investment in relation to cultivator households' short term consumption needs and requirements to service the loans.

Fisher and Sriram identify three post-independence phases in rural credit provision. First, the 1950's up to the mid-1960's when cooperatives were the institutional vehicles of choice; second, the 1970's and 1980s when attention shifted to commercial banks and RRBs and third, the reform period in the early 1990's which saw the re-structuring of the banking system, the emergence of SHGs and a growing number of MFIs. In terms of scale, spread, costs, risks, and the inter-temporal nature of credit markets, financial institutions and agents in India face formidable challenges in meeting the diverse financial service needs of the country's rural population.

The present rural financial infrastructure comprises a wide variety of formal, semi-formal and informal financial service providers, with distinctive cultures and characteristics. The number of organisations and agents is very substantial: 33,553 rural and semi-urban branches of commercial banks, 13,932 rural and semi-urban branches of Regional Rural Banks, 1.09 lakh primary cooperatives, 1,000 NGO-MFIs and around 20 MFIs registered as companies and nearly three million SHGs. Even more numerous are the myriad of informal agents constituting a great range of financial service providers across the country.

Different segments of the financial infrastructure have not developed uniformly or simultaneously, and their relative standing in terms of government policy and intervention has changed over time.

Moreover, financial institutions have themselves influenced government policy. In the following paragraphs, an attempt is made to trace the forces and compulsions that have led to the development of particular rural financial institutions in the country, to outline the changing fortunes and shares of these different systems, to show the present gap between rural financial needs and provisions, and to assess policy options to reduce this gap through institutional development, linkages and reform.

Evolution of Commercial Banks

The foundation for building a broad base of agricultural credit structure was laid by the Report of the All-India Rural Credit Survey of 1954. The provision of cultivator credit in 1951-52 was less than 1% for commercial banks. In the report it was observed that agricultural credit fell short of the right quantity, was not of the right type, did not fit the right purpose and often failed to go to the right people. With a view to give an impetus to commercial banks, particularly, in the sphere of investment credit, the nationalization of the Imperial Bank of India and its redesignation as the State Bank of India was recommended.

Growth in Outreach 1951-91

From the position prevalent in 1951-52, commercial banks came a long way with a substantial spread of 32,224 branches in rural and semi-urban areas comprising 68% of their total outlets as on 31 March 1991. The outstanding deposits of such branches at Rs.67,855 crore as on the same date constituted around 35% of their total deposits, while loans outstanding at Rs. 43,797 crore comprised 36% of outstanding credit. The agricultural advances of the commercial banking system aggregated Rs. 16,687 crore and constituted 14% of total advances in March 1991. The rural and semi-urban branches of commercial banks covered 17.6 crore deposit accounts while the number of loan accounts serviced aggregated 3.7 crore.

Growth Buring 1991-92 to 2003-04

The period since 1991-92 has seen a fairly rapid expansion of credit to agriculture. Available data indicate that the flow of credit to agriculture by commercial banks and RRBs taken together increased to Rs. 60,022 crore in 2003-04. This implies a compounded annual growth rate of 22.2%. In fact, as compared with commercial banks, the flow of credit from the cooperative sector was much slower through this period. The compounded annual growth rate of credit for agriculture from cooperative institutions was only 13.7%. Further, the proportion of agriculture credit to total credit came down because of the rapid growth in nonagriculture credit. The Government took some major initiatives during the period to boost agriculture production and productivity through enhanced credit flow and by way of building agricultural infrastructure, particularly irrigation and connectivity in rural areas.

Special Agricultural Credit Plan was introduced by RBI for Public Sector Commercial Banks in 1994-95. Credit growth for agriculture and allied sectors under this caption reflected a CAGR of 36.45% during 2001-02 to 2005-06. SACP has since been extended to Private Sector Commercial Banks from 2005-06.

The SHG - Bank Linkage Programme was started as a pilot project by NABARD in 1992. It led to the evolution of a set of RBI approved guidelines to banks to enable SHGs to transact with banks. Initially there was slow progress in the programme up to 1999 as only 32,995 groups were credit linked during the period 1992 to 1999. Since then the programme has been growing rapidly and the cumulative number of SHGs financed increased from 4.61 lakhs on 31 March 2002 to 10.73 lakhs on 31 March 2004 and further to 29.25 lakh groups as on 31 March 2007.

Rural Infrastructure Development Fund was set-up in NABARD by GoI during 1995-96 with an initial corpus of Rs.2000 crore, to accelerate the completion of on-going projects of rural infrastructure. Banks which did not fulfill the priority sector credit requirement and agriculture credit mandate were required to contribute to this Fund. The fund has been strengthened every year with additional allocations in the Union Budget. A large number of irrigation and rural connectivity projects could get completed under RIDF.

RBI scaled down its contribution to the Rural Credit funds with NABARD to a token amount of Rs.1 crore per annum since 1993-94. However to enable NABARD to have reasonably strong leverage for accessing market funds, the share capital of NABARD was strengthened and increased to Rs.2000 crore from Rs.100 crore at the time of its formation in 1982. Contributions to enhanced share capital have come from GoI and RBI. By prudent funds management, the institution has also built a strong base of reserves and has been using it in its business operations judiciously to keep lending rates to rural financial institutions at significantly lower than market costs.

Developments - Post 2003-04

Since 2003-04, there has been a substantial increase in the flow of credit to agriculture through commercial banks. Disbursements have increased from Rs. 52,441 crore in 2003-04 to Rs. 1,16,447 crore in 2005-06, reaching an annual growth of 43% each year. As envisaged in the GoI's strategy for "doubling of credit", 95 lakh new farmers have been brought under the institutional fold and 1,383 agri-clinics opened. Commercial banks have also played a major role in the promotion of the SHG - bank linkage movement with more than 11.88 lakh groups being linked to banks for provision of credit. Reforms in the commercial banking system include removal of procedural and transactional bottlenecks including elimination of Service Area Approach, reducing margins, redefining overdues to coincide with crop cycles, new debt restructuring policies, one time settlement and relief measures for farmers indebted to non-institutional sources.

THE TASK AHEAD

Commercial banks are now slowly coming to appreciate the business potential in financial inclusion and also the need for better involvement. RRBs who are expected to function with the social heart of cooperatives and financial acumen of commercial banks have a significant role to play in financial inclusion, especially in the post-amalgamation scenario. The vast postal network, leveraging on their immense outreach, could also be an effective vehicle for purveying financial services.

While, there is evidence that commercial banks have been cognizant of their social responsibility in regard to small farmers, their focus on marginal and submarginal farmers, tenants, share croppers, oral lessees and non-cultivator households, viz., the very poor and disadvantaged sectors has been found wanting. In the circumstances, there is a need to evolve conscious strategies for providing easier access to affordable credit to the marginal, sub-marginal and other disadvantaged groups in the rural sector. Such strategies should combine using a variety of delivery channels, intermediaries and IT solutions apart from the traditional brick and mortar branch network.

The specific recommendations of the Committee for achieving targets under the NRFIP by leveraging the existing commercial bank branch network in rural areas are as follows

Targets for Rural/Semi-urban Branches

Currently, there are 33,478 commercial bank branches in rural and semi-urban centres in the country. Out of these, there are about 12,340 branches in the rural and semi urban areas of the Central, Eastern and North-Eastern Regions, where the majority of the financially excluded population live. It is understood that each branch of Grameen Bank in Bangladesh services at least 4,000-5,000 borrowers, with 6-7 field officers per branch. Given the existing staff strength, it should be possible for commercial banks to provide access to credit to at least 250 hitherto excluded households per annum at each of their existing rural and semi-urban branches. For this, banks will have to strengthen their staff and use a variety of delivery mechanisms.

Targeted Branch Expansion in Identified Districts

In several districts, the population per branch office is much higher than the national average, particularly in rural and semi urban areas. The list of such districts has already been circulated by RBI among banks. The DLCCs in these districts may identify centres for opening branches by commercial banks and RRBs. in the next three years.

For the North-Eastern Region, the financial sector plan has already identified such centres and branch expansion plan as laid out therein may be implemented. SLBC may monitor the branch expansion plan for each State.

Product Innovation

The excluded segments of the population require products which are customised, taking into consideration their varied needs. Their banking requirements being small, the issue of servicing and delivery in a cost-effective manner assumes significance.

The need for savings by these groups require special attention, e.g. for meeting life cycle needs, creating assets, repaying high cost borrowings, meeting emergencies etc. The saving products offered at present do not effectively meet these needs.

The services offered are also not suitable because of the spatial spread of the excluded people and also the small quantum of finance involved:

- *Savings:* Savings products to meet the specific requirements of the poor need to be evolved. One way of meeting this would be to utilize SHGs for tapping the small savings by providing incentives to the SHGs with suitable back-end technology support. The banks can develop medium and long term savings instruments by issue of pre-printed deposit receipts to the SHGs which in turn can be sold to the SHG members. Banks could be given the freedom to develop their own products, suiting local requirements and felt needs of the poor.
- *Credit:* With regard to credit products, the savings linked financing model can be adopted for these segments. The approach should be kept simple which should guarantee the beneficiaries a credit limit, subject to adherence to terms and conditions. The credit within the limit can be made available in 2-3 tranches, with the second and subsequent tranches disbursed based on repayment behaviour of the first tranche. This is to ensure that the vulnerable groups do not get into a debt trap; it also ensures good credit dispensation.
- *Insurance:* Banks can play a vital role in this regard – by distributing suitable micro-insurance products.

Incentivising Human Resource – Measurable Performance indicators

Lending to low income groups and increasing financial inclusion need motivated bank staff. Such motivation is a function of attitudes and beliefs as also a system of incentives/ disincentives put in place by the bank's management for special efforts/failures to achieve desired levels of financial inclusion.

The Committee debated the issue of creating a separate cadre of rural bank employees. While the arguments in favour were supported by the large proportion of rural branches, quantum of deposits and credit, the arguments against were the high costs involved and compulsions regarding rotation of staff.

It was, therefore, felt that existing staff posted to rural branches can be incentivised within a framework of performance parametres including covering of new households through deposit and loan accounts, increase in business in existing and new small loan/deposit accounts, increase in number of SHGs/Joint Liability Groups formed and credit linked, efforts put in for promotion of asset management skills and developing linkages to promote credit absorption.

Funding

The Committee recognized that there is a cost involved in providing credit plus services and technology applications. Such costs may come down over a period of time with the resultant business expansion. Banks are expected to meet a part of the costs. However, in the initial stages some funding support thru' specially constituted Funds may be extended to them.

This funding support, envisaged as a mechanism to reduce costs, may be provided to the banks on two counts:

1. Promotional and developmental initiatives that will lead to better credit absorption capacity among the poor and vulnerable parts and
2. Application of technology for facilitating the mandated levels of inclusion.

Financial Inclusion Funds

The Committee proposes the constitution of two funds – the Financial Inclusion with NABARD, for meeting the cost of developmental and promotional interventions indicated below and the Financial Inclusion Technology Fund, with NABARD, to meet the costs of technology adoption. Each Fund will have an initial corpus of Rs. 500 crore, with a start-up funding of Rs. 250 crore each, to be contributed in equal proportion by GoI/RBI/NABARD and with annual accretions thereto.

Banks will be eligible for support from the Funds on a matching contribution of 50% from the Fund in regard to districts other than tribal districts and 75% in case of branches located in tribal districts identified under the Tribal Sub Plan.

Financial Inclusion Promotion and Development Fund

The Financial Inclusion Promotion and Development Fund will focus on financing the following interventions:

Farmers' Service Centres

With the creation of and support to FSCs a host of financial and farm advisory services are to be provided to the new/hitherto excluded customer segments. The Centres will network on the technology front with Agricultural Universities/KVKs, farmers clubs, the formal extension machinery of the State Governments, technical staff of banks, portals of national level commodity exchanges etc. Such FSCs can be financed by the banks on the pattern of agri clinics. In the initial stages, it may be necessary to provide them some support by way of viability gap funding.

Promoting Rural Entrepreneurship

Commercial banks may consider setting up institutions like farmer training centres and Rural Development and Self Employment Training Institutes for developing skills among farmers/rural entrepreneurs for effectively managing the assets financed.

Self-Help Groups

The process of financial inclusion can be greatly facilitated through the medium of linking SHGs with the formal sector. It has been observed elsewhere in the Report that the SHG movement is yet to catch up on a big scale in regions manifesting high levels of exclusion. The funding support for promotion, nurturing and credit linking of SHGs can be extended.

Developing HR – Addressing Attitudinal Issues Thru' Training

Various studies have confirmed that lending to the poor raises a number of issues ranging from sources and reliability of their incomes to lack of suitable bank projects for them to the elitist approach of the formal institutional credit delivery apparatus. These factors are the outcome of attitudes towards the poor, as generally not viable and profitable customers of the bank. Experience indicates that the poor, if guided properly, not only succeed as entrepreneurs, but are also good "repayers". However, changing this attitude or mindset is a challenge.

In a study conducted in Madhya Pradesh, it was found that attitudes of branch managers shape the branch lending behaviour. Two other important findings which emerged were that a majority of the branch managers held negative attitudes towards lending to the poor and about themselves, their work roles and situations and exhibited a general lack of motivation and confidence. Secondly, there was a positive correlation between the training received by the branch managers and their overall attitudes. Branch managers felt that in terms of frequency, and relevance to their work, training was inadequate, too theoretical, inappropriate for rural assignment, outdated and in some case a mere formality.

Keeping in view the impact that training has on attitudes, a training module has been developed and tested for commercial banks and RRBs in the College of Agricultural Banking, Pune. The Committee recommends that banks use/adapt this programme for bringing about the right mindset amongst their branch staff posted to districts having a high share of population excluded from access to financial services.

Resource Centres

Resource Centres, apart from facilitating members of mature SHGs to graduate to micro-enterprises, also helps in ensuring long term sustainability of SHGs. The cost of setting up such centres can be met out of this Fund and/or the MFDEF. This is discussed in detail later in the report.

Federations

As indicated later in the report, funding support may also be extended from this Fund and/or MFDEF for voluntary establishment of federations.

Capacity building of BFs/BCs

Funding support, on priority basis, to be extended to specialized institutions which provide capacity building inputs to BFs/BCs, as discussed later in the Report.

Financial Inclusion Technology Fund

Technology Applications for Greater Financial Inclusion

Extending outreach on a scale envisaged under NRFIP would require the application of low-cost technology solutions, which have been discussed in greater detail elsewhere in the Report. This may also call for certain levels of funding support for rolling out such IT-based inclusive financial sector plan.

Guidelines for Operationalising the Funds

NABARD, in consultation with RBI, may prepare detailed guidelines based on consulatations with commercial banks and technology service providers for operationalising both the Funds.

Procedural Changes

Simplifying Mortgage Requirements

The Talwar Committee had recommended acceptance of

a simple declaratory charge as equitable mortgage. Enabling legislation has been passed in some States. This may be done by all the State Governments as it would simplify documentation processes considerably.

Exemption from Stamp Duty for Loans to Small and Marginal Farmers

Stamp duty adds to transaction costs incurred by farmers. Non-availability of stamps in required denominations results in borrowers paying higher than the prescribed stamp duty. The Committee recommends waiver of stamp duty requirements for loan documents of small/marginal farmers and tenant cultivators.

Saral Documentation for Agricultural Loans

NABARD, in cooperation with a core group of bankers, has prepared a one page document for agricultural loans up to Rs.1 lakh. This document has been circulated among the scheduled commercial banks with the approval of the Indian Banks' Association. The Committee recommends that this simplified document be adopted by all banks with a view to deepening credit outreach among the disadvantaged parts of the rural poor.

Nodal Branches

Taking cognizance of the fact that the marginal and sub-marginal farmers require credit plus services in the form of extension services, in all districts identified as having the largest number of excluded people, the Committee recommends that one branch of the lead bank or the bank having the largest presence at the block/taluka level may be identified as the nodal branch to address the issue of exclusion. Lead banks or banks having the largest presence may strengthen these nodal branches with technical staff to provide agricultural/business development services in the farm and non-farm sectors respectively, comprising of technical inputs and extension services to the banks/farmers. These could either be provided by regular officers of the bank or local consultants/

practitioners/agri-business clinics on a retainer basis. As the services of the nodal branch would be available to all other branches in the vicinity, an appropriate cost sharing arrangement may be worked out between various banks.

It is possible that in some districts the dominant presence is of the RRBs in which case sponsor banks may assist the RRBs in putting in place arrangements for technical staff for providing credit plus services for facilitating financial inclusion. NABARD may defray the cost of such technical staff, particularly, in the North- Eastern Region.

Business Facilitators/Business Correspondents

With the objective of ensuring greater financial inclusion and increasing the outreach of the banking sector, the RBI has permitted banks to use the services of NGOs/SHGs, MFIs and other civil society organisations as intermediaries in providing financial and banking services through the use of BF and BC Models vide their Circular of 25 January 2006.

Business Facilitator Model

Under the BF Model, banks may use intermediaries such as NGOs, farmers' clubs, cooperatives, community based organisations, IT-enabled rural outlets of corporate entities, post offices, insurance agents, well functioning Panchayats, village knowledge centres, agri-clinics/agri-business centres, Krishi Vigyan Kendras and KVIC/KVIB units for providing facilitation services. It has been clarified that such services may include:

Identification of borrowers and fitment of activities:

- Collection and preliminary processing of loan applications,
- Creation of awareness about savings and other products, education and advise on managing money and debt counseling,
- Processing and submission of application to banks,
- Promotion and nurturing of SHGs/JLGs,
- Post sanction monitoring,

- Monitoring and hand holding of SHGs/JLGs/credit groups/others, and
- Follow-up for recovery.

Business Correspondent Model

Under the BC Model, NGOs/MFIs set up under the Societies/Trust Act, Societies registered under Mutually Aided Cooperative Societies Acts or the Cooperative Societies Acts of States, *Section 25 Companies,* Registered NBFCs not accepting public deposits and post offices may performance as BCs. Banks have been advised to conduct due diligence on such entities and ensure that they are well established, enjoy good reputation and have the confidence of local people.

In addition to the activities listed under the BF Model, the scope and activities to be undertaken by BCs will include:

- Disbursal of small value credit,
- Recovery of principal/collection of interest,
- Collection of small value deposits,
- Sale of micro-insurance/mutual fund products/ pension products/other third party products, and
- Receipt and delivery of small value remittances/other payment instruments.

The activities to be undertaken by the BCs would be within the normal course of the banks' business, but conducted through the entities indicated above at places other than the banks' premises.

Operating Norms

Banks have been permitted to pay reasonable commission/ fees to the BFs/BCs, the rate and quantum of which is to be reviewed periodically. Such costs have to be borne entirely by the banks. Initially, it may affect operational margins, but over time, on account of the incremental business brought in, the arrangement is expected to become viable and self-sustaining. Further, banks have been advised that the agreement with the BCs should specifically prohibit them from charging any fee to the customers directly for services rendered by them on behalf of the bank.

It has been clarified that the arrangements with the BCs shall specify:

- Suitable limits on cash holding by intermediaries as also limits on individual customer payments and receipts,
- The requirements that the transactions are accounted for and reflected in the banks' books by end of the day or next working day,
- All agreements/contracts with the customer shall specify that the bank is responsible to the customer for acts of omission and commission of the BF/BC.

It was explained to the Committee that notwithstanding the dispensation given to banks, the response of the banking system was somewhat low key and that the model is yet to be fully grounded.

Discussions with a cross section of bankers revealed that the muted response was in part due to:

- Disinclination on part of banks to absorb the costs involved on grounds of its impact on viability of operations,
- Lack of clarity regarding certain procedural complexities.

Taking the totality of circumstances into account, specially the need to facilitate greater financial inclusion, the Committee makes the following recommendations insofar as the BF/BC Model is concerned

Business Facilitators

Originally, only individuals who were insurance agents could performance as BFs while no individuals could be placed as BC. This was later on widened to include retired officials, viz., Government servants like postmasters, school teachers and headmasters, who were considered eligible by RBI to performance as BF. These people have a standing in the local community and provide the needed comfort level to the banks. The banks may make use of this relaxation and use individuals.

Ex-servicemen in rural areas have the comforting support, not only of the institutionalized ex-servicemen's fraternity but also of their Regional Centres. These Centres performance as guide and monitor both serving and retired armed forces personnel. During discussions with the Committee, it was indicated that ex-servicemen would volunteer to performance as BCs in selected districts having a high concentration of ex servicemen. The Committee is of the view that, initially, banks may appoint exservicemen

Further, after identification and placement of BFs, the banks should ensure that the banking awareness created and potential identified by BFs get translated into business propositions by providing suitable banking services in the area. This could be attempted thru' mobile outlets, which could visit the various locations, as per a scheduled programme, so as to purvey banking services to the excluded.

To facilitate easy roll-out of this mobile banking model, banks should simplify and rationalize back-end processes and front-end procedures so that banking operations are made more customer-friendly.

Business Correspondents

With increasing competition, banks are getting to be quite wary of the reducing margins available to them on financial intermediation. Banks are, therefore, hesitant to opt for increasing their physical presence in upcountry/ remote locations entailing considerable capital/ operating costs. Under the present dispensation, small value clients in remote locations get very little preference in accessing financial services.

It is, therefore, imperative to have in place an arrangement which can cater to a large number of clients having irregular and low value transactions ensuring at the same time full protection of the interests of depositors. Such an arrangement is possible only by having a BC touchpoint in each of the 6 lakh plus villages serving as a customer interface at the front-end and backed by appropriate technology for its integration with the mainframe banking at the bank level. Keeping this in view, the following recommendations for the BC Model are made.

In addition to the institutions presently allowed by RBI to function as BCs, individuals like locally settled retired Government servants like postmasters, school teachers, ex-servicemen and ex-bank staff whose relationship with the banking system, through a pension account, has already been established, may be permitted to performance as BCs.

Further, MF-NBFCs may be allowed to performance as limited BCs of banks for only providing savings and remittance services.

The Committee recognizes the fact that technology has to be an integral part in sustaining outreach efforts thru' the BC model. Ultimately, banks should endeavour to have a BC touch point in each of the six lakh villages in the country. This is discussed in detail later in the Report.

With a view to encouraging the BCs to widen their client-base, a suitable incentive mechanism may be formulated by the banks, appropriately linked to the number of accounts opened/transactions put thru' by the BCs. This will go a long way in stabilizing the arrangement between the Banks and the BCs. Further, banks may consider identifying BCs even in areas where they have their own branches, so as to supplement their efforts in widening outreach and addressing access issues.

The Committee also observed that certain banks have already put in place intermediaries in the form of loan agents, who are akin to the BCs, but in addition, also partake a certain element of risk/responsibility in case of loan defaults. In the intial stages, the BC model as envisaged by RBI could be implemented widely. In due course, when the BCs reach a higher level of turnover, they should bear commensurate financial responsibilities.

Banks may, at their discretion, appoint any individual/ institution of its choice as Business Correspondent, after exercising due diligence. This will facilitate greater acceptance of the BC Model by banks.

Funds may be provided to specialized institutions which provide capacity building inputs to BCs. Such funding support could be extended on priority basis to most excluded areas/ sectors of the society and met out of the Financial Inclusion

Promotion and Development Fund. SLBC convener banks may initiate discussion with their respective State Governments regarding routing government payments through BCs using the smart card or other relevant technology on a pilot basis.

SLBCs may undertake a study to identify organisations having the capacity to serve as customer service points and BC. In States like Andhra Pradesh and Kerala the VOs and Kudumbashree structures already exist and these can be used as customer service points. Training modules for BFs/BCs may be prepared in vernacular and in culture sensitive pictorial forms.

Role of Commercial Banks in Microfinance

Deepening the outreach of the microfinance programme is an effective way in reaching out to the excluded segments. Commercial Banks have played a very important role in the SHG-Bank Linkage Programme. As at the end of March 2007, as many as 50 Commercial Banks are involved in the programme, having linked 15.95 lakh SHGs, forming more than 54% of the total SHGs credit-linked in the country. This programme should be strengthened and carried further, playing a key role in financial inclusion.

Financing Poor Farmers

Joint Liability Groups of the poor such as landless, share croppers and tenant farmers is another innovative mechanism towards ensuring greater financial inclusion. This mechanism has already been operationalised in a few regions under a Pilot Project of NABARD. Commercial Banks can actively promote such groups for effectively purveying credit and other facilities to such clients. RBI may encourage banks to adopt the JLG model for lending to SF/MF, tenant cultivators, share croppers and oral lessees.

Making Marginal Farm Holdings Viable and Enabling their Financial Inclusion

The Committee examined the credit absorption capacity among marginal farm holdings and is of the view that:

- Farm aggregation models including contract farming fully protecting the interests of farmers could be an option for enhanced viability. Credit-marketing linkage can also be effected through appropriate agreements.
- Access to irrigation will make a substantial difference on viability of small farms. A massive programme for financing minor irrigation structures may be undertaken specifically targeting marginal farm households.
- Supplementary activities like dairy, small poultry, sheep-rearing, etc. have to be specifically targeted for marginal farmers, tenants and non-cultivator households. In this context, the Committee notes that against an estimated production of 91 million tons of milk in 2004-05, the demand for milk in 2021-22 would increase to 172 million tons as per estimates of the Planning Commission. To meet the demand, milk production should continue to grow at 4% per annum for the next 15 years. The growth of milk production could be augmented through a two pronged approach focusing on improving production in major milk producing areas and expanding infrastructure for procurement, processing, marketing and quality assurance. A National Dairy Plan has been prepared to target production enhancement in 323 potential districts. Under the NDP the following has been envisaged:
  - Financing dairy animals and dairy infrastructure to individuals, SHGs, cooperative societies, corporates, NGOs, etc after ensuring input and marketing linkages.
  - Establishment and encouragement of viable institutional structures through grants for institutional development, incentivising reforms by cooperatives.
  - Reform of existing dairy cooperatives.
  - Study of low potential districts to assist State

Governments for developing dairy activities and evolving suitable plans.

- Development of road and power infrastructure and watershed development in the identified areas under the NDP through RIDF loans to state governments.
- The NDP would be implemented through a consortium of NABARD, the National Dairy Development Board and the National Cooperative Development Corporation. The funds required for breeding, nutrition and milk handling are estimated to be Rs. 18,500 crore over the next three five-year plan periods. The assistance from the GoI would be Rs. 225 crore for the first year.
- It is recommended that similar initiatives may be considered for other sectors also like poultry, horticulture, etc.
- Technical counseling and farm advisory services have to be extended to such farms which are provided finance for undertaking the activities.

5

International Capital Markets

AN OVERVIEW

Investors in the surplus countries have become more selective about the kind of claims they wish to acquire in the deficit countries, resulting in a change in the nature of financial intermediation. The trend in capital market liberalization, the spread of innovative techniques and the development of derivative products have facilitated better matching of investors' preferences and debtors' needs.

Yet, the developments of the mid-1980s, that culminated in the equity market crash of October 1987, delineated the significance of macroeconomic policies that create market confidence and promote intermediation through international capital markets.

Lapses on this count can lead to adverse consequences for exchange and interest rates as well as abrupt and unwelcome shifts in financial flows. They can also weaken the market confidence and lead to situations like that seen in 1987. International trade in goods and services recorded impressive increases in the 1980s.

The volume of world trade increased by 50 per cent, while in value terms it increased by three-quarters. During the mid-1980s, the external imbalances among the major industrialized countries were large and reached $168 billion in 1986 and $183 billion in 1987. The current account deficits of the developing countries, which had declined from their high level of 1982, registered a tiny surplus in the overall current account balances in 1987 before moving into the red in 1988. These imbalances are important because they are considered to be an indicator of the required net movement of capital through the financial system. Coupled with progress in financial market liberalization, the imbalances were to a great extent responsible for capital flows during these years.

The macroeconomic environment in which these flows took place was characterized by a good deal of financial uncertainty associated with an upswing in interest rates in 1987, renewed concern about inflation, and sizeable official market interventions that followed the Plaza Agreement of 22 September 1985. Interest rates, that had started falling during late 1982, began to firm up in 1987. At the beginning of the year, they were at their lowest levels since the late 1970s in the USA, Japan, Canada and Italy.

However, in late 1987 they began to rise in most of the major industrial economies except Japan, a trend that was to continue during the following year. The LIBOR on six-month dollar deposits increased from 6.4 per cent in the first half of 1987 to 9.4 per cent in December 1988. In Japan, in the aftermath of the Plaza Agreement, interest rates kept on declining until the discount rate reached its lowest ever level in 1989.

Some commentators of the international financial scene argued that rising long-term interest rates in the industrial countries, especially in the USA, reflected the changing expectations regarding the stability of exchange rates among the major currencies. In fact, the depreciation of the dollar during this period was accompanied by an increase in the premium in dollar interest rates over interest rates on instruments denominated in the yen or deutsche mark. The continued depreciation of the dollar against other SDR currencies during this period was in accordance with the Plaza Agreement between the G5 countries.

A falling dollar led investors to avoid the somewhat illiquid securities of the Eurobond market in favour of the domestic bond markets. The Eurobond investors became reluctant to acquire dollar-denominated debt. The interna-©tional securities markets also remained depressed during

1987, particularly during the third and fourth quarters. At the beginning of 1988, the dollar started to recover against the other SDR currencies and in the second quarter the exchange rate movement between the dollar, yen and deutsche mark became much less volatile. The subdued volatility partly reflected the public commitment made by the G5 countries to promote exchange rate stability. There was a marked improvement in world trade and economic activity in 1988. The output growth in most industrial countries was strong and inflation remained moderate.

The growth rate of real GNP in the industrial countries was 4.4 per cent which was the second highest in the 1980s. The stable macroeconomic conditions in 1988 and 1989 brought about a rebound in the capital markets from their previous somewhat depressed levels. The Eurobond market recovered faster than expected.

The buoyant activity level reflected settled market conditions, market resilience and generally higher expectations of stability in the main economic variables. Some of the favourable developments in the international economy were a reduction in the fiscal deficits in major industrial economies during 1988 and 1989, a reduction in claims on developing countries, a high level of investment activity leading to strong economic expansion in most industrial countries and an environment of relatively stable prices and exchange rates.

In the aftermath of the Plaza Agreement, a period of exchange rate stability began, although the Agreement was not wholly responsible for it. Therefore, nominal interest rate differentials started having a greater influence on the financial flows. The apprehension that inflation might come back made the industrial economies take a tight monetary stand which was reflected in a widespread increase in short-term interest rates in 1988. As opposed to this, the longer-term interest rates by and large remained stable. Their yield curve flattened and even became inverted, partly reflecting the confidence in inflation control measures as well as anti-inflationary commitments of the governments.

During this period the interest rate differentials gradually widened in favour of the dollar, in particular *vis-à-vis* the yen. But from the second quarter of 1989 the inflationary pressures began to recede in the USA, leading to a fall in the US interest rates and a reversal of interest rate differentials against other currencies.

The recovery in the nominal value of the US dollar against the other major SDR currencies during the period 1988-9 had started after three years of decline. Because of relatively stable exchange markets, official intervention was not necessary after 1988 and financing of the imbalances was more or less autonomous through the capital accounts.

The stability of the international currency markets inspired private capital flows to respond to interest rate differentials more strongly than in 1987. Before this point in time, large-scale intervention by central banks was needed to do the same job. At the end of the decade, intervention played a minor role in the major industrialized countries, with the notable exception of the UK.

The return to autonomous financing was made possible by sharp increases in net direct investment and net financing through international bond markets. The former was partly associated with the high level of merger and acquisition (M&A) activity.

Such outflows were particularly high in the case of Japan, with a good deal of these flows directed to the USA, which was the major deficit country. It saw a significant increase in inward capital flows with respect to direct investment as well as through bond markets. Both of these are private-sector-dominated channels.

THE GENERAL MARKET AND SECTOR TRENDS

The noteworthy developments of the mid-1980s included the collapse of the perpetual FRN market which was largely due to the concern of investors about the liquidity of the instruments. These concerns were heightened by the equity market crash and for a few months thereafter there was a virtual halt in the issue of new equity-linked bonds. An increase in awareness of the systemic risk was natural and logical. A strong recovery in the international bond markets was observed after the crash and the gross issuance of fixed rate bonds during 1988 began to rise, with the issuance of equity-related fixed rate bonds also reaching a high level. Likewise the bond markets perked up and large net inflows were recorded for the USA, particularly through purchases of US Treasury bonds. Japan and the FRG continued to record net outflows.

The portfolio investment in corporate equities played less of a role in the financing of current account imbalances during 1988 and 1989 than in the past. Also, there was a major change in the direction of investment, i.e. both the UK and the USA shifted from being net importers of capital through the equity markets in 1987 to net exporters in 1988 and 1989. As for lending through the banking system, net inflows in the USA and Japan declined substantially after reaching record levels in 1987. This reversal was the counterpart of the reduced reliance on official intervention. The reduction lowered the need for banks to readjust their positions through interbank activities. The other causes included the impact of the new Basle ratios regarding capital adequacy and flat or inverted yield curves.

The structure of the bond market was considerably influenced by changing currency valuations and interest rate variations during the mid-1980s. The international bond market activity expanded in 1988-9 with the help of swaps. In this case, the flat yield curve and the relative stability of exchange rates served to stimulate growth in fixed rate bond investments. Investors had a clear preference for currencies with high nominal interest rates, particularly the US dollar. The need for official intervention in support of the dollar declined in 1988-9 because, first, there was a decline in the US current account deficit and, second, foreign direct investment rose significantly. Accordingly, the acquisition of liabilities by foreign monetary authorities declined substantially. During these years, net capital inflows into the USA through portfolio investments in securities markets rose moderately, although there were variations in the performance of the different market segments. For instance, owing to the interest rate differential in favour of the USA and the relative strength of the dollar, net purchases of public sector bonds by foreigners, particularly German and Japanese investors, increased substantially. Despite the inward direct investment surge, the acquisition of corporate equity in the USA dwindled over 1988-9. Net inflows through the banking sector also declined because the short-term borrowings of the US banks fell. This was partly because of the withdrawal of dollar deposits from the Eurodollar market by foreign monetary authorities.

In Japan, the current account surpluses and foreign exchange reserves were rising. Net foreign exchange reserves increased by $39 billion in 1987, which corresponded to 45 per cent of the current account surplus; in 1986, such reserve accumulation had accounted for only 18 per cent of the current account surplus. During 1988, foreign exchange reserves expanded more slowly, at a rate of $16 billion, or 20 per cent of the Japanese current account surplus. Japan's current account surpluses, net of direct investment outflows, declined significantly in 1989 and the rate of accumulation of the official reserves was also reduced, while net financing to the rest of the world through financial markets did not rise.

However, there was a change in the composition of such financing, i.e. outflows through the securities markets declined and the net flow through the banking system rose. For the reasons given in the preceding paragraph, Japan was a big purchaser of US Treasury bonds and its net capital outflows through bond markets rose dramatically. These outflows were more than offset by equally dramatic inflows through the stock market. In 1988, foreigners switched to heavy purchasing of Japanese stocks which was opposite to the past trend. The stock market had also rebounded to its pre-crash levels, reflecting confidence of the investors in the Japanese economy. The banking sector in Japan experienced a large amount of inflows because the Japanese investors tried to cover their long-term investment by short-term borrowing. The inflows of short-term capital increased considerably in 1987, which mainly reflected the borrowing of the Japanese banks. But Japan continued to be a net lender of long-term capital and a net borrower of short-term capital.

Germany, like Japan, recorded a large increase in the long-term outflows of capital through securities markets. This was the net result of reduced purchases of domestic securities by foreigners and a sharp increase in purchase of foreign bonds by German investors. The cause behind these outflows is the same, namely, widening of interest differentials in favour of the dollar. Despite large surpluses, the central bank had to intervene to support the deutsche mark because of strong outflows. Between 1987 and 1988, net flows of private capital doubled, partly reflecting a sharp decline in foreign purchases of German securities. This development is partly associated with changes in the exchange rate expectations and partly with investors' concerns about a new German tax on interest income.

The banking sector witnessed a net inflow of long-term capital over 1988 and 1989 which occurred because of the German banks' issuance of bonds and placing of the proceeds on long-term deposits in German banks, thereby taking advantage of the lower interest rates on foreign bonds. With respect to short-term capital, there was a small net increase which corresponded to the purchases by the Bundesbank of deutsche marks in the exchange market and to an increase in the net interbank claims of German banks.

In recent years, the UK has become a major source of external finance to the USA. Of late, substantial capital outflows have taken place through security markets. The increased demand for foreign securities by British investors was directed towards both bond and corporate securities. This was a reversal of the disinvestment trend of the final months of 1987. Also, while short-term interest rates provided a significant premium on sterling assets, the long-term picture was less favourable. It was because of the former that the current account deficit of the UK was largely financed through a massive increase in net inflows of funds through the banking system. These inflows were supported by official intervention.

International Bank Leadings

International bank lendings are overwhelmingly dominated by borrowers in the industrial countries. International bank claims on these countries expanded from $210 billion in 1985 to $547 billion in 1987. After this spurt, the flows moderated substantially. This sector is dominated by interbank activities, i.e. interbank loans and interbank deposits account for three-quarters or more of flows. The 1988 slowdown in the activities of the banks extended to non-banks as well. Bank claims on non-bank entities in industrial countries, which had more than doubled between 1985 and 1986 and had again risen in 1987, plunged sharply in 1988. The reasons for contraction in interbank lending include new capital adequacy requirements by the BIS which forced the banks to slow the expansion of their balance sheets, particularly in activities with low profit margins relative to their risk weighting.

Second, these flows swelled in 1987 as a result of the opening of the Japan Offshore Market in December 1986. Third, the relatively flat yield curve mentioned earlier reduced the incentives for financing medium- and long-term investment through short-term interbank borrowing. As opposed to this, bank lendings to non-bank entities in the industrialized economies went ahead with the same pace as in the past and picked up somewhat in 1989. Fourth, investor interest in the international bond market was rekindled by somewhat reduced uncertainty regarding the behaviour of exchange rates and bond yields. The same uncertainty benefited the international banking activity in 1987 because banks provided suitable instruments and investors were led to borrow from them in order to finance purchases of hedging instruments.

An interesting change was observed in long-term bank credit commitments which rose sharply in 1988 due to high merger-related lending. It represented over 30 per cent of new syndicated Eurocredits. Corporate borrowings for debt consolidation was also heavy. However, lending to sovereign borrowers remained subdued because the creditworthy developing country borrowers were able to raise funds more cheaply through swap-related Eurobond issues.

International Bond Markets

In the aftermath of the Plaza Agreement, the new bond issues moved away from bonds denominated in dollars towards those denominated in yen, Swiss francs and pounds sterling. The dollar-denominated bonds declined from 55 per cent of the total in 1986 to 37 per cent in 1987 and subsequently stabilized around this level. Since the yen's strong appreciation was expected, the share of bonds denominated in yen increased from 10 per cent in 1986 to 15 per cent in 1987. Because of low interest rates in Japan and high interest rates in the UK and the USA, this trend did not continue. Over the period 1984-7, several significant changes took place in the type of instruments used for new bond issues. While the issuance of fixed interest rate bonds accounted for a growing share of total international bonds issued during this period, the relative importance of FRNs and equity-related bonds varied sharply.

FRNs, which accounted for about 35 per cent of total international bond issues in 1984-5, declined sharply to only 7 per cent in 1986-7. At the same time, issuance of equity-related bonds, which accounted for about 9 per cent of total international bond issues in 1984-5, rose sharply to reach 24 per cent of total issues in 1987. The reduction in the use of FRNs reflected liquidity problems resulting from the collapse of the market for perpetual FRNs, which has been noted earlier, in December 1986. As opposed to this, on a number of national markets the equity-related bonds expanded during the first nine months of 1987, when equity prices were rising. In 1988. despite increasing competition from Eurocommercial paper and fixed rate note swaps, the issuance of FRNs started to recover fast. This was largely due to rising interest rates, which made floating rates more attractive for investors. The fixed interest rate bonds declined after several years of sustained growth. Despite the equity market crash of 1979, the issuance of equity- related bonds-convertibles and bonds with equity warrants attached-expanded sharply during 1987. This was due to large issuance activity in the first three-quarters of the year. The activity encompassed both a fall in the sales of convertible bonds and an increase in the use of bonds with equity warrants.

After a contraction, the international bond markets sharply expanded in 1988. They recovered to their former peak level activity which was reached in 1986. Their recovery was assisted by strong expansion in the swap market and continued during 1989 when the Japanese borrowers issued equity warrants. Other market segments remained subdued because of the flattening of the yield curve for several currencies which has been alluded to earlier. Besides, liquidity in the secondary markets for international bonds has increasingly been viewed as limited.

The investors showed a preference for the bonds issued by top-quality sovereign borrowers where the risk was rated as low. Little wonder that these issues were dominated by industrial countries. In 1988 and 1989, their issues accounted for 87 per cent of the total issues of international bonds. The share of the developing countries was miniscule-4 per cent of the total in 1988 and 2 per cent in 1989.

Early repayment of bonds, which had become a market style, slowed down in 1989. Rising interest rates prevented many borrowers from refinancing the existing debt. As regards the currency composition, the scene continued to change and the share of dollar-denominated bonds which was 37 per cent during 1987 and 1988 went up to 50 per cent the following year. The dollar's gaining strength and declining interest rate were the reasons behind this development. Bonds denominated in yen fell from 15 to 10 per cent of the total between 1987 and 1989, owing to uncertainties about the exchange rate as well as movements in differentials between Japanese and US interest rates.

Fears about the depreciation of the deutsche mark and the Swiss franc also led to low issuance of bonds denominated in these currencies. The types of instruments used in the international bond markets further underwent a significant change. Issues in fixed rate bonds increased by 32 per cent in

1988 due to the credibility of anti-inflationary programmes. The favourable terms available in the swap markets also assisted the growth.

Markets dampened in 1989 because of the flattening of the yield curve, which reduced the demand for medium-term bonds *vis-à-vis* short-term bonds. Borrowers from the USA and the UK were the most important in this market segment. Although the use of floating rate instruments had declined in 1987, it later picked up a little because of borrowing by the mortgage institutions and building societies from the UK.

The equity-related bond issues, after a moderate decline in 1988, rose again in 1989. These market segments were overwhelmingly dominated by the Japanese issuers who accounted for 87 per cent of the new issues in 1988 and 96 per cent the following year. The issues were the bonds denominated in US dollars with equity warrants. The investors were attracted to them because of the profit opportunities provided by the strong performance of the Tokyo stock market.

A noteworthy development of 1989 was the successful issue by the World Bank of the first global bond which was launched simultaneously in Europe and the USA. We shall see in the next section that liberalization and elimination of controls in a number of markets has blurred the line between the domestic markets and Euromarkets. The market segmentation is made mainly by divergent market traditions and practices. The global bond of the World Bank was an attempt to reconcile these practices and overcome the differences because, if they could be overcome, the borrower would have simultaneous access to a large pool of investors, thus reducing his cost. Another advantage that the Bank expected to have was to tap the most liquid market segments in the USA by being classified with the US government agencies.

FUNDAMENTAL CHANGES IN MARKET TRENDS

The developments and changes that have taken place in financial markets in the recent past have been influenced by two fundamental processes: first, the strengthening of the linkages between the individual markets which tended to integrate national economies and provide a deeper market for instruments of different kinds; second, in so far as the market participants operate with increasing freedom in the various segments of the international financial system, the international financial markets are globalized-the decision-maker can increasingly think of them as an integrated whole.

MARKET INTEGRATION

An integration process between countries, between different market sectors, between institutions, between maturities and between instruments gained momentum during the 1980s. It brought the capital markets closer together and linked them, enabling the intermediation process between saving and investment to become more efficient and thereby reducing the cost of capital to firms and increasing returns to savers. Better integrated markets facilitate the reallocation of a broadening spectrum of risks, thus enhancing the scope and efficiency of international and intertemporal resource allocation. The flip-side of this coin is that this process may be creating new risks that are not fully understood as yet.

The integration of capital markets followed the policy initiatives to liberalize restrictions and deregulate the domestic markets in all the major industrialized economies. For instance, in the US financial markets the dividing line between banking and the securities business has become increasingly nebulous. Several restrictions have been eliminated between Eurocurrency markets in Germany and the UK, encouraging the merging of domestic and offshore capital markets. The most recent steps in this direction were taken by the Japanese authorities who have freed interest rates through a reduction in the minimum size of deposits bearing full market rates. Steps to liberalize Euro-yen lending and encourage the development of domestic money markets are also under way. Dismantling of restrictions on the entry of foreign banks and financial institutions in domestic markets stimulated the market integration process. Since the foreign banks lack the base of retail business, they do most of their business with other customers and other banks, yet they do make the domestic markets more competitive. In this context, it should be noted that the OECD has a code regarding the freedom of capital movement and the industrial countries are party to this code. However, some industrial countries are still opposed to the idea of allowing the takeover of large domestic banks and securities houses by non-residents.

An economic integration process in the EC is at present under way and several dramatic strides have been made towards the integration of financial markets. Likewise, under the US-Canada Free Trade Agreement similar efforts are under way in North America. In the EC, the Second Banking Directive allows a Community bank to perform throughout the Community all the functions it is authorized to perform in its home country. Since several important measures have already been taken and there is a high degree of commitment to integrating financial services in the Community, the remaining restrictions will fizzle away gradually. In addition, the freedom of capital movements will pressurize the authorities to harmonize taxes and other regulations.

The blurring of distinctions between different instruments is another characteristic feature of the current capital markets. Although the distinction between syndicated loans and bonds exists, syndicate banks are becoming more like underwriters because they tend to sell off almost all the loan participation to other banks and financial institutions. The note issuing programmes adopted by corporate borrowers used to be a prerogative of banks in the past. The integration process in the financial markets has been assisted by growth and expansion of the derivative products. They have managed to increase the efficiency of the financial markets at both national and international levels. Integration of the international financial markets leads to globalization of investor and borrower behaviour. Let us look at that now.

Globalization

Over the 1980s, large institutional investors dominated the

assets issued on international capital markets. A large proportion of assets were issued by insurance companies, pension funds, mutual funds and other investment trusts. The institutional investors have a markedly different behavioural pattern from that of individual investors which, in turn, has important implications for the development of capital markets. They are under intense competitive pressure and are better placed to use the derivative products to adjust their portfolios than individual investors are.

They also respond more rapidly to market developments and their moves are well researched, which implies that the institutional investors have a shorter time horizon than the individual investors.

There has been a strong tendency among institutional investors to turn to foreign assets to reduce the volatility of their returns and steady their earnings. For instance, the share of foreign equities and bonds in the total portfolio of UK pension funds rose from 5 per cent in 1979 to 20 per cent in 1988. The foreign securities in total securities holdings of life insurance companies rose from 15 per cent in 1981 to 31 per cent in 1988. However, most countries for prudential reasons regulate and limit the amount of foreign assets that can be acquired, although these regulations are now dwindling.

The globalization trend in the financial markets was assisted by the advances in financial information and telecommunications technology and the emergence of the derivative products markets. Together they changed their roles of institutional investors and financial intermediaries. The large market power of these investors increased the scope and reduced the cost of financial engineering, i.e. the creation of customised products for both borrowers and investors. At present, in many markets large institutional investors can obtain tailor-made assets that are not available to the general public. The telecommunications technology now also allows these investors to circumvent the middleman function of the securities houses and have a direct real-time access to capital markets and bid on securities directly as they are issued. In fact, 'disintermediation' became a buzz word of the late 1980s.

INTERNATIONAL EQUITY MARKETS

During the 1980s, the equity markets expanded rapidly all over the world and there was a concomitant increase in international trade in them, i.e. transactions in domestic stocks involving non-residents soared. The international equity issues entail underwriting and distribution of equity securities to investors in one or more markets outside the issuers' home country by national or international underwriting syndicates, e.g. Canadian fund managers investing in Japanese stock or British investment trusts selling Germany equity. The growth in international trading in equities suffered in 1987 and fell in 1988, yet the annual average growth rate for the period 1979-88 was 18 per cent. The average annual growth of share prices was 16 per cent during this period. By 1988, international equity trading amounted to over $1.2 trillion and, in one out of every nine equity tradings, the buyer or the seller was a non-resident.

The reason behind such a brisk growth in international equity markets was an attempt by portfolio managers to reduce risk through international portfolio diversification. It also reflected a tendency to cash in on international arbitrage opportunities emerging from changing macroeconomic and regulatory environments. The portfolio diversification trend was facilitated by a reduction in barriers to both international capital movements and international provision of financial services. Towards the end of the decade, about 10 per cent of investment portfolios in the large industrial countries consisted of foreign assets.

With expansion in trade in international equities, the international stock markets have grown more interdependent. This is reflected in an increase in correlation between the price movements in different market centres. The correlation coefficient between stock price indices in the USA and other industrialized countries increased, on average, from 0.35 in 1975-9 to 0.62 in 1985-8. The greater interdependence reflects greater market efficiency, i.e. funds can freely flow from markets where assets are overvalued to those where they are undervalued. Eventually, the stock prices tend to be based on risk-return criteria, making the most productive use of resources feasible. The flip-side of this coin is that interdependence makes market shocks easily transferable.

The incidents of October 1987, as we shall see, demonstrated the speed with which adverse market developments can spread through equity markets almost all over the world. As stated, the expansionary trend in international equity trading was interrupted by the events of October 1987 and the value of trading dropped by 10 per cent in 1988. The number of traded shares showed a more precipitous fall of 26 per cent. However, these flows recovered strongly in 1989. The gross international equity investment from the FRG, Japan, the UK and the USA reached an annualized flow of $584 billion in the first quarter of 1989, compared with $485 billion in the previous year and $546 billion in 1987.

Although the equity market crash of 1987 has been factually, if somewhat euphemistically, referred to in the preceding paragraphs, we need to dwell on it further to bring out its real and comparative dimensions. The severity of this shock has been compared with the collapse of equity prices in October 1929. What was unique about the October 1987 decline in equity prices was not the scale of decline but the speed with which it took place and spread from one market to another-the panic selling was almost global in nature. Countries with short settlement periods reported exceptional pressure from foreign market participants seeking to utilize the liquidity of their markets to meet obligations elsewhere.

It was observed that the effect of trading halts or price limits in one market spilled over into other markets. With the multiple listings of stocks and instruments on a number of exchanges, such phenomena are not surprising. There were several reasons behind the collapse, many of which lay in the macroeconomic factors and the structural characteristics of equity markets. Large and persistent external payments and fiscal imbalances in some of the large industrial countries have been viewed by many analysts as being incompatible with stable financial and foreign exchange market conditions.

Although these imbalances created pressures on financial and foreign exchange markets, the short-term developments in equity markets in the months preceding the crash were viewed as most directly affected by:

- The interest and exchange rate movements and
- Perceived policy conflicts between the authorities in some of the major industrialized countries.

The new or primary international equity issues, other than equity-linked bonds, soared from $300 million in 1984 to $18 billion in 1987. The interruption of 1987 was squarely reflected by a sharp decrease in new international issues of equity to $7.7 billion in 1988. The decline was particularly sharp in the issues of Euroequities and issues related to privatizations. Although the Euroequities dominate the international equity market, privatization-related issues have also grown large in volume. Judged by the 1988 performance, investors in the UK were the most active in international equity markets.

The value of their trade was estimated at $224 billion, or 18 per cent of the total value of international equity trade. The USA and Japan came next each with 12 per cent of the total value of the international equity market transactions, while investors from Europe accounted for 27 per cent. Among the Europeans, the Swiss investors were the most active and accounted for 11 per cent of global equity turnover. As for the benefits of these flows, the USA was the largest recipient of international equity investment. Europe has been of increasing importance, partly as a result of the corporate restructuring that has taken place in relation to the planned establishment of a unified European market by 1992. International interest in Japan has been strong and it has been estimated that non-residents own as much as 4 per cent of the Japanese equity securities.

M&As were a significant source of cross-border equity flows. In 1988, they generated about $125 billion in cross-border flows through 2,500 international M&A deals. Again, firms in the UK were the most aggressive in this arena, acquiring foreign firms with a total value of $44 billion, three-quarters of which were accounted for by the acquisition of US firms. The value of international acquisitions by the European companies was $37 billion, almost half of it involving acquisitions of US firms. The M&As in the USA remained the most attractive target for international portfolio investors in other industrialized economies.

DEVELOPMENT AND GROWTH IN DERIVATIVE PRODUCTS

Exchange rates and interest rates remained highly volatile during the 1970s and the early 1980s and created a need for hedging instruments which in turn stimulated the search for new products and techniques to transform and reallocate financial risks. The environment of financial liberalization, market innovation and relaxation of controls in the industrial countries made this search easier. Consequently, the interest rate and currency fluctuation hedging instruments came into being and their use expanded rapidly.

A significant development was the use of exchange-traded contracts as opposed to over the counter (OTC) contracts. These contracts had the advantage that their associated secondary markets were far more liquid. Since the exchange acted as counterparty in such contracts and the margin requirements had to be maintained on a daily basis, exchange-traded instruments had much less credit risk than the OTC instruments. On exchanges around the world, this trading activity continued to expand vigourously not only in terms of the variety of instruments offered but also in terms of trading volume.

The Euro-dollar interest rate future contracts began life on the Chicago Mercantile Exchange (CME) in 1981 and expanded rapidly. By 1987, the average monthly trading volume at the CME had risen by 88 per cent to 1.8 million contracts having a face value of $1.8 billion, and the expansion continued. Of late, the LIFFE and SIMEX also expanded their trading in the Euro-dollar interest rate futures but the volumes traded on these exchanges were modest compared with those on the CME. Likewise, trading in Euro-dollar options contracts, which began in 1985 at the CME and the LIFFE, also expanded sharply. The SIMEX Euro-dollar options, however, have shown limited growth because of excessive premia.

The interest rate futures and options contracts have also traded actively on the major exchanges. For instance, the volume of futures contracts on US Treasury bonds on the LIFFE recorded a dramatic increase from a monthly average of 23,628 contracts in 1984 to 127,360 contracts in 1987 and has continued to expand.

In August 1987, the LIFFE also began futures contracts on Japanese government bonds which began strongly but the market stabilized thereafter at a moderate level of about 11,000 contracts a month. The volume of trading of futures contracts on ninety-day US Treasury bills has also been large at CME but the average volumes have contracted recently. The same trend has been observed in options contracts on US Treasury bills.

The trading activity in currency futures has been concentrated in the CME and other exchanges in the USA, as noted in the preceding paragraph, and has expanded considerably. Of late, trading in yen futures experienced the highest growth rate. Similarly, trading currency options began in 1982 on the Philadelphia Stock Exchange (PHLX) and it has remained the most active centre for currency options. The trading volumes in the yen and the deutsche mark have recorded the highest expansion rates.

Since the early 1980s, an important OTC hedging instrument has emerged and its use has grown in significance and volume. It is the medium-term swap which is used to arbitrage differences in borrowing costs across financial markets and to reallocate the interest rate and exchange rate risks contained in medium-term financial transactions. The access to swaps is limited by creditworthiness considerations. Borrowers in industrial countries use interest rate swap markets to convert their floating interest rate debt into the equivalent of fixed interest rate debts, both measured on the same notional principal amount and the same maturity. The interest rate and currency swaps have been among the fastest growing financial instruments of the 1980s.

By the end of 1987, the total amount of outstanding swap transactions reached the $1.1 trillion mark. Interest rate swaps account for 80 per cent of the total outstanding swap transactions while currency swaps account for the remaining 20 per cent. A large part of the latter involves the dollar and the yen swaps. A study of the International Swap Dealers Association (ISDA), New York, revealed a very low incidence of losses. Of the seventy-one major firms covered, only eleven had any losses to report, which reflects the general creditworthiness of counterparties engaged in swaps. The expansion of OTC markets for derivative products has continued and by the end of 1988 the market volume for interest rate and currency swaps reached $1.3 trillion. Of this, about $1.0 trillion were the interest rate swaps and $317 million were currency swaps. The annual report of the ISDA revealed that, at the end of 1988, 72 per cent of the interest rate swaps were in dollars and 8 per cent in yen.

For currency swaps, 86 per cent involved dollars and 42 per cent yen. It should be noted that the percentage of swaps denominated in all currencies total 200 per cent because each currency swap involves two currencies. Other OTC derivative products, namely interest rate caps, floors, collars and 'swaptions', accounted for $327 billion of notional principal at the end of 1988.

Developing Countries In The Capital Markets: When measured in terms of net or gross capital flows, the degree of integration of developing countries in the international financial system was less at the end of the 1980s than at the beginning. This was the result of the development of the debt crisis and the resultant reappraisal of the risks involved in the bank lending to the public sectors of the highly indebted LDCs. The spontaneous flows have declined and remained limited to the developing countries that have not restructured their debt in the recent past. The bond markets experienced the same and the volume of bonds issued by LDCs declined dramatically. As opposed to this, foreign direct investment in these countries rose, which was partly a consequence of debt-equity conversion schemes. Interest in the LDC portfolio investment also rose and several investment funds were established. The Asian newly industrializing economies (ANIEs) expanded their links with the international financial markets as both users and suppliers of capital, and integrated themselves better than most other LDCs.

A clear polarization can be observed in recent trends in bank claims. LDCs without debt-servicing problems recorded increases in bank claims as well as bond issues, whereas the claims on fifteen heavily indebted countries witnessed a decline. According to the Fund's *International Banking Statistics* (IBS), the estimated cash flow from banks to the latter group of LDCs during 1985-8 was $14 billion compared with a net repayment of $15 billion, measured by the exchange-rate-adjusted change in stocks. During the first three quarters of 1988, despite minor increases in disbursements, bank claims on this group of LDCs declined by an estimated $11.3 billion. Total disbursements under the conceited lending arrangements during 1988 were $6.0 billion, marginally above the 1987 level of $5.7 billion.

Attempts to resolve the LDC debt riddle continued and the terms of rescheduling were relatively more favourable to LDCs in 1988 when the average maturities extended up to eighteen years and the average spreads above the LIBOR contracted to 83 points. The use of exit bonds also increased substantially. The banks found them more acceptable in the case of Brazil than they had in the past for Argentina. More attractive pricing was the main reason behind it. Several Latin American debtors made special efforts to reduce their debt.

In their eagerness to bring down the exposure to debt-ridden LDCs, banks accelerated the rate of disposing of claims on them in 1988. The US banks' claims declined by $12.7 billion in 1988, which followed a decline of $10 billion the year before. The smaller and regional US banks accounted for a major part of this decline. Banks in other countries, except Germany and Japan, bent with the wind and reduced their LDC exposures as well. Coupled with the strengthening of bank capital bases, this trend improves the ratio of LDC debt to bank capital in all major banking systems.

Likewise, the nine US money-centre banks strengthened their capital bases considerably, although it should be noted that their levels of exposure in relation to capital were generally among the highest in the world. The trend in making provisions against LDC exposure continued in 1988, but it was much smaller than in the past. Japan was a late starter in this respect and the Japanese banks were allowed to raise their provisioning levels from 5 per cent to 15 per cent only in early 1989. Canada also raised the mandatory provisioning standards. However, in the USA and Japan, the mandatory provisioning standards remained at the lowest level in the world.

The debt of LDCs with servicing problems tended to be traded at a discount to its face value and gradually a secondary market developed in LDC debt. The exact size of the secondary market is not known but the 1988 transactions were in the vicinity of $40 billion, far above the $5 billion mark reached in 1985.

Although there was a decline in turnover in the first two months of 1989 to about one-half of the 1988 level, the announcement of the Brady Plan in March 1989 by the US Treasury caused the turnover to recover strongly. The participating banks anticipated more debt-restructuring agreements and the resumption of a debt-equity programme.

Two kinds of transactions dominate the secondary market:

1. Debt swaps, which help banks restructure their LDC loan portfolios to their advantage, and
2. Cash transactions, which include purchases by countries of their own debt at a discount and conversion of debt into equity. Such transactions have grown in importance with the increase in debt conversion schemes.

The secondary market prices of LDC debt had a declining trend in the latter half of the 1980s, and they fell further sharply between July 1988 and March 1989. The weighted average price for the debt of fifteen heavily indebted LDCs came down to 33 cents per dollar of the face value. The 1985 level was 70 per cent of the face value.

In 1986 and 1987 the declines were largely due to the combination of the introduction of a moratorium by Brazil and the provisioning decision by Citibank. The recent fall reflected the market's tendency to respond sharply to changes in perceptions of the general outlook of the debt strategy possibly a sign of a thin market. The short-term movements in the secondary market prices were fuelled essentially by opportunities for debt-equity transactions.

The non-bank financial institutions have not shown a great deal of interest in LDC debt and efforts to repackage LDC loans as marketable securities have so far met little success. According to the estimates of the IMF, the total volume of debt conversion under officially recognized schemes was as low as $4.6 billion in 1987 and $8.2 billion in 1988.

It took about five years after the eruption of the LDC debt crisis for the capital market to evolve its strategy towards the secondary LDC debt market. Since this market has increased considerably in volume, banks now recognize that the secondary market prices contain a certain amount of information and that at these prices some of their claims could be liquidated. They have also become more aware of the possibilities that the secondary market offers them for reorganizing and streamlining their portfolios. That the secondary debt market is the market-oriented solution of a long-festering debt crisis is more widely accepted in the international capital market and several large banks have reorganized their LDC debt operations to merge with their asset-trading operations. These banks are actively reducing their LDC debt exposures through the secondary market.

In order to integrate themselves better with the international capital markets, LDCs will need to ensure that their policies foster and encourage an attractive financial environment for investors. Besides, domestic savers and investors can benefit from a more global outlook and the investment opportunities abroad. We have seen that the international capital movements have become easier because of financial liberalization and technological developments; therefore, there is an all the more pressing need to improve the standards of the domestic financial markets in LDCs. If this does not happen, capital flight will increase.

In addition, to attract capital from both residents and foreign investors, well-functioning domestic financial systems are indispensable. Since the rates of return on many investment projects in LDCs are high, if their financial markets are integrated with those in the rest of the world many LDCs stand a reasonably good chance of attracting the much needed capital. The only conditional clause here is that these LDCs have to see that their country risk factor does not offset the high return factor.

The emerging stock markets: The emerging stock markets in India, Indonesia, Korea, Malaysia, Taiwan, Thailand, Brazil, Chile and Mexico performed well over the 1980s, the bulk of gains coming since 1985. The stock markets in these LDCs have come to be known as the emerging stock markets. Low oil prices, the booming world trade and relatively successful economic policies in the key emerging market developing countries helped share prices rise strongly. With the exception of Brazil, where large devaluations against the US dollar more than eroded gains in the local market, other emerging markets did extraordinarily well over the 1985-9 period.

In Taiwan, the market recorded outstanding growth and roughly doubled each year. The majority of the key emerging stock markets are in outward-oriented economies which prospered faster on the back of sustained export growth, particularly in manufacturing. In Asia, for instance, Taiwan, Korea, Thailand and Malaysia were highly successful on the export front throughout the 1980s. Indonesia saw no growth in the dollar value of its exports between 1980 and 1989 but this conceals a 40 per cent increase in exports since the halving of oil prices in 1986. The Latin American three, Brazil, Chile and Mexico, showed less impressive growth during the 1980s than those in Asia but could still be judged to be exporting successes. India is not considered to be an export success.

Two factors, namely higher rates of share price appreciation and prospects of gains from diversification, make a strong case for investing in the emerging markets. The IFC data suggest that a portfolio with a mix of emerging and developed market securities will show lower variability than one with only the latter. Some investors and fund managers see emerging markets as a growth area that cannot be ignored. An indicator of potential growth is that their market capitalization in aggregate is only about 5 per cent of world stock market capitalization, despite a 12 per cent share in the world GDP. However, fund managers believe that they need to be cautious in buying because company valuations in the embryonic markets may not fairly reflect the best forecast on earnings growth. Their emphasis is not to be on buying the market as a whole but on picking the specific stocks.

After several good years, 1990 has been a difficult period for these markets and by October 1990 market capitalization was down by an average of 39 per cent on their end 1989 levels (weighted by market capitalization). The relatively poor performance is also visible in the market prices of traded country funds. With only a few exceptions, their quoted prices fell during 1992. Some of the declines can be explained as being market corrections after rapid rises over the past few years had taken prices to unsustainable levels.

Risk Management In The International Financial Institutions: Inasmuch as competitive pressure in the international financial markets has increased as a result of a dynamic growth in innovative products and the use of derivative instruments and the advancement in telecommunications technology, the general level of risk has *pari passu* soared. Apparently, it is necessary to control it and keep it within prudent limits. To be sure, increased competition and market liberalization have had a favourable effect on the market efficiency because competition is considered as value creating. However, along with that the financial markets should remain sound and supportive of growth in the real economy and confidence in them must not waiver. Therefore, supervisory authorities in a number of countries are reassessing the adequacy of prudential arrangements, at both national and international levels.

There are two principal kinds of risks: credit risk and liquidity risk. The former implies that a counterparty is not able to reimburse the bank when an obligation falls due. The general perception is that the credit risk in the international banking system has been increasing and that banks have stumbled into riskier areas in search of higher rates of return on assets so that stock prices and capital can be raised. Second, there is evidence that liquidity risk has also increased. It refers to the inability of the banks to have, or to be able to raise, enough liquid assets to meet current needs. Some of the innovative products have turned out to be less liquid than initially believed.

Besides, banks have moved into securities business and changes in securities market conditions can suddenly transform short-term credits into illiquid assets. This tendency has forced banks to examine each other's credit rating a little more carefully and look for new mechanisms for limiting exposure. Third, due to a gradual elimination of interest rate controls and a reduction in the sources of low cost funding, banks could become more exposed to interest rate risk if their interest rate in liabilities is not matched with that in assets. Funding raised on floating rates and lending on a similar basis reduces interest risk to an extent but effectively converts it into increased credit risk. A mismatch of currency composition in assets and liabilities can create an additional risk which exposes banks to the possibility of adverse changes in exchange rates.

Lastly, although the derivative products were designed to control risk through various hedging techniques, these new instruments as alluded to earlier are not without their own risk characteristics. It is difficult to know what they are until sufficient experience has been gained regarding how they function, and in particular how they function during an economic downturn. With so many banks and financial institutions using innovative products, it is felt that the risk involved is at times inadequately appreciated. It is partly due to the arcane nature of some of the new instruments and computerized strategies that often drive their use. The Basle capital adequacy standards have begun to take such multiple exposures into account.

The newest standards for banks, in fact, have been designed to achieve three objectives:

1. To harmonize the competitive conditions under which international banks operate,
2. To bring indirect financial commitments within a general prudential framework, and
3. To inject more capital into the banking system. We shall return to this issue a little later.

The securities houses are not being left out of supervision and relative responsibilities of the parent company and of branches are being defined. Having uniform standards for securities houses is difficult because there are considerable differences in the structures of securities businesses in different countries. In addition, the focuses and objectives of securities market regulations differ from country to country. With financial markets becoming more fully integrated, the need for an internationally consistent supervision approach is greater than it was in the past. Deliberations are under way in the International Organization of Securities Commissions (IOSCO), the OECD and other fora on these and related aspects. Attention is also being paid to the safety and efficiency of the securities transactions.

The work of the regulatory authorities has become increasingly difficult with the gradual breakdown of functional barriers within the financial services industry. While the most apparent trend is in the integration of banking and securities businesses, there is also a gradual trend towards the integration of banking, insurance and other financial services. Regulating and supervising diversified financial conglomerates is therefore onerous but necessary because a problem in one area can quickly spread from one financial sector to another. Therefore, functional rather than institutional supervision is becoming more relevant. This approach was taken by the Financial Services Act of the UK which regulates specific lines of business, ignoring the fact of whether it is a bank or a security house that is involved.

In the ultimate analysis, the supervisory authorities have to establish a level of regulation that maximizes market competition without jeopardizing safety and soundness. With deepening market integration, the problem of striking a balance between the two prime objectives is becoming more complex. The over-arching challenge for the supervisory authorities lies in finding the appropriate level of prudential supervision in a liberalized regulatory environment.

The latest measures taken by the BIS and endorsed by the G10 in July 1988 were rather significant. They fixed a minimum capital base for international banks at 8 per cent of risk-weighted assets and off-balance-sheet commitments. These are the minimum capital requirements but national authorities are free to impose more stringent requirements.

The general reaction of the banks was:

- To raise more capital,
- To shed or restructure assets and
- To endeavour to generate higher returns by improvising margins.

The first measure has already led banks all over the world to increase their primary and secondary capital. The shedding of LDC debt or reducing their LDC exposure has been favourably received by the financial market. The pressure for higher capital ratios has led many banks either to securitize their claims or to sell to non-bank financial institutions and investors. It has also led some banks to rein in the growth of their assets. Many international banks have adjusted their balance sheets to switch the relative weight of capital-absorbing assets in favour of those with low-risk weights. The need to raise returns on assets and generate more funds has encouraged banks to move towards earning more fee income.

This movement has been necessitated by a squeeze in margins in regular banking business due to an excess capacity in the industry:

- Quantifying International Capital Mobility in The 1980s

Feldstein and Horioka upset conventional wisdom in 1980 when they concluded that changes in countries' rates of national saving had a very large effect on their rates of investment, and interpreted this finding as evidence of low capital mobility. Although their regressions have been subject to a great variety of criticisms, their basic finding seems to hold up. But does it imply imperfect capital mobility?

Let us begin by asking why we would ever expect a shortfall in one country's national saving *not* to reduce the overall availability of funds and thereby crowd out investment projects that might otherwise be undertaken in that country. After all, national saving and investment are linked through an identity. (The variable that completes the identity is, of course, the current account balance.)

The aggregation together of all forms of 'capital' has caused more than the usual amount of confusion in the literature on international capital mobility. Nobody ever claimed that international flows of foreign direct investment were large enough that a typical investment project in the domestic country would costlessly be undertaken directly by a foreign company when there was a shortfall in domestic saving. Rather, the argument was that the typical American corporation could borrow at the going interest rate in order to finance its investment projects and, if the degree of capital mobility were sufficiently high, the going interest rate would be tied down to the world interest rate by international flows of *portfolio* capital. If portfolio capital were a perfect substitute for physical capital, then the difference would be immaterial; but the two types of capital are probably not in fact perfect substitutes.

A number of alternative ways of quantifying the degree of international capital mobility are examined. One conclusion is that the barriers to cross-border flows are low enough that, by 1989, financial markets can be said to be virtually completely integrated among the large industrial countries (and among some smaller countries as well). But this is a different proposition from saying that real interest rates are equalized across countries, which is still different from saying that investment projects in a country are unaffected by a shortfall in national saving. We shall see that there are several crucial links that can, and probably do, fail to hold.

In many cases, notably the UK and Japan (and perhaps now Italy and France as well), the finding of high integration with world financial markets is a relatively new one, attributable to liberalization programmes over the last ten years. Even in the case of financial markets in the USA, integration with the Euromarkets appears to have been incomplete as recently as 1982. The USA is that the current account deficits of the 1980s have been large enough, and by now have lasted long enough, to reduce estimates of the correlation between saving and investment significantly. The increased degree of world-wide financial integration since 1979 is identified as one likely factor that has allowed such large capital flows to take place over the past decade. But even if US interest rates are now viewed as tied to world interest rates, there are still other weak links in the chain. The implication is that crowding out of domestic investment can still take place.

FOUR ALTERNATIVE DEFINITIONS OF INTERNATIONAL CAPITAL MOBILITY

By the second half of the 1970s, international economists had come to speak of the world financial system as characterized by perfect capital mobility. In many ways, this was 'jumping the gun'. It is true that financial integration had been greatly enhanced after 1973 by the removal of capital controls on the part of the USA, Germany, Canada, Switzerland and the Netherlands; by the steady process of technical and institutional innovation, particularly in the Euromarkets; and by the recycling of OPEC surpluses to developing countries. But almost all developing countries retained extensive restrictions on international capital flows, as did a majority of industrialized countries. Even among the five major countries without capital controls, capital was not perfectly mobile by some definitions.

There are at least four distinct definitions of perfect capital mobility that are in widespread use:

1. The *Feldstein-Horioka definition:* Exogenous changes in national saving (i.e. in either private savings or government budgets) can be easily financed by borrowing from abroad at the going real interest rate, and thus need not crowd out investment in the

originating country (except perhaps to the extent that the country is large in world financial markets).

2. *Real interest parity:* International capital flows equalize real interest rates across countries.
3. *Uncovered interest parity:* Capital flows equalize expected rates of return on countries' bonds, despite exposure to exchange risk.
4. *Closed interest parity:* Capital flows equalize interest rates across countries when contracted in a common currency.

These four possible definitions are in ascending order of specificity. Only the last condition is an unalloyed criterion for capital mobility in the sense of the degree of financial market integration across national boundaries.

Each of the first three conditions, if it is to hold, requires an auxiliary assumption in addition to the condition that follows it. Uncovered interest parity requires not only closed (or covered) interest parity, but also the condition that the exchange risk premium is zero. Real interest parity requires not only uncovered interest parity, but also the condition that expected real depreciation is zero. The Feldstein-Horioka condition requires not only real interest parity, but also a certain condition on the determinants of investment. But even though the relevance to the degree of integration of financial markets decreases as auxiliary conditions are added, the relevance to questions regarding the origin of international payments imbalances increases. We begin our consideration of the various criteria of capital mobility with the Feldstein-Horioka definition.

FELDSTEIN-HORIOKA TESTS

The Feldstein-Horioka definition requires that the country's real interest rate is tied to the world real interest rate by criterion:

- It is, after all, the real interest rate rather than the nominal interest rate on which saving and investment in theory depend. But for criterion
- To hold, it is also necessary that any and all determinants of a country's rate of investment *other*

than its real interest rate be uncorrelated with its rate of national saving. Let the investment rate be given by where *I* is the level of capital formation, *Y* is national output, *r* is the domestic real interest rate and *u* represents all other factors, whether quantifiable or not, that determine the rate of investment. Feldstein and Horioka (1980) regressed the investment rate against the national saving rate,

The saving-investment literature Feldstein and Horioka's finding that the coefficient *B* is in fact closer to unity than to zero has been reproduced many times. Most authors have not been willing, however, to follow them in drawing the inference that financial markets are not highly integrated. There have been many econometric critiques, falling into two general categories.

The point most commonly made is that national saving is endogenous, or in our terms is correlated with *ui*. This will be the case if national saving and investment are both procyclical, as they are in fact known to be, or if they both respond to the population or productivity growth rates. But Feldstein and Horioka made an effort to handle the econometric endogeneity of national saving, more so than have some of their critics. To handle the cyclical endogeneity, they computed averages over a sufficiently long period of time that business cycles could be argued to wash out. To handle other sources of endogeneity, they used demographic variables as instrumental variables for the saving rate.

The other econometric critique is that, if the domestic country is large in world financial markets, r^* will not be exogenous with respect to (NS/*Y*)*i*, and therefore, even if $r=r^*$, *r* and in turn *(I/Y)i* will be correlated with (NS/*Y*)*i*. In other words, a shortfall in domestic savings will drive up the world interest rate and thus crowd out investment in the domestic country as well as abroad. This 'large-country' argument has been made. An insufficiently appreciated point is that the large-country argument does not create a problem in cross-section studies, because all countries share the same world interest rate r^*. Since r^* simply goes into the constant term in a cross-section regression, it cannot be the source of any correlation with the right-hand-side variable. The large-country problem cannot explain why the countries that are high-saving relative to the average tend to coincide with the countries that are high-investing relative to the average.

If the regressions of saving and investment rates were a good test for barriers to financial market integration, one would expect to see the coefficient falling over time. Until now, the evidence has if anything showed the coefficient rising over time. This finding has emerged both from cross-section studies, which typically report pre- and post-1973 results, and from pure time-series studies for the USA. The econometric endogeneity of national saving does not appear to be the explanation for this finding, because it holds equally well when instrumental variables are used.

The easy explanation for the finding is that, econometric problems aside, real interest parity-criterion (2) above-has not held any better in recent years than it did in the past. For example, found even more significant rejections of real interest parity among major industrialized countries for the floating rate period after 1973.

Some of the major industrialized countries in the 1980s moved farther from real interest parity than they had been in the 1970s. In the early 1980s, the real interest rate in the USA, in particular, rose far above the real interest rate of its major trading partners, by any of a variety of measures. If the domestic real interest rate is not tied to the foreign real interest rate, then there is no reason to expect a zero coefficient in the saving-investment regression. We discuss in a later section the factors underlying real interest differentials.

The US Saving-Investment Regression Updated

Since 1980 the massive fiscal experiment carried out under the Reagan Administration has been rapidly undermining the statistical finding of a high saving-investment correlation for the case of the USA. The increase in the structural budget deficit, which was neither accommodated by monetary policy nor financed by an increase in private saving, reduced the national saving rate by 3 per cent of GNP relative to the 1970s. The investment rate-which, like the saving rate, initially fell in the 1981-2 recession-in the late 1980s approximately re-attained its 1980 level at best.

The saving shortfall was made up, necessarily, by a flood of borrowing from abroad equal to more than 3 per cent of GNP-hence the current account deficit of $161 billion in 1987. By now, the divergence between US national saving and investment has been sufficiently large and long lasting to show up in longer-term regressions of the Feldstein-Horioka type. If one seeks to isolate the degree of capital mobility or crowding out for the USA in particular, and how it has changed over time, then time-series regression is necessary. Decade averages are used for each variable, which removes some of the cyclical variation but gives us only twelve observations.

As before, the coefficient is statistically greater than zero and is not statistically different from unity, suggesting a high degree of crowding out. But the point estimate of the coefficient (when correcting for possible serial correlation) drops from 0.91 in the earlier study to 0.79 in the longer sample. We can allow for a time trend in the coefficient; it drops from *plus* 0.01 a year in the earlier study to *minus* 0.01 a year (or plus 0.001, when correcting for serial correlation) in the longer sample. Thus the additional years 1980-7 do show up as anticipated: as exhibiting a lower US degree of crowding out, even if the change is small. (The trend is not statistically significant, but this is not surprising given the small number of observations.)

A data set that begins later would seem more promising than the twelve decade averages. Much of the variation in the yearly data is cyclical. (The cyclical adjustment of each is accomplished by first regressing it on the GNP gap, defined as the percentage deviation from the Bureau of Economic Analysis's 'middle expansion trend' of GNP, and then taking the residuals.)

In previous work with a sample period of 1956-84, the coefficient in a regression of cyclically adjusted saving and investment rates was estimated at 0.80, statistically indistinguishable from unity. But now the coefficient has dropped essentially to zero, suggesting a zero degree of crowding out, or a zero degree of 'saving-retention'. This finding is the result of the addition to the sample of another three years of record current account deficits, a period also in which the cyclically adjusted national saving rate was historically low. When the equation is estimated with an allowance for a time trend in the coefficient, the trend is negative (though statistically insignificant), whereas the earlier sample that stopped in 1984 showed a time trend that was positive (and insignificant).

To verify that the 1980s experience is indeed the source of the precipitous fall in the saving-investment coefficient, the sample period is split at 1980. For the period 1955-79, not only is the coefficient statistically indistinguishable from unity, but the point estimate is slightly *greater* than unity. It is clearly the unprecedented developments of the present decade that have overturned the hitherto-robust saving-investment relationship for the case of the USA.

It is likely that financial liberalization in Japan, the UK and other countries, and continued innovation in the Euromarkets (and perhaps the 1984 repeal of the US withholding tax on borrowing from abroad), have resulted in a higher degree of capital mobility, and thereby facilitated the record flow of capital to the USA in the 1980s. But the magnitude of the inflow is in the first instance attributable to the unprecedented magnitude of the decline in national saving.

DIFFERENTIALS IN EXPECTED RATES OF RETURN, AND EXPECTED REAL DEPRECIATION

If the goal is to measure the degree of integration of capital markets, rather than the degree to which decreases in national saving have crowded out investment, then it is better to look at differences in rates of return across countries rather than looking at saving-investment correlations. But measuring *real* interest differentials will not do the trick. An international investor, when deciding which country's assets to buy, will not compare the interest rates in different countries each expressed in terms of expected purchasing power over that country's goods. When he or she thinks to evaluate assets in terms of purchasing power, all assets will be evaluated in terms of the same basket, the one consumed by that particular investor. The expected inflation rate then drops out of differentials in expected rates of return among assets.

The differential in expected rates of return on two countries' bonds is the uncovered interest differential, the nominal interest differential minus the expected change in the exchange rate: (Ds$^{)}$. If asset demands are highly sensitive to expected rates of return, then the differential will be zero, which gives us uncovered interest parity:

To distinguish this parity condition from the other definitions, it has often been designated 'perfect substitutability': not only is there little in the manner of transactions costs or government-imposed controls to separate national markets, but also domestic-currency and foreign-currency bonds are perfect substitutes in investors' portfolios.

The enormous real appreciation of the dollar in the early 1980s and the subsequent real depreciation have by now convinced the remaining doubters, but abundant statistical evidence against PPP was there all along. For example, computed for the floating rate period from July 1973 to December 1976 standard deviations of the (logarithmic) real exchange rate equal to 6.0 per cent for the pound-dollar rate and 8.4 per cent for the mark-dollar rate. He also computed serial correlation coefficients for PPP deviations of 0.897 and 0.854, respectively, on a monthly basis, equal to 0.271 and 0.150 on an annual basis. The serial correlation coefficient is of interest because it is equal to one minus the speed of adjustment to PPP. It may be best not to rely exclusively on the standard deviation of the real exchange rate as a summary statistic for the degree of integration of goods markets, because it in part reflects the magnitude of monetary disturbances during the period.

The real exchange rate between the USA and Great Britain. During the floating rate period 1973-87, though there is no significant time trend, there is a large standard error of 15.6

per cent. The serial correlation in the deviations from PPP is estimated at 0.687, with a standard error of 0.208. This means that the estimated speed of adjustment to PPP is 0.313 per year and that one can easily reject the hypothesis of instantaneous adjustment.

From the ashes of absolute PPP, a phoenix has risen. In response to findings such as those reported here, some authors have swung from one extreme, the proposition that the tendency of the real exchange rate to return to a constant is complete and instantaneous, to the opposite extreme, that there is no such tendency at all. The hypothesis that the real exchange rate follows a random walk is just as good as the hypothesis of absolute PPP for implying *ex ante* relative PPP. But there is even less of an *a priori* case why PPP should hold in rate-of-change form rather than in the level form.

Even though *ex ante* relative PPP has little basis in theory, if does appear to have some empirical support. Typically, the estimated speeds of adjustment during the floating rate period, while not so low as to be implausible as point estimates, are nevertheless low enough that one statistically cannot reject the hypothesis that they are zero. In other words, one cannot reject the random walk hypothesis that the autoregression coefficient is unity. A 95 per cent confidence interval on the autoregressive coefficient AR covers the range 0.27-1.10. If the null hypothesis is an autoregressive coefficient of unity, one cannot legitimately use the standard t test derived from a regression where the right-hand side variable is the level of the real exchange rate, because under the null hypothesis the variance is infinite. There are a number of ways of dealing with this non-stationarity problem. Here one simply applies the corrected Dickey-Fuller 95 per cent significance level, 3.00. The 0.31 estimate for the floating rate period is insignificantly different from zero.

A more promising alternative is to choose a longer time sample to get a more powerful estimate. The entire post-war period 1945-87. PPP held better for the Bretton Woods years than it did after 1973, as measured either by the mean absolute deviation and standard deviation of the real exchange rate or by the ability to reject the hypothesis of zero auto-correlation. But, despite the longer time sample, one is only at the borderline of being able to reject the random walk. The 95 per cent confidence interval for AR runs from 0.64 to 1.02 and the *t* ratio of 1.85 falls short of the Dickey-Fuller 95 per cent significance level of 2.93.

The asymptotic standard error of an estimate of AR is approximately the square root of (1"AR)/ *N*. So if the true speed of adjustment is of the order of 30 per cent a year a simple calculation suggests that we might require at least forty-nine years of data to be able to reject the null hypothesis of AR =1. It is not very surprising that forty-three years of data are not enough, much less the fifteen years of data used in most studies. (Econometricians consider the asymptotic standard error on which this calculation is based to be a bad approximation in small samples. But the correct power calculation suggests that, if anything, the sample required to reject a random walk would be even larger than forty-nine.)

With a time sample this long, the standard error is reduced considerably. The rejection of no serial correlation in the real exchange rate is even stronger than in the shorter time samples. More importantly, one is finally able to detect a statistically significant tendency for the real exchange rate to regress to PPP, at a rate of 16 per cent a year. The confidence interval for AR runs from 0.75 to 0.94, safely less than unity, and the *t* ratio of 3.12 exceeds the Dickey-Fuller significance level of 2.89.

The motivation for looking at PPP in this section has been to obtain insight into the expected rate of real depreciation, because that is the variable that can give rise to real interest differentials even in the presence of uncovered interest parity. In rejecting the random walk description of the real exchange rate, one has rejected the claim that the rationally expected rate of real depreciation is zero. To take an example, in 1983-4, when the dollar had appreciated some 30 per cent above its PPP value, survey data show expected future real depreciation of 4.3 per cent per year. It is thus not difficult to explain the existence of the US real interest differential, even without appealing to any sort of risk premium.

If the failure of *ex ante* relative PPP could, in itself, explain the failure of real interest parity, then it could also, by itself, explain the failure of saving and investment to be uncorrelated. In the recent US context, a fall in national saving could cause an increase in the real interest differential and therefore a fall in investment, even if financial markets are perfectly integrated and even if the fall in saving is truly exogenous, provided that the real interest differential is associated with expected real depreciation of the dollar.

Demonstrating that the failure of *ex ante* relative PPP is *capable* of producing a correlation between saving and investment is, of course, not the same thing as asserting that this in fact is the explanation for the observed correlation. Plenty of other competing explanations have been proposed. But some support for the idea that the existence of expected real depreciation *is* key to the observed correlation comes from Cardia (1988). She simulates saving and investment rates in a sequence of models featuring shocks to fiscal spending, money growth and productivity, in order to see which models are capable, for empirically relevant magnitudes of the parametres, of producing saving-investment correlations as high as those observed. To get at some of the explanations that have been most prominently proposed, she constructs models both with and without PPP, both with and without endogenous response of fiscal policy to current account imbalances and both with and without the small-country assumption. The finding is that the model that allows for deviations from PPP is able to explain saving-investment correlations as high as unity, while the various models that impose PPP are generally not able to do so.

Further empirical support for the idea that the Feldstein-Horioka results may in fact be due to imperfect integration of goods markets, rather than imperfect integration of financial markets, is provided by a test. They compute the correlation of saving and investment across regions within the UK, reasoning that these regions-unlike nations-are highly integrated with respect to their goods markets, and find no positive correlation.

A DECOMPOSITION OF REAL INTEREST DIFFERENTIALS FOR TWENTY-FIVE COUNTRIES

Because there are so many competing definitions of the degree of international capital mobility, it would be worth knowing if the sort of countries that register high by one criterion are also the sort that register high by the others. In this section we look at rates of return in the 1980s across a sample of twenty-five countries. We begin with the broadest measure of barriers to international capital mobility. We call it the political or country premium because it captures all barriers to integration of financial markets across national boundaries: transactions costs, information costs, capital controls, tax laws that discriminate by country of residence, default risk and risk of future capital controls. The second term could be described as the real forward discount. We call it the currency premium because it captures differences in assets according to the currency in which they are denominated, rather than in terms of the political jurisdiction in which they are issued. As we shall see, the currency premium can in turn be decomposed into two factors, the exchange risk premium and expected real depreciation.

The decomposition of the real interest differential would not be possible without the use of data on forward exchange rates. Many previous studies have used forward rate data to test covered interest parity, but only for a few countries. The present study uses forward rate data for a panel of twenty-five countries, The set of twenty-five includes countries both large and small, industrialized and developing, Atlantic and Pacific. The forward rate data for most of the countries come from Barclays Bank in London, via Data Resources Inc.

Real Interest Differentials

The twenty-five countries, expressed in each case as the local interest rate measured relative to the Eurodollar interest rate. For local interest rates we use the interbank market rate or, where no market rate exists, the most flexibly determined interest rate available.

We use, to begin with, the realized inflation rates during the *ex post* three-month period. The first column reports the mean real interest differential during the sample period, September 1982 to January 1988. (In this and subsequent tables the statistics go up to April 1988 because the *ex post* data run three months behind the *ex ante* expectations.) The numbers are negative for a majority of countries, averaging "1.74 across all twenty-five, which reflects the high level of real dollar interest rates during this period.

The countries are classified into five groups chosen on *a priori* grounds. The group with real interest rates farthest below the world rate includes Bahrain, Greece, Mexico, Portugal and South Africa.

These five (very diverse) countries bear the burden of representing a wide class of LDCs in our sample. Altogether there are eight countries classified as LDCs that happen to have forward rate data available, and thereby appear in our sample; three of these are East Asian countries (Hong Kong, Singapore and Malaysia) that are thought to have open financial markets in the 1980s and so are here classified separately.

One might object that the large negative real interest differentials in the group of five reflect administered local interest rates that are kept artificially low by 'financial repression'. But countries cannot maintain artificially low interest rates without barriers to capital outflow. These statistics reflect a low degree of capital mobility precisely as we want them to. In this respect our group of five is typical of LDCs. A number of studies, including much larger LDC samples than are available here, have shown the extremes to which real interest rates can go, particularly some very negative levels in the 1970s.

As with the other measures of interest rate differentials that we shall be considering below, the mean is not always the most useful statistic. A small mean over a particular sample period may hide fluctuations in both directions. Even if a mean is statistically significant, it is useful to know in addition the variability of the differential. We also report the root mean squared error in the third column. (This would be a superior measure of how closely the rates are tied together if, for example, we are worried about the possibility of a large differential that is fairly constant over time because of government administration of interest rates.) Finally we report in the fourth column how big a band would be needed to encompass 95 per cent of the deviations from real interest parity.

Country-group comparisons of the measures of real interest differential variability in some respects suit *a priori* expectations: the five closed LDCs constitute the group with the highest variability and the five open Atlantic countries the group with the lowest.

But there are some results that are anomalous if the real interest differential is taken as a measure of financial market integration. France, for example, had stringent capital controls in place during our sample period (at least until the latter part) and yet appears, by the criterion of real interest differential variability, to have a *higher* degree of capital mobility than Japan, which announced liberalization of its capital controls before our sample period (1979-80). One might conceivably argue that the Japanese liberalization must not have been genuine. But the French real interest differential is smaller and less variable even than those of the Netherlands and Switzerland, major countries that are known to be virtually free of capital controls. Only Canada shows a smaller and less variable real interest differential than France.

Because the realized inflation rates could not have been precisely known *a priori*, it is necessary to project them onto contemporaneously known variables. Three such variables were used: the forward discount, the nominal interest differential and the lagged inflation differential. (The results are reported in NBER Working Paper 2856, but are omitted here to save space.) In a majority of cases, a statistically significant amount of the variation in the real interest differential turned out to be forecastable.

The standard deviation of the projected differential gives us our final measure of variability. The results for the *ex ante* real interest differential are mostly similar to those for the *ex post* data. France, for example, still shows a lower degree of variability than the Netherlands.

Covered Interest Differentials: the Country Premium

We now use the Barclays forward rate data to decompose the real interest differential into one part due to country factors and another part due to currency factors. The first component, the covered interest differential, encompasses all factors related to the political jurisdiction in which the asset is issued. Its size and variability measures barriers to international capital mobility in the most narrow and proper definition of the term.

A good rule of thumb, when the absolute magnitude of the mean or the variability of the differential indicates the existence of significant barriers, is as follows: a negative differential *vis-à-vis* the Eurocurrency market indicates that, to the extent that barriers exist, there are capital controls or transactions costs currently operating to discourage capital from flowing out of the country. Investors would not settle for a lower return domestically if they were free to earn abroad the higher return covered to eliminate exchange risk. This is the case for all the LDCs in the sample with the exception of Hong Kong and for all of the traditionally 'closed' European countries with the exceptions of Austria and Belgium (which should by now probably be classified with the 'open' countries). The negative differential that existed for the UK before Margaret Thatcher removed capital controls in 1979 is now extremely small. Similarly, Canada's differential is effectively zero.

Germany and several other neighbouring European countries (Switzerland, the Netherlands, Austria and Belgium) show higher interest rates locally than offshore, which suggests some barriers discouraging capital *inflow:* investors would not settle for a lower mark return in the Euromarket if they were free to get the higher return in Germany. But the magnitude is quite small, as it has been observed to be ever since Germany removed most of its controls on capital inflow in 1974. Japan has a covered differential that by all measures is smaller and less variable than those of Switzerland and Germany, let alone France and most of the other countries.

This might come as a surprise to those accustomed to thinking of Japanese financial markets in terms of the large barriers to capital inflow that were in place in the 1970s. The liberalization of Japanese markets, which has been documented elsewhere, continued during our sample period. Australia and New Zealand, while lagging well behind Japan, also show signs of liberalization during the course of our sample period.

The covered interest differential for France is much larger and more variable than that for the other major industrialized countries known to be free of capital controls. This is the reverse of the finding from the criterion of real interest differentials. It supports the value of the criterion of covered interest differentials as the proper test of financial market integration.

The differential, with its negative sign signifying controls on French capital outflows, has been previously studied, especially its tendency to shoot up shortly before devaluations of the franc. Our data indicate that the last major occurrence of thisphenomenon was February 1986; since then the differential has been close to zero.

Similarly, the samė phenomenon for Italy, which has also been previously studied, appears to have ended after the February 1986 realignment. France and Italy apparently dismantled their capital controls quickly enough to meet a 1990 deadline for liberalization set by the EC Twelve. Of four countries that required a later deadline, Spain and Portugal have by our measures already been liberalizing (plots show that the magnitude of the covered interest differential fell sharply in 1987 for these two countries), but Greece and Ireland have not. Sweden is one non-EC European country that appears to have moved towards liberalization during our sample period, while Norway does not. All of these European countries show up with negative mean differentials, which implies that the remaining controls act to discourage capital outflow rather than inflow. For the EC countries, this finding supports records of the European Commission which report more freedom for short-term inflows than short-term outflows.

Registering impressively open financial markets are our three East Asian LDCs (which, especially in the case of Singapore, have rapidly outgrown the appellation 'less developed'). Hong Kong and Singapore show even smaller covered differentials than some open European countries like Germany. Malaysia's differential has been considerably higher, particularly in 1986, but still compares favourably with some European countries.

Not surprisingly, our remaining LDCs show by far the largest and most variable covered interest differentials. Again, the results are precisely what one would expect if covered interest differentials are the proper criterion for capital mobility, but the reverse of what the saving-investment criterion shows.

Why does the covered differential criterion give such different answers from the saving-investment criterion, which shows a high degree of saving retention among industrialized countries? Feldstein and Horioka argue that financial markets are less well integrated at longer-term maturities, as compared with the three-month maturities used in tests of covered interest parity such as those reported above: It is clear from the yields on short-term securities in the Eurocurrency market and the forward prices of those currencies that liquid financial capital moves very rapidly to arbitrage such short-term differentials. There are however reasons to be sceptical about the extent of such long-term arbitrage.

Studies of international interest parity have been restricted by a lack of forward exchange rates at horizons going out much further than one year. But even without the use of forward rate data, there are ways of getting around the problem of exchange risk. Data on currency swap rates can be used in place of forward exchange rates to test the long-term version of interest rate parity. Popper finds that the swap-covered return differential on five-year US government bonds versus Japanese bonds averaged only 1.7 basis points from 3 October 1985 to 10 July 1986, and that the differential on seven-year bonds averaged only 5.3 basis points. The means mask some variation in the differential. But a band of 46 basis points is large enough to encompass 95 per cent of the observations for the five-year bonds. The band is 34 basis points for the seven-year bonds. The means on five-year bonds for some other major countries are as follows: Canada, 15.9; Switzerland, 18.7; UK 51.1; and Germany, 28.4. The magnitude of these long-term differentials compares favourably with the magnitude of the short-term differentials. The implication is that Feldstein and Horioka are wrong in their conjecture that there is a term-structure wedge separating national capital markets. The most relevant distinction appears to be not long term versus short term, but rather real versus nominal.

'Real Forward Discounts': The Currency Premium

Even for those countries that exhibit no substantial country premium, as reflected in covered interest parity there may still be a substantial currency premium that drives real interest differentials away from zero. If real interest differentials are not arbitraged to zero, then there is in turn no reason to expect saving-investment correlations to be zero.

Germany, Switzerland, the Netherlands, Austria and Japan, for example, all have substantial real forward discounts (or-more precisely-real forward premia) which constitute approximately the entirety of their real interest differentials. These are countries with currencies that have experienced a lot of exchange rate variability, both nominal and real, *vis-à-vis* the dollar since 1973 and especially since 1980.

As a consequence, some combination of exchange risk premia and expected real depreciation-factors pertaining to the currency, not to the political jurisdiction-produces the gap in real interest rates. For these five financially open industrialized countries, and for Hong Kong as well, the currency factors produce a *negative* real interest differential, while the covered interest differential (though small) is *positive:* the small regulations or frictions that remain in these countries are, if anything, working to resist capital inflow (at least at the short end of the maturity spectrum) and not outflow as one would mistakenly conclude from the real interest differential criterion. The other countries all have highly variable currency premia as well. Indeed the real forward discount (currency premium) is more variable than the covered interest differential (country premium) for all but three of our twenty-five countries (Greece, Mexico and France). The average variability across all countries is higher for the currency premium than for the country premium.

We can project the real forward discount on the same three variables as we did for the real interest differential (the forward discount, nominal interest differential and lagged inflation differential) to get an *ex ante* measure. Its standard deviation now shows six countries for whom the currency premium is less variable than the country premium (Greece, Mexico, Portugal, France, Italy and Spain). But the currency premium remains the major obstacle to real interest parity for most countries.

Further Decomposition into Exchange Risk Premium and Expected Real Depreciation

Our decomposition so far has lumped together two terms, the exchange risk premium and expected real depreciation, into the currency premium:

In this section we attempt to complete the decomposition by separating these two terms. To do so requires a measure or model of expected depreciation. The usual approach is to use the *ex post* changes in the spot rate (Ds) as a measure of *ex ante* expectations (Ds), and to argue that under rational expectations the expectational error should be random (uncorrelated with information currently available at time *t*). The mean value of fd-Ds for each of our countries. Most of the means are positive, showing that the weak dollar period dominates over the strong dollar period.

But only three currencies have mean risk premia, of either sign, that are statistically significant. Furthermore, in a majority of cases (sixteen out of twenty-five), the sign of the mean return differential is the *opposite* of the sign of the mean real interest differential during the same period. So this measure of the exchange risk premium does not explain any positive part of the real interest differential. The measures of the variability of fd-Ds show up very large in the second, third and fourth columns. These are measures of the variability of *ex post* return differentials and not *ex ante* return differentials.

They tell us little about the variability of the exchange risk premium. But the high variability of the exchange rate does tell us two things. First, it provides an obvious explanation-low power-of why the first moments might not be statistically significant. On the other hand, the existence of substantial uncertainty regarding the future spot rate suggests, via the theory of optimal portfolio diversification, that a non-zero exchange risk premium must exist to reward risk-averse investors for holding currencies that are perceived as risky or that are in oversupply. To estimate the *ex ante* exchange risk premium, we can project fd-depr onto our same three variables: the forward discount, the interest differential and the inflation differential.

The regression is statistically significant for a majority of currencies, as many others have found. The standard deviation shows that the most variable exchange risk premia belong to Mexico and New Zealand, but the UK, the Netherlands, Austria, Germany and Switzerland follow close behind. The statistics for the other component of the currency premium, expected real depreciation. As noted earlier, given the widely accepted failure of PPP on levels, there is no theoretical reason to expect it necessarily to hold in terms of expected rates of change, the hypothesis sometimes known as *ex ante* relative PPP.

The statistics for *ex post* real depreciation. The means in the first column are negative, indicating real appreciation of the currency against the dollar, for all European countries and for most other countries as well. The only five exceptions, countries that experienced real depreciation against the dollar, were our three East Asian developing countries, Australia and Bahrain. Bahrain was the only one, of either sign, that was statistically significant. We already know, from the results reported above for the 119 years of US-UK data, that we cannot expect to reject *ex ante* relative PPP on just a few years of data: new disturbances to the real exchange rate are so large that one needs a much longer time sample to find evidence of systematic movement. But the signs of the mean real depreciations are usually (in twenty out of twenty-five cases) the same as the signs of the mean real interest differentials, suggesting a high correlation of the real interest differential and expected real depreciation across countries.

To estimate *ex ante* expected real depreciation, we project *ex post* real depreciation, again, on the same three contemporaneous variables. The standard deviations for the various currencies are quite similar to those for the projected exchange risk premium. In most cases (eighteen out of twenty-five) the projected exchange risk premium is slightly more variable than projected real depreciation.

6

Financial Innovation and Risk Sharing

FINANCIAL INNOVATION

There are several interpretations of the phrase financial innovation. In general, it refers to the creating and marketing of new types of securities.

WHY DOES FINANCIAL INNOVATION OCCUR?

Economic theory has much to say about what types of securities should exist, and why some may not exist but little to say about why new types of securities should come into existence.

One interpretation of the Modigliani-Miller theorem is that taxes and regulation are the only reasons for investors to care what kinds of securities firms issue, whether debt, equity, or something else. The theorem states that the structure of a firm's liabilities should have no bearing on its net worth. The securities may trade at different prices depending on their composition, but they must ultimately add up to the same value.

Furthermore, there should be little demand for specific types of securities. The capital asset pricing model, first developed by Markowitz, suggests that investors should fully diversify and their portfolios should be a mixture of the "market" and a risk-free investment. Investors with different risk/return goals can use leverage to increase the ratio of the market return to the risk-free return in their portfolios. However, Richard Roll argued that this model was incorrect, because investors cannot invest in the entire market. This implies there should be demand for instruments that open up new types of investment opportunities but not for instruments that merely repackage existing risks.

If the world existed as the Arrow-Debreu model posits, then there would be no need for financial innovation. The Arrow-Debreu model assumes that investors are able to purchase securities that pay off if and only if a certain state of the world occurs. Investors can then combine these securities to create portfolios that have whatever payoff they desire. The fundamental theorem of finance states that the price of assembling such a portfolio will be equal to its expected value under the appropriate risk-neutral measure.

THE ROLE OF TECHNOLOGY IN FINANCIAL INNOVATION

Some types of financial innovation are driven by improvements in computer and telecommunication technology. For example, Paul Volcker suggested that for most people, the creation of the ATM was a greater financial innovation than asset-backed securitization. Other types of financial innovation affecting the payments system include credit and debit cards and online payment systems like PayPal.

These types of innovations are notable because they reduce transaction costs. Households need to keep lower cash balances — if the economy exhibits cash-in-advance constraints then these kinds of financial innovations can contribute to greater efficiency. Alvarez and Lippi using data on Italian households' use of debit cards, find that ownership of an ATM card results in benefits worth €17 annually.

These types of innovations may also have an impact on monetary policy by reducing real household balances. Especially with the increased popularity of online banking, households are able to keep greater percentages of their wealth in non-cash instruments. In a special edition of 'International Finance' devoted to the interaction of electronic commerce and central banking, Goodhart and Woodford express confidence in the ability of a central bank to maintain its policy goals by affecting the short-term interest rate even if electronic money has eliminated the demand for central bank liabilities, while Friedman is less sanguine.

CRITICISM

Some economists argue that financial innovation has little to no productivity benefit: Paul Volcker states that "there is little correlation between sophistication of a banking system and productivity growth," that there is no "neutral evidence that financial innovation has led to economic growth", and that financial innovation was a cause of the financial crisis of 2007–2010, while Paul Krugman states that "the rapid growth in finance since 1980 has largely been a matter of rent-seeking, rather than true productivity."

GLOBALIZATION AND RISK SHARING

Globalization and risk sharing are closely inter-linked. Economic globalization is defined as the incorporation of national economy into international economy through factors like capital inflow, migration, trade and foreign direct investment. Risk sharing basically means the risks associated with any enterprise is distributed among the various participants in the enterprise. The current trend of globalization has encouraged many entrepreneurs and manufacturers to explore the market beyond their own inhabited territories. The liberal economic policies and the changing consumerism are the two major factors that have encouraged investors to invest in markets abroad. It goes without saying that globalization and risks sharing also go hand in hand.

ADVANTAGES OF GLOBALIZATION

One of the primary benefits of globalization is that it has allowed certain evolutions in the risk sharing pattern. Trade with other countries has definitely become easier than it was before. Due to globalization there is a higher likelihood of developed countries investing in developing countries and this can bring about a dynamic change in developing the economy of a country. Globalization has ensured that corporates have a higher flexibility in operating across borders. As a result of this, there has emerged a greater interdependence of nation-states.

GLOBALIZATION AND INTERNATIONAL RISK SHARING

Credit inflow from around the globe can be used as an insurance against adverse financial crisis that may hamper an economy.

It is better for the investors if risk sharing is distributed with other countries. Studies suggest that globalization and international risk sharing is very small. It is likely that there are more unexploited gains of international risk sharing for developing countries.

Generally, people prefer to have steady consumption yearly rather than widely fluctuating amounts. This helps them to counter any adverse economic situation that they may encounter. There are three things that need to be considered for international risk sharing.

They are:

- To ask for a unified investigation in the risk sharing economies and to analyse the emerging markets in developing countries
- To examine changes caused due to the globalization and risk sharing programmes in different countries and then correlate them with the growth rate of financial inflows.
- To evaluate different cyclical actions undertaken by risk sharing programmes with the help of research.

DISADVANTAGE OF GLOBALIZATION AND RISK SHARING

One of the primary disadvantages of risk sharing in globalization is that the age old patterns of risk sharing have not been replaced in the global market with newer ones. The steps currently being followed for risk management is not conducive to all developing and emerging economies. Every market is different and generally the risk sharing welfare programmes are not suitable for these varied economies. Studies have indicated that the openness of financial inflows improves risk sharing in a country's economy; however this is not a global phenomenon. It has been seen that developing economies have attained better benefits from the risk sharing plans.

FUTURES MARKETS

'Futures trading has a long history, both in the U.S. and around the world. Futures trading on a formal futures exchange in the U.S. originated with the formation of the Chicago Board of Trade in the middle of the Nineteenth Century. Grain dealers in Illinois were having trouble financing their grain inventories. The risk of grain prices falling after harvest made lenders reluctant to extend grain dealers credit to purchase grain for subsequent sale in Chicago.

To reduce their risk exposure, grain dealers began selling "To Arrive" contracts, which specified the future date a specified quantity of grain would be delivered to a particular location at a price identified in the contract. Fixing the price in advance of delivery reduced the grain dealer's risk exposure and made it easier to obtain credit to finance grain purchases from farmers. The "To Arrive" contracts were a forerunner of the futures contracts traded today. Although dealers found it advantageous to trade what essentially were forward cash contracts in various commodities, they soon found these forward cash contract markets inadequate and formed futures exchanges.

The first U.S. futures exchange was the Chicago Board of Trade formed in 1848. Other U.S. exchanges also have their origin in the last half of the 1800s. For example, the Kansas City Board of Trade traces its roots to January 1876 when a precursor to today's hard red wheat futures contract was first traded. Similarly, a forerunner of the Chicago Mercantile

Exchange was formed in 1874 when the Chicago Product Exchange was organized to trade butter. In each case the exchanges were formed because commercial dealers in corn, wheat and butter needed a mechanism whereby they could reduce some of their unwanted price risk, which hampered the day-to-day management of their business. Sellers wanted to rid themselves of the price risk associated with owning inventories of grain or butter and buyers wanted to establish prices for these same products in advance of delivery. In recent years futures contracts have proliferated, particularly in the financial arena, as businesses become more aware of the price risks they face and seek ways to reduce those risks.

WHAT IS A FUTURES CONTRACT?

A futures contract is a binding agreement between a seller and a buyer to make and to take delivery of the underlying commodity at a specified future date with agreed upon payment terms. Most futures contracts don't actually result in delivery of the underlying commodity. Instead, most traders find it advantageous to settle their futures market obligation by selling the contract or by buying it back. The trader then completes the actual cash transaction in his or her local cash market.

Futures contracts are standardized with respect to the delivery month; the commodity's quantity, quality, and delivery location; and the payment terms. The fact that futures contracts terms are standardized is important because it enables traders to focus their attention on one variable, namely price. Standardization also makes it possible for traders anywhere in the world to trade in these markets and know exactly what they are trading.

This is in sharp contrast to the cash forward contract market, in which changes in specifications from one contract to another might cause price changes from one transaction to another. One reason futures markets are considered a good source of commodity price information is because price changes are attributable to changes in the commodity's price level, not changes in contract terms.

In contrast to a forward cash contract market, futures exchanges provide:

- Rules of conduct which traders must follow or risk expulsion;
- An organized market place with established trading hours by which traders must abide;
- Standardized trading through rigid contract specifications, which ensure that the commodity being traded in every contract is virtually identical;
- A focal point for the collection and dissemination of information about the commodity's supply and demand, which helps ensure all traders have equal access to information;
- A mechanism for settling disputes among traders without resorting to the costly and often slow U.S. court system; and
- Guaranteed settlement of contractual and financial obligations via the exchange clearinghouse.

CHANGES IN A FUTURES CONTRACT'S VALUE

A futures contract's value is simply the number of units in each contract times the current price. The volume of grain or livestock covered by a futures contract is specified in each contract. Both Chicago and Kansas City Board of Trade grain and oilseed futures contracts cover 5,000 bushels. The CME's live cattle futures contract covers 40,000 pounds of live weight steers. The lean hogs futures contract covers 40,000 pounds of carcass weight pork and the feeder cattle futures contract covers 50,000 pounds of feeder steers.

To determine both contract value and changes in contract value, examine the July KCBT wheat futures contract on a day when the settlement price is $3.00 per bushel. The total contract value would simply be 5,000 bushels times $3.00 or $15,000. If the July KCBT wheat futures price changes to $3.10 per bushel the next day, the new contract value is 5,000 bushels times $3.10 or $15,500. The change in contract value is $15,500 minus $15,000, or $500. Alternatively, you can compute the change in contract value by simply multiplying the price change per unit times the number of units in the contract.

The impact of a change in contract value depends on whether you previously sold or purchased a futures contract. A decrease in contract value is a loss to anyone who previously purchased a futures contract, but a gain for a trader who previously sold a futures contract. Conversely, an increase in contract value is a gain to anyone who previously purchased a futures contract but is a loss for a trader who previously sold a futures contract. One trader's loss is another trader's gain. For example, in the previous wheat futures example a trader who purchased July KCBT wheat futures at $3.00/ bushel saw the value of his futures market account increase by $500 when the price rose to $3.10; a trader who sold a futures contract at $3.00/bushel saw the value of his futures market account decline by $500. The $500 gain earned by the futures contract buyer came from the futures contract seller's $500 loss via the exchange clearinghouse, as outlined in Figure.

Buyer (Long)			Seller (Short)		
Date	Action	Price	Date	Action	Price
Day 1	Buy at	$ 3.00/bu.	Day 1	Sell at	$ 3.00/bu.
Day 2	No Action (But Price Increases)	$ 3.10/bu. $0.10/bu. gain X 5,000 bu $ 500 gain Fror day 1	Day 2	No Action (But Price Increases)	$ 3.10/bu. $0.10/bu. loss X 5,000 bu $ 500 loss Fror day 1

Fig. Markeing-to-Market Buyer and Seller Accounts at Exchange Clearinghouse.

Futures contract performance is guaranteed by the exchange through an institution known as the exchange clearinghouse, which tracks the value of each trader's position and ensures that sufficient funds are available to cover each trader's obligations. The exchange clearinghouse requires that traders deposit money at the outset of the trade to ensure contract performance. This deposit is usually referred to as the initial margin deposit. Each trader's margin money is maintained in a separate margin account, which is adjusted daily to reflect the gain or loss in contract value that occurred that day. This process is sometimes referred to as "Marking-to- Market," because the account is adjusted to reflect its current market value based upon that day's closing or settlement price. Although the margin requirements are small relative to the total value of the contract, traders of futures contracts are relieved of the responsibility of worrying that the trader on the other side of the contract will default on his financial obligations by the mark-to-market margin system and by a series of checks and balances put in place by the exchange to ensure that sufficient funds are available to cover each account's risk exposure.

FUTURES TRADING TERMINOLOGY

Trading futures contracts requires that you become familiar with the terminology used in the trade. A short definition of some of the terms used in the trade: .

Long A buyer of a futures contract. Someone who buys a futures contract is often referred to as being long that particular contract. Short A seller of a futures contract. Someone who sells a futures contract is often referred to as being short that particular contract. Bull A person who expects a commodity's price to increase. If you are bullish about wheat prices you expect them to increase. Bear A person who expects a commodity's price to decline. If you are bearish about wheat prices you expect them to decline.

Market order An order to buy or sell a futures contract at the best available price. A market order is executed by the broker immediately. "Sell one July KCBT wheat, at the market" is an example of a market order. Limit order An order to buy or sell a futures contract at a specific price, or at a price that is more favourable than the price specified. For example, "Buy one March KCBT wheat at $3.30 limit" means buy one March KCBT wheat contract at $3.30 or less. In this example, the order will not be executed at a price higher than $3.30. Stop order An order which becomes a market order if the market reaches a specified price. A stop order to buy a futures contract would be placed with the stop price set above the current futures price. Conversely, a stop order to sell a futures contract would be placed with the stop price set below the current futures price.

USING FUTURES CONTRACTS IN A FARM MARKETING PROGRAMME

There are a number of ways futures contracts can be used in a farm marketing programme. Futures contracts can be useful when marketing grain or livestock because they can be a temporary substitute for an intended transaction in the cash market that will occur at a later date. This is a working definition of hedging. For example, if you plan on selling cash wheat at harvest, but would like to lock in the futures price ahead of harvest, you could sell a KCBT July wheat futures contract as a temporary substitute for the cash grain you plan to sell in the future. When you actually make the cash grain sale at harvest, you will no longer need the "temporary substitute," which was your sale of the wheat futures contract. Thus, as soon as you sell the cash wheat you would exit your "temporary substitute contract" by buying a KCBT July wheat futures contract. Doing so means you no longer have an open position on the futures exchange. Your actual net sale price for the wheat would be the amount you received for the cash wheat at the elevator, plus any gain or minus any loss on the futures transaction.

Futures contract prices also can be used as a source of price forecasts. A futures contract price represents today's opinion of a commodity's value at the time the futures contract will expire. If a history of the difference between a commodity's futures contract and cash prices, for a particular grade and specific location of interest is available, it can be used to estimate a futures market-based cash price forecast. For example, assume that on March 15 the KCBT July wheat futures contract is trading at $3.00 per bushel, and your local cash market price at harvest is generally $0.40/bushel below the KCBT July wheat futures contract price. In this case, a futures-based local cash price forecast at harvest time would be $2.60/bushel. This forecast can be compared with price forecasts from other sources such as university Extension economists, market advisory services, and the U.S. Department of Agriculture when preparing budgets and making marketing decisions.

ROLE OF FINANCIAL FUTURE

A financial future is a futures contract on a short term interest rate. Contracts vary, but are often defined on an interest rate index such as 3-month sterling or US dollar LIBOR.

They are traded across a wide range of currencies, including the G12 country currencies and many others.

Some representative financial futures contracts are:

United States:

- 90-day Eurodollar
- 1 mo LIBOR
- Fed Funds 30 day

Europe:

- 3 mo Euribor
- 90-day Sterling LIBOR
- Euro Sfr

Asia:

- 3 mo Euroyen
- 90-day Bank Bill

Where:

- IMM is the International Money Market of the Chicago Mercantile Exchange
- CBOT is the Chicago Board of Trade
- TOCOM is the Tokyo Commodity Exchange
- SFE is the Sydney futures exchange

As an example, consider the definition of the International Money Market eurodollar interest rate future, the most widely and deeply traded financial futures contract.

- There are four contracts per year: March, June, September, December
- They are listed on a 10 year cycle. Other markets only extend about 2–4 years.
- Last Trading Day is the second London business day preceding the third Wednesday of the contract month

- Delivery Day is cash settlement on the third Wednesday.
- The minimum fluctuation is half a basis point or 0.005%.
- Payment is the difference between the price paid for the contract multiplied by the "tick value" of the contract which is $12.50 per tick.
- Before the Last Trading Day the contract trades at market prices. The Final Settlement Price is the British Bankers Association percentage rate for Three–Month Eurodollar Interbank Time Deposits, rounded to the nearest 1/10000th of a percentage point at 11:00 London time on that day, subtracted from 100..

Financial futures are extensively used in the hedging of interest rate swaps.

CURRENCY SWAP

A currency swap is a foreign-exchange agreement between two parties to exchange aspects of a loan in one currency for equivalent aspects of an equal in net present value loan in another currency. Currency swaps are motivated by comparative advantage. A currency swap should be distinguished from a central bank liquidity swap.

Currency swaps are over-the-counter derivatives, and are closely related to interest rate swaps. However, unlike interest rate swaps, currency swaps can involve the exchange of the principal.

There are three different ways in which currency swaps can exchange loans:

The most simple currency swap structure is to exchange the principal only with the counterparty, at a rate agreed now, at some specified point in the future. Such an agreement performs a function equivalent to a forward contract or futures. The cost of finding a counterparty and drawing up an agreement with them, makes swaps more expensive than alternative derivatives as a method to fix shorter term forward exchange rates. However for the longer term future, commonly up to 10 years, where spreads are wider for alternative derivatives, principal-only currency swaps are often used as a cost-effective way to fix forward rates. This type of currency swap is also known as an FX-swap.

Another currency swap structure is to combine the exchange of loan principal with an interest rate swap. In such a swap, interest cash flows are not netted before they are paid to the counterparty because they are denominated in different currencies. As each party effectively borrows on the other's behalf, this type of swap is also known as a back-to-back loan.

Last here, but certainly not least important, is to swap only interest payment cash flows on loans of the same size and term. Again, as this is a currency swap, the exchanged cash flows are in different denominations and so are not netted. An example of such a swap is the exchange of fixed-rate US Dollar interest payments for floating-rate interest payments in Euro. This type of swap is also known as a cross-currency interest rate swap, or cross-currency swap.

Currency swaps have two main uses:

1. To secure cheaper debt.
2. To hedge against exchange rate fluctuations.

Currency swaps were originally conceived in the 1970s to circumvent foreign exchange controls in the United Kingdom. At that time, UK companies had to pay a premium to borrow in US Dollars. To avoid this, UK companies set up back-to-back loan agreements with US companies wishing to borrow Sterling. While such restrictions on currency exchange have since become rare, savings are still available from back-to-back loans due to comparative advantage.

Cross-currency interest rate swaps were introduced by the World Bank in 1981 to obtain Swiss francs and German marks by exchanging cash flows with IBM. This deal was brokered by Salomon Brothers with a notional amount of $210 million dollars and a term of over ten years.

During the global financial crisis of 2008, the currency swap transaction structure was used by the United States Federal Reserve System to establish central bank liquidity swaps. In these, the Federal Reserve and the central bank of a developed or stable emerging economy agree to exchange domestic currencies at the current prevailing market exchange rate and agree to reverse the swap at the same exchange rate at a fixed future date. The aim of central bank liquidity swaps is "to provide liquidity in U.S. dollars to overseas markets." While central bank liquidity swaps and currency swaps are structurally the same, currency swaps are commercial transactions driven by comparative advantage, while central bank liquidity swaps are emergency loans of US Dollars to overseas markets, and it is currently unknown whether or not they will be beneficial for the Dollar or the US in the long-term.

The People's Republic of China has multiple year currency swap agreements of the Renminbi with Argentina, Belarus, Hong Kong, Indonesia, Malaysia, and South Korea that perform a similar function to central bank liquidity swaps.

FLEA MARKET

A flea market or swap meet is a type of bazaar where inexpensive or secondhand goods are sold or bartered. It may be indoors, such as in a warehouse or school gymnasium; or it may be outdoors, such as in a field or under a tent. The flea market vendors may range from a family that is renting a table for the first time to sell a few unwanted household items to a commercial operation including a large variety of used merchandise, scouts who rove the region buying items for sale from garage sales and other flea markets, and several staff watching the stalls.

Many flea markets have food vendors who sell snacks and drinks to the patrons, and may be associated with carnivals or concerts. Some have become infamous as outlets for bootleg movies and music or knockoff brand clothing, accessories, or fragrances.

The origins of the term are disputed, but some have observed that buyers and sellers may be as active as fleas, or that the original people and goods were infested. Word and Phrase Origins, the term was derived from the "Vallie Market" of Manhattan.

The original flea market may be the Marché aux puces of

Saint-Ouen, Seine-Saint-Denis, in the northern suburbs of Paris. It is a large, long-established outdoor bazaar, one of four in Paris. From the late 17th century, the makeshift open-air market in the town of Saint-Ouen began as temporary stalls and benches among the fields and market gardens where ragpickers exchanged their findings for a small sum.

INTEREST RATE

An interest rate is the price a borrower pays for the use of money they borrow from a lender, for instance a small company might borrow capital from a bank to buy new assets for their business, and the return a lender receives for deferring the use of funds, by lending it to the borrower. Interests rates are fundamental to a capitalist society. Interest rates are normally expressed as a percentage rate over the period of one year.

Interest rates targets are also a vital tool of monetary policy and are taken into account when dealing with variables like investment, inflation, and unemployment.

In the past two centuries, interest rates have been variously set either by national governments or central banks. For example, the Federal Reserve federal funds rate in the United States has varied between about 0.25% to 19% from 1954 to 2008, while the Bank of England base rate varied between 0.5% and 15% from 1989 to 2009, and Germany experienced rates close to 90% in the 1920s down to about 2% in the 2000s. During an attempt to tackle spiraling hyperinflation in 2007, the Central Bank of Zimbabwe increased interest rates for borrowing to 800%.

The interest rates on prime credits in the late 1970s and early 1980s were far higher than had been recorded – higher than previous US peaks since 1800, than British peaks since 1700, or than Dutch peaks since 1600; "since modern capital markets came into existence, there have never been such high long-term rates" as in this period.

REASONS FOR INTEREST RATE CHANGE

- *Political short-term gain*: Lowering interest rates can

give the economy a short-run boost. Under normal conditions, most economists think a cut in interest rates will only give a short term gain in economic activity that will soon be offset by inflation. The quick boost can influence elections. Most economists advocate independent central banks to limit the influence of politics on interest rates.

- *Deferred consumption*: When money is loaned the lender delays spending the money on consumption goods. Since according to time preference theory people prefer goods now to goods later, in a free market there will be a positive interest rate.
- *Inflationary expectations*: Most economies generally exhibit inflation, meaning a given amount of money buys fewer goods in the future than it will now. The borrower needs to compensate the lender for this.
- *Alternative investments*: The lender has a choice between using his money in different investments. If he chooses one, he forgoes the returns from all the others. Different investments effectively compete for funds.
- *Risks of investment*: There is always a risk that the borrower will go bankrupt, abscond, or otherwise default on the loan. This means that a lender generally charges a risk premium to ensure that, across his investments, he is compensated for those that fail.
- *Liquidity preference*: People prefer to have their resources available in a form that can immediately be exchanged, rather than a form that takes time or money to realise.
- *Taxes*: Because some of the gains from interest may be subject to taxes, the lender may insist on a higher rate to make up for this loss.

REAL VS NOMINAL INTEREST RATES

The nominal interest rate is the amount, in money terms, of interest payable. For example, suppose a household deposits

$100 with a bank for 1 year and they receive interest of $10. At the end of the year their balance is $110. In this case, the nominal interest rate is 10% per annum.The real interest rate, which measures the purchasing power of interest receipts, is calculated by adjusting the nominal rate charged to take inflation into account.

If inflation in the economy has been 10% in the year, then the $110 in the account at the end of the year buys the same amount as the $100 did a year ago. The real interest rate, in this case, is zero.

After the fact, the 'realized' real interest rate, which has actually occurred, is given by the Fisher equation, and is,

$$r = \frac{1+i}{1+p} - 1$$

where p = the actual inflation rate over the year. The linear approximation,

$$r \approx i - p$$

is widely used.

The expected real returns on an investment, before it is made, are:

$$i_r = i_n - p_e$$

where:

i = nominal interest rate

r = real interest rate

p_e = expected or projected inflation over the year

MARKET INTEREST RATES

There is a market for investments which ultimately includes the money market, bond market, stock market and currency market as well as retail financial institutions like banks. Exactly how these markets function is a complex question.

However, economists generally agree that the interest rates yielded by any investment take into account:

- The risk-free cost of capital
- Inflationary expectations

- The level of risk in the investment
- The costs of the transaction

This rate incorporates the deferred consumption and alternative investments elements of interest.

Inflationary Expectations

The theory of rational expectations, people form an expectation of what will happen to inflation in the future. They then ensure that they offer or ask a nominal interest rate that means they have the appropriate real interest rate on their investment. *This is given by the formula:*

$$i_n = i_r + p_e$$

where:

i_n = offered nominal interest rate

ir = desired real interest rate

p_e = inflationary expectations

Risk

The level of risk in investments is taken into consideration. This is why very volatile investments like shares and junk bonds have higher returns than safer ones like government bonds. The extra interest charged on a risky investment is the risk premium. The required risk premium is dependent on the risk preferences of the lender. If an investment is 50% likely to go bankrupt, a risk-neutral lender will require their returns to double. So for an investment normally returning $100 they would require $200 back. A risk-averse lender would require more than $200 back and a risk-loving lender less than $200. Evidence suggests that most lenders are in fact risk-averse.

Generally speaking a longer-term investment carries a maturity risk premium, because long-term loans are exposed to more risk of default during their duration.

Liquidity Preference

Most investors prefer their money to be in cash than in less fungible investments. Cash is on hand to be spent immediately if the need arises, but some investments require time or effort to transfer into spendable form. This is known as liquidity preference. A 1-year loan, for instance, is very liquid compared to a 10-year loan. A 10-year US Treasury bond, however, is liquid because it can easily be sold on the market.

A Market Interest-rate Model

A basic interest rate pricing model for an asset,

$$i_n = i_r + p_e + rp + lp$$

Assuming perfect information, p_e is the same for all participants in the market, and this is identical to:

$$i_n = i_n^* + rp + lp$$

where,

i_n is the nominal interest rate on a given investment

i_r is the risk-free return to capital

i^*_n = the nominal interest rate on a short-term risk-free liquid bond.

rp = a risk premium reflecting the length of the investment and the likelihood the borrower will default

lp = liquidity premium.

Interest Rate Notations

What is commonly referred to as the interest rate in the media is generally the rate offered on overnight deposits by the Central Bank or other authority, annualised. The total interest on an investment depends on the timescale the interest is calculated on, because interest paid may be compounded. In finance, the effective interest rate is often derived from the yield, a composite measure which takes into account all payments of interest and capital from the investment.

In retail finance, the annual percentage rate and effective annual rate concepts have been introduced to help consumers easily compare different products with different payment structures. Money market mutual funds quote their rate of interest as the 7 Day SEC Yield.

INTEREST RATES IN MACROECONOMICS

Output and Unemployment

Interest rates are the main determinant of investment on

a macroeconomic scale. Broadly speaking, if interest rates increase across the board, then investment decreases, causing a fall in national income.

A government institution, usually a central bank, can lend money to financial institutions to influence their interest rates as the main tool of monetary policy. Usually central bank interest rates are lower than commercial interest rates since banks borrow money from the central bank then lend the money at a higher rate to generate most of their profit.

By altering interest rates, the government institution is able to affect the interest rates faced by everyone who wants to borrow money for economic investment. Investment can change rapidly in response to changes in interest rates and the total output.

Open Market Operations in the United States

The Federal Reserve implements monetary policy largely by targeting the federal funds rate. This is the rate that banks charge each other for overnight loans of federal funds, which are the reserves held by banks at the Fed.

Open market operations are one tool within monetary policy implemented by the Federal Reserve to steer short-term interest rates. Using the power to buy and sell treasury securities.

Money and Inflation

Loans, bonds, and shares have some of the characteristics of money and are included in the broad money supply.

By setting i^*_n, the government institution can affect the markets to alter the total of loans, bonds and shares issued. Generally speaking, a higher real interest rate reduces the broad money supply.

Through the quantity theory of money, increases in the money supply lead to inflation.

MATHEMATICAL NOTE

Because interest and inflation are generally given as percentage increases, the formulae are approximations.

For instance,

$$i_n = i_r + p_e$$

is only approximate. In reality, the relationship is,

$$(1+i_n) = (1+i_r)(1+p_e)$$

so

$$i_r = \frac{1+i_n}{1+p_e} - 1$$

The two approximations, eliminating higher order terms, are:

$$(1+x)(1+y) = 1+x+y+xy \qquad \approx 1+x+y$$

$$\frac{1}{1+x} = 1-x+x^2-x^3+\cdots \approx 1-x$$

The formulae are exact if logarithms of indices are used in place of rates.

NEGATIVE INTEREST RATES

Interest rates are usually positive, but not always. Given the alternative of holding cash rather than lending it out, profit-seeking lenders will not lend below 0%, as they will guarantee a loss, and a bank offering a negative deposit rate will find few takers, as savers will instead hold cash.

However, central bank rates can be negative; in July 2009 Sweden's Riksbank was the first central bank to use negative interest rates, lowering its deposit rate to “0.25%, a policy advocated by deputy governor Lars E. O. Svensson. This negative interest rate is possible because Swedish banks, as regulated companies, must hold these reserves with the central bank – they do not have the option of holding cash.

Negative interest rates have been proposed in the past, notably in the late 19th century by Silvio Gesell. A negative interest rate can be described as a "tax on holding money"; he proposed it as the Freigeld component of his Freiwirtschaft system.

To prevent people from holding cash, Gesell suggested issuing money for a limited duration, after which it must be exchanged for new bills – attempts to hold money thus result in it expiring and becoming worthless.

CURRENCY COUPON SWAP

A variant on the standard currency or interest rate swap in which the interest rate in one currency is fixed, and the interest rate in the other is floating. The only difference between a traditional interest rate swap and a currency coupon swap is the combination of the currency and interest rate features. Also called Circus Swap, Cross-Currency Swap. A special case of CUrrency Protected Swap.

7

International Stock Exchanges

NEW YORK

The New York Stock Exchange is a stock exchange located at 11 Wall Street in lower Manhattan, New York City, USA. It is the world's largest stock exchange by market capitalization of its listed companies at US$28.5 trillion as of May 2008. Average daily trading value was approximately US$153 billion in 2008.

The NYSE is operated by NYSE Euronext, which was formed by the NYSE's 2007 merger with the fully electronic stock exchange Euronext. The NYSE trading floor is located at 11 Wall Street and is composed of four rooms used for the facilitation of trading. A fifth trading room, located at 30 Broad Street, was closed in February 2007. The main building, located at 18 Broad Street, between the corners of Wall Street and Exchange Place, was designated a National Historic Landmark in 1978, as was the 11 Wall Street building.

The origin of the NYSE can be traced to May 17, 1792, when the Buttonwood Agreement was signed by 24 stock brokers outside of 68 Wall Street in New York under a buttonwood tree on Wall Street. On March 8, 1817, the organization drafted a constitution and renamed itself the "New York Stock and Exchange Board". Anthony Stockholm was elected the Exchange's first president.

The first central location of the Exchange was a room, rented in 1792 for $200 a month, located at 40 Wall Street. After that location was destroyed in the Great Fire of New York in 1835, the Exchange moved to a temporary headquarters. In

1863, the New York Stock and Exchange Board changed to its current name, the New York Stock Exchange. In 1865, the Exchange moved to 10-12 Broad Street.

The volume of stocks traded increased sixfold in the years between 1896 and 1901, and a larger space was required to conduct business in the expanding marketplace. Eight New York City architects were invited to participate in a design competition for a new building; ultimately, the Exchange selected the neoclassic design submitted by architect George B. Post. Demolition of the Exchange building at 10 Broad Street, and adjacent buildings, started on May 10, 1901.

The new building, located at 18 Broad Street, cost $4 million and opened on April 22, 1903. The trading floor, at 109 x 140 feet, was one of the largest volumes of space in the city at the time, and had a skylight set into a 72-foot -high ceiling. The main façade of the building features six tall Corinthian capitals, topped by a marble sculpture by John Quincy Adams Ward, called "Integrity Protecting the Works of Man". The building was listed as a National Historic Landmark and added to the National Register of Historic Places on June 2, 1978.

In 1922, a building for offices, designed by Trowbridge and Livingston, was added at 11 Broad Street, as well as a new trading floor called the Garage. Additional trading floor space was added in 1969 the Blue Room, and in 1988 the EBR or Extended Blue Room, with the latest technology for information display and communication. Yet another trading floor was opened at 30 Broad Street called the Bond Room in 2000. As the NYSE introduced its hybrid market, a greater proportion of trading came to be executed electronically, and due to the resulting reduction in demand for trading floor space, the NYSE decided to close the 30 Broad Street trading room in early 2006. As the adoption of electronic trading continued to reduce the number of traders and employees on the floor, in late 2007, the NYSE closed the rooms created by the 1969 and 1988 expansions.

The Stock Exchange Luncheon Club was situated on the seventh floor from 1898 until its closure in 2006.

The NYSE announced its plans to acquire Archipelago on April 21, 2005, in a deal intended to reorganize the NYSE as a publicly traded company. NYSE's governing board voted to acquire rival Archipelago on December 6, 2005, and become a for-profit, public company. It began trading under the name NYSE Group on March 8, 2006. A little over one year later, on April 4, 2007, the NYSE Group completed its merger with Euronext, the European combined stock market, thus forming the NYSE Euronext, the first transatlantic stock exchange.

Presently, Marsh Carter is Chairman of the New York Stock Exchange, having succeeded John S. Reed and the CEO is Duncan Niederauer, having succeeded John Thain.

The exchange was closed shortly after the beginning of World War I, but it partially re-opened on November 28 of that year in order to help the war effort by trading bonds, and completely reopened for stock trading in mid-December.

On September 16, 1920, a bomb exploded on Wall Street outside the NYSE building, killing 33 people and injuring more than 400. The perpetrators were never found. The NYSE building and some buildings nearby, such as the JP Morgan building, still have marks on their facades caused by the bombing.

The Black Thursday crash of the Exchange on October 24, 1929, and the sell-off panic which started on Black Tuesday, October 29, are often blamed for precipitating the Great Depression of 1929. In an effort to try to restore investor confidence, the Exchange unveiled a fifteen-point programme aimed to upgrade protection for the investing public on October 31, 1938.

On October 1, 1934, the exchange was registered as a national securities exchange with the U.S. Securities and Exchange Commission, with a president and a thirty-three member board. On February 18, 1971 the non-profit corporation was formed, and the number of board members was reduced to twenty-five.

One of Abbie Hoffman's well-known protests took place on August 24, 1967, when he led members of the Yippie movement to the gallery of the New York Stock Exchange. The protesters threw fistfuls of dollars down to the traders below, some of whom booed, while others began to scramble frantically to grab the money as fast as they could. Hoffman claimed to be pointing out that, metaphorically, that's what NYSE traders"were already doing.""We didn't call the press," wrote Hoffman,"at that time we really had no notion of anything called a media event." The press was quick to respond and by evening the event was reported around the world. Since that incident, the stock exchange has spent $20,000 to enclose the gallery with bulletproof glass.

On October 19, 1987, the Dow Jones Industrial Average dropped 508 points, a 22.6% loss in a single day, the second-biggest one-day drop the exchange had experienced, prompting officials at the exchange to invoke for the first time the"circuit breaker" rule to halt all trading. This was a very controversial move and led to a quick change in the rule; trading now halts for an hour, two hours, or the rest of the day when the DJIA drops 10, 20, or 30 per cent, respectively. In the afternoon, the 10% and 20% drops will halt trading for a shorter period of time, but a 30% drop will always close the exchange for the day. The rationale behind the trading halt was to give investors a chance to cool off and reevaluate their positions. Black Monday was followed by Terrible Tuesday, a day in which the Exchange's systems did not perform well and some people had difficulty completing their trades.

Consequently, there would be another major drop for the Dow on October 13, 1989; the Mini-Crash of 1989. The crash was apparently caused by a reaction to a news story of a $6.75 billion leveraged buyout deal for UAL Corporation, the parent company of United Airlines, which broke down. When the UAL deal fell through, it helped trigger the collapse of the junk bond market causing the Dow to fall 190.58 points, or 6.91 per cent.

Similarly, there was a panic in the financial world during the year of 1997; the Asian Financial Crisis. Like the fall of many foreign markets, the Dow suffered a 7.18% drop in value on October 27, 1997, in what later became known as the 1997 Mini-Crash but from which the DJIA recovered quickly.

On January 26, 2000, an altercation during filming of the music video for Sleep Now in the Fire, which was directed by Michael Moore, caused the doors of the exchange to be closed and the band, Rage Against the Machine, to be escorted from the site by security, after band members attempted to gain entry into the exchange. Trading on the exchange floor, however, continued uninterrupted.

On May 6, 2010, the Dow Jones Industrial Average posted its largest intraday percentage drop since the October 19, 1987 crash, with a 998 point loss later being called the Flash Crash. The SEC and CFTC published a report on the event, although it did not come to a cease as to the cause. The regulators found no evidence that the fall was caused by erroneous orders.

The New York Stock Exchange provides a means for buyers and sellers to trade shares of stock in companies registered for public trading. The NYSE is open for trading Monday through Friday between 9:30am – 4:00pm ET, with the exception of holidays declared by the Exchange in advance.

On the trading floor, the NYSE trades in a continuous auction format, where traders can execute stock transactions on behalf of investors. They will gather around the appropriate post where a specialist broker, who is employed by an NYSE member firm acts as an auctioneer in an open outcry auction market environment to bring buyers and sellers together and to manage the actual auction. They do on occasion facilitate the trades by committing their own capital and as a matter of course disseminate information to the crowd that helps to bring buyers and sellers together.

As of January 24, 2007, all NYSE stocks can be traded via its electronic Hybrid Market. Customers can now send orders for immediate electronic execution, or route orders to the floor for trade in the auction market. In the first three months of 2007, in excess of 82% of all order volume was delivered to the floor electronically.

The right to directly trade shares on the exchange is conferred upon owners of the 1366 "seats". The term comes from the fact that up until the 1870s NYSE members sat in chairs to trade. In 1868, the number of seats was fixed at 533, and this number was increased several times over the years. In 1953, the exchange stopped at 1366 seats. These seats are a sought-after commodity as they confer the ability to directly trade stock on the NYSE. Seat prices have varied widely over the years, generally falling during recessions and rising during economic expansions. The most expensive inflation-adjusted seat was sold in 1929 for $625,000, which, today, would be over six million dollars. In recent times, seats have sold for as high as $4 million in the late 1990s and $1 million in 2001. In 2005, seat prices shot up to $3.25 million as the exchange was set to merge with Archipelago and become a for-profit, publicly traded company. Seat owners received $500,000 cash per seat and 77,000 shares of the newly formed corporation. The NYSE now sells one-year licenses to trade directly on the exchange.

In the mid-1960s, the NYSE Composite Index was created, with a base value of 50 points equal to the 1965 yearly close. This was done to reflect the value of all stocks trading at the exchange instead of just the 30 stocks included in the Dow Jones Industrial Average. To raise the profile of the composite index, in 2003 the NYSE set its new base value of 5,000 points equal to the 2002 yearly close.

In 1792, The NYSE acquires its first traded securities. In 1817, The constitution of the New York Stock and Exchange Board is adopted. In 1867, The First Stock Ticker. In 1896, Dow Jones Industrial Average first published in The Wall Street Journal. In 1903, NYSE moves into new quarters at 18 Broad Street. In 1906, Dow exceeds 100 on January 12. In 1907, Panic of 1907. In 1914, World War I causes the longest exchange shutdown: four months, two weeks; re-opening December 12 brings the largest one-day percentage drop in the DJIA. In 1915, Market price is given in dollars. In 1929, Central quote system established; Black Thursday, October 24 and Black Tuesday, October 29 signal the end of the Roaring Twenties bull market. In 1943, Trading floor is opened to women. In 1949, Longest bull market begins.

In 1954, Dow surpasses its 1929 peak in inflation-adjusted dollars. In 1956, Dow closes above 500 for the first time on March 12. In 1966, NYSE creates the Common Stock Index;

floor data fully automated lli. In 1967, Protesters led by Abbie Hoffman throw mostly fake dollar bills at traders from gallery, leading to the installation of bullet-proof glass. In 1970, Securities Investor Protection Corporation established. In 1971, NYSE recognized as Not-for-Profit organization. In 1972, Dow closes above 1,000 for the first time on November 14. In 1977, Foreign brokers are admitted to NYSE. In 1980, New York Futures Exchange established. In 1982, Longest bull market in DJIA history begins. In 1987, Black Monday, October 19, sees the second-largest one-day DJIA percentage drop in history. In 1991, Dow exceeds 3,000. In 1995, Dow exceeds 5,000. In 1996, Real-time ticker introduced. In 1999, Dow exceeds 10,000 on March 29. In 2000, Dow peaks at 11,722.98 on January 14; first NYSE global index is launched under the ticker NYIID. In 2000, January 26,filming of the music video for "Rage against the machine - Sleep Now in the Fire", caused the doors of the New York Stock Exchange to be closed.

In 2001, Trading in fractions ends, replaced by decimals; September 11, 2001 attacks occur, closing NYSE for 4 sessions. In 2003, NYSE Composite Index relaunched and value set equal to 5,000 points. In 2006, NYSE and ArcaEx merge, creating NYSE Arca and forming the publicly owned, for-profit NYSE Group, Inc.; in turn, NYSE Group merges with Euronext, creating the first trans-Atlantic stock exchange group; DJIA tops 12,000 on October 19. In 2007, US President George W. Bush shows up unannounced to the Floor about an hour and a half before a Federal Open Market Committee interest-rate decision on January 31. NYSE announces its merger with the American Stock Exchange; NYSE Composite closes above 10,000 on June 1; DJIA exceeds 14,000 on July 19 and closes at a peak of 14,164.53 on October 9. This was the peak of the early-to-mid 2000s boom before the 2008-2009 bust.

In 2008, On September 15, the DJIA loses more than 500 points amid fears of bank failures, resulting in a permanent prohibition of naked short selling and a three-week temporary ban on all short selling of financial stocks; in spite of this, record volatility continues for the next two months, culminating at 5 1/2-year market lows. In 2009, Dow closes at

6547.05 on March 9 reaching a 12 year low. Returns to 10,015.86 on October 14. *2010 - Dow suffers largest intraday point decline in its history during a massive selloff believed to have been sparked by a single sell order of Procter and Gamble sent to the NYSE.

LONDON STOCK EXCHANGE

The London Stock Exchange or LSE, is one of the world oldest stock exchanges with a rich history dating back to 1698. The exchange began its life in the coffee houses of 17th century London when John Castaing began issuing "at this Office in Jonathan's Coffee-house" a list of stock and commodity prices called "The Course of the Exchange and other things."

HISTORY OF THE LONDON STOCK EXCHANGE

In 1773, the brokers erected their own building in Sweeting's Alley, with a dealing room on the ground floor and a coffee room above. This location was briefly known as "New Jonathan's," but members soon change the name to "The Stock Exchange".

The Stock Exchange Tower, which was located on Threadneedle Street/Old Broad Street was opened by Queen Elizabeth II in 1972 and housed the Trading Floor where traders would traditionally meet to conduct business. In July 2004, the London Stock Exchange moved from Threadneedle Street to its present location in Paternoster Square close to St Paul's Cathedral, which is still within the "Square Mile" also known as the City of London.

LONDON STOCK EXCHANGE STRATEGY

The stated strategy of the London Stock Exchange is to compete globally in the market for financial transaction services and become the stock market of choice. The Exchange intends to grow their existing business and the reach and scale of their operations, through business development initiatives, acquisitions, joint ventures and alliances where appropriate.

CORE BUSINESS AREAS

As it is organized today, the LSE has four core business areas or offerings to the market:

- *Equity Markets*: Enabling companies from around the world to raise capital needed to grow and by listing securities in a well regulated market. Access to these markets is provided through the Main Market and AIM.
- *Trading Services*: Providing a fast and efficient trading platform to be used by brokers and firms around the world to buy and sell securities.
- *Market Information Services*: Supplying high quality, real-time information and news to the financial community.
- *Derivatives*: Expanding to become the world's most efficient and liquid market for equity derivatives. The EDX London hopes to move the LSE beyond their core equities markets.

LONDON STOCK EXCHANGE FACTS AND FIGURES

The following are some of the facts and figures available for the London Stock Exchange that should give you a feel for the size the exchange:

- There are more than 380 firms worldwide trade as members of the London Stock Exchange.
- The exchange claims to be the most international of all stock exchanges with companies from over 84 countries admitted to trading in their markets.
- The exchange is arguably the largest stock exchange in Europe.
- The LSE accounts for 63% of all European initial public offerings.
- In 2008, there were roughly 55 million trades involving 2.2 trillion British Pounds.
- Approximately 3,500 companies are listed on the London Stock Exchange with a total market value of 2.9 trillion British Pounds.

LONDON STOCK EXCHANGE HOLIDAY SCHEDULE

Since most Europeans do not celebrate the exact same holidays as Americans, the following table contains the 2007, 2008 and 2009 holiday schedules for the London Stock Exchange.

Table. LSE Holiday Schedule 2010

Holiday	Date
New Year	January 1, 2010
Good Friday	April 2, 2010
Easter Monday	April 5, 2010
May	May 3, 2010
Spring	May 31, 2010
Summer	August 30, 2010
Christmas Day	December 27, 2010
Boxing Day	December 28, 2010

Market hours for the LSE's trading services and markets will, unless stated otherwise, commence at their normal scheduled times and will close from 12:30 GMT on Christmas Eve and New Years Eve.

Table. LSE Holiday Schedule 2009

Holiday	Date
New Year	January 1, 2009
Good Friday	April 10, 2009
Easter Monday	April 13, 2009
May	May 4, 2009
Spring	May 25, 2009
Summer	August 31, 2009
Christmas Day	December 25, 2009
Boxing Day	December 28, 2009

Market hours for the LSE's trading services and markets will, unless stated otherwise, commence at their normal scheduled times and will close from 12:30 GMT on Christmas Eve and New Years Eve.

Table. LSE Holiday Schedule 2008

Holiday	Date
New Year	January 1, 2008
Good Friday	March 21, 2008
Easter Monday	March 24, 2008
May	May 5, 2008
Spring	May 26, 2008
Summer	August 25, 2008
Christmas Day	December 25, 2008
Boxing Day	December 26, 2008

Market hours for the LSE's trading services and markets will, unless stated otherwise, commence at their normal scheduled times and will close from 12:30 GMT on Christmas Eve and New Years Eve.

LSE HOURS OF OPERATION

Hours of operation/trading occurs on the London Stock Exchange's in accordance with the schedule appearing on the following table.

Table.LSE Hours of Operation

Trade Reporting	07:15 - 07:50
Opening Auction	07:50 - 08:00
Continuous Trading	08:00 - 16:20
VWAP	16:20 - 16:30
Closing Auction	16:30 - 16:35
Order Maintenance	16:35 - 17:00
Trade Reporting Only	17:00 - 17:15

Note: UK Time is in the Western European Time Zone, which is the same as Greenwich Mean Time. Summer Time is observed in UK Time, where the time is shifted forward by 1 hour; 1 hours ahead of Greenwich Mean Time.

HOSTILE TAKEOVER BY MACQUARIE

On December 15, 2005 a consortium lead by Macquarie announced an unsolicited cash offer to shareholders of the London Stock Exchange.

At writing, the LSE Board was recommending rejection of the offer on the following grounds:

- The offer does not reflect the Exchange's present value, let alone any takeover premium.
- Macquarie's offer disregards the LSE's unique position in global capital markets and strong growth prospects.
- The Exchange has delivered significantly higher volume growth than Macquarie claims in its cash offer.
- Macquarie claims the Exchange is overvalued and the cash offer under-represents the true value of the exchange.

LUXEMBOURG STOCK EXCHANGE

In the year 1927,the Luxembourg Stock Exchange was created. Since the time Luxembourg Stock Exchange was founded it has been successful in acquiring a particular ability of trading and listing in securities from an extended chain of areas. With more than four thousand issuers across 100 countries and more than eighty years of experience Luxembourg Stock Exchange copes with capital market players' demands through better services and outputs along with secure fast and flexible processes. The Luxembourg Stock Exchange entered into an understanding with Euronext in November 2000.

The broad listing opportunities are offered through two ways in Luxembourg stock Exchange.

They are:

- The main market in the European Union list of regulated markets is the Main Regulated Market or Bourse de Luxembourg. A European passport is offered by Luxembourg Stock Exchange who looks to expand their chance for international investors.
- The Euro MTF market or the exchange-regulated market,inaugurated in the year 2005 for those issuers who do not want European Union Passport and for

those also who do not set up financial information according to IFRS or equal accounting standards.

No restrictions are applied on the security types to be listed on both the exchange regulated market and the main market. The issuers in accordance to their chosen market, just need to follow the requirements that it comprises of. Official responsibilities are applicable for listings in both markets.

Key features and requirements needed to get enlisted in Luxembourg Stock Exchange main market:

- A system of training along with a lasting execution place while trading. Transparency features for both pre and post trades for the securities enlisted in accordance with IFRS.
- Simple and easy method for offers of securities across the border.
- The prospectuses should be looked after by the CSSF.

Key features and requirements needed to get enlisted in Luxembourg Stock Exchange, exchange regulated market:

- Luxembourg Stock Exchange in association with MiFID directive operate MTF or Multilateral Trading Facility
- Conditions for listing are very much the same compared to the main market of Luxembourg Stock Exchange with same fees for listing.
- Trading systems are the same with a lasting execution venue keeping the pre-trade and post-trade transparency.
- The Luxembourg Stock Exchange has two stock indexes. They are:
- Luxembourg Stock Price Index is adjusted for normal transactions other than dividends.
- Luxembourg Stock Return Index is adjusted for payments in dividends and including the dividends that are paid to the current market.

8

International Monetary System

Historically, any commodity that was generally accepted as a medium of exchange could be used as money. Various objects have been used as money over time, including human skulls, cows, wine, shells, and mainly metals. Even today in the Yap island of the Pacific, large stones (*fei*) are used as money.

Cows were used as money in ancient Greece or Hellas, Egypt, China, Italy, and Britain. In Southern Sudan, even today, people use cattle and goats as a standard of value. Thus, "a reasonably sound wife costs about 40 head of cattle, with perhaps a few goats and chickens thrown in."

From recent discoveries in Dispilio, near Kastoria, Greece, the most ancient signs of written words, fishing and other instruments, and vases were dated back to 5260 B.C. Also, shapes of coins, similar to talents used in ancient Greece and Rome and existing now in the Museum of Heracleion, Crete, were found to belong to the same ancient times (7,260 years ago). Such discoveries put an end to the myths about the Phoenician alphabet and the Indo-European race. Hellenes (Greeks) were living in that area and the rest of Greece at that time. The research continues and is financed by the European Union (LIFE Programme), whereas a museum is under construction near the lake of Kastoria where such monuments and tools were found. Moreover, human fossil bones and tools were discovered by French and Greek archeologists in Triglia, Halkidikis (*homo erectus trigliensis*), as ancient as 11–12 million years old, compared to 2.5-million-year-old tools found in Africa.

Lending operations for commodities predates money itself, as for example during the Minoan (Cretan) and Mycenean civilizations (earlier than 3000 B.C.), when values were expressed in terms of cows and oxen. Also, the Code of Hammurabi (about 1800 B.C.) deals with mortgages and debts. However, the use of coins and other monetary units, away from the inefficient barter system, later necessitated the establishment of banks.

In addition to cattle, during the Homeric period (about 1200 B.C.), certain pieces of gold called talents were used as money. Recent research in Mycenae (Greece) discovered a copper ingot 2.5 feet long in a shape of ox-hide, dated around the fourteenth century B.C. Moreover, certain pieces of gold (talents) were in circulation but were expressed mainly in terms of cows. An alternative name to euro, suggested in the European Union (EU), was the talent, used in ancient Greece and classical Rome, which are considered as the common roots of the EU member states. It was considered as a hard currency with a value of 26 kg of silver.

In ancient Sparta, large iron disks were introduced by Lycurgus as money units (ninth century B.C.). The Spartan monetary units had a face value higher than the intrinsic or metal value. This system of debased money is used even today by advanced money societies. Later, gold and silver were deposited by the Lacedaemonians with the Arcadians for safekeeping.

Silver coins (drachmas) replaced previous tortoise-shell currency in Corinth, the island of Aegina, and mainly Athens (seventh–fifth century B.C.). They were stamped to indicate their value on the one side, and with an owl (the wisdom bird of Athens) on the other side. According to Aristotle, commodities have a use value and an exchange value measured in drachmas, which can be used for exchanges and storage of wealth.

Plato proposed, in the *Laws*, that token money be used for domestic transactions and gold and silver for transactions with foreigners. In that way, money was internationalized by the Hellenes at that time. However, Aristophanes noted in

"The Frogs" (405 B.C.) that "in our Republic bad citizens are preferred to good, just as bad money circulates while good money disappears." This concept is very near to Gresham's law, after Sir Thomas Gresham, Queen Elizabeth's Chancellor of the Exchequer (A.D. 1559).

As domestic and foreign trade increased, mainly between Athens-Piraeus and Phoenicia, Egypt, Sicily, and other neighbouring countries, banking transactions developed. A number of arcades, the most famous called Degma, were used for exhibitions and exchanges of commodities from all the markets of the eastern Mediterranean and beyond. Moreover, regulations similar to our antitrust laws were enacted by the city government.

Other important monetary units used in ancient times were the Pu money, in the shape of a shirt, as well as knives and other metallic instruments, in China around 700 B.C. Also, the first paper or parchment money was issued in China in 140 B.C. In Egypt, the first coinage was established under the Ptolemies at the end of the fourth century B.C.

ROMAN PERIOD

Money and credit opened new freedoms and opportunities during the period of the Roman Empire. Financiers and profiteers flourished while trade enterprises were growing, and money interest began to play an important role in trade and finance.

The Romans used a common currency to help military cooperation and to stimulate free economic transactions with the regions under their domain. Such common currencies were used later by the United States (the dollar) and the European Union (the euro).

Copper bars or ingots were the first monetary units in ancient Rome. Silver coins, called denarii, similar to those previously used in Greece and mostly debased, were introduced after 269 B.C. Furthermore, with the use of gold later, three metals were used together and serious problems of trimetalism or bimetalism appeared as the relative values of the various metals (gold, silver, copper) changed over time.

During the Roman Empire (31 B.C. to A.D. 476), the creation of a new commercial class, the patricians, increased transactions in the cities and necessitated a body of laws that later had a profound influence on legal and economic institutions, including banks and other financial firms. The recognition of juristic or artificial persons by the Roman laws was important for the creation and expansion of the corporate form of modern enterprises.

The Romans, with their efficient administration of justice and the security of life and property, created many trading, financial, and shipping centres in their dominion and promoted international transactions.

Nevertheless, Rome suffered at times from too little or too much gold and silver and the frequent debasement of its metal money. The rudimentary banking system was inadequate to deal with price changes in the absence of a paper or check system.

MIDDLE AGES AND LATER

Moral corruption, slavery, and decline of the silver and gold mines of Spain and Greece were the main reasons for the fall of the Roman Empire.

During the Byzantine Empire (330–1453) and the Middle Ages (476 to about 1500), gold was the main currency used, but there were problems of debasement of currencies and price fluctuations, mainly from changes in the supplies of gold and silver.

Tax reductions and other administrative reforms stimulated trade and made Constantinople, the capital of Byzantium, a commercial and financial centre for southeastern Europe and the Middle East. However, commercially minded Venetians, who were better organized in foreign trade and finance, managed to settle in a number of ports around the Balkan and other areas and to control customs revenue and banking activities. In competition with the Genoese, another commercial people, they exploited the lucrative trade and financial markets of the Golden Horn, the Black Sea, and other neighbouring regions.

In the Middle Ages, early financial operations were carried on by monasteries, but any interest was considered immoral by Church law and was considered unnatural by Aristotle (two dimes cannot beget a baby dime).

After the Renaissance, modern banking activities were conducted at the old Fairs and monasteries and by the Lombard bankers in England, as well as by financial houses such as the Bardi, the Medici, the Peruzzi, and the Strozzi of Italy, based mainly in Florence, and the Fuggers and the Rothschilds in Germany. They were exempted from the ban on usury and made loans to kings and even to the Pope. Goldsmiths or jewelers in Lombard Street (London) and other places accepted deposits for safekeeping, giving the proper receipts, which were payable to the bearer. The depositors could hand the receipts over to their creditors, performing the same functions as in modern banking. Thereafter, important banks appeared, such as the Bank of Sweden (1694), the Bank of France (1800), and the German Reichs Bank (1873).

The British silver coin initially was a pound of standard (sterling) silver (divided into 240 pennies). Also, the French livre was one pound of silver (ninth century A.D.), and both represented one of the early international monetary units. Other countries, mainly Mexico, China, and India, developed a silver standard.

During the period of Mercantilism (1550–1776), emphasis was given:

- On foreign trade as a means of accumulating precious metals, primarily gold and silver, as the most desirable form of national wealth, and
- On the supremacy of the state over the individual. Gold and silver could be used to finance trade or pay large armies for foreign wars or be retained as luxuries.

As Columbus said (1503), with gold one can get even souls into paradise. The state should support foreign trade and establish colonies to increase national wealth. Commercial expansion occurred by monopolies, such as the Merchant Adventurers, the Eastland Company, the Muscovy Company, and the East India Company. Towards the end of the Mercantilistic period, the physiocratic school appeared (1756–1778) in France. The school was based on the natural order, which prevailed over all the economic activities in a harmonious way, similar to that of the planetary system. This laissez-faire system was further developed by Adam Smith (1776) and other classical economists and is considered as the basis of capitalism. Later, Eugen Von Böhm Bawerk (1891) and other Austrian economists stressed the justification of interest payment, based mainly on the productivity of capital, which helps the worker and the entrepreneur to increase production.

The gold standard, first introduced in Britain in 1821, was also adopted by Portugal (1854), Germany (1871), and other European countries later. Britain abandoned gold from 1914 to 1925 and permanently in 1931.

During the classical gold era, roughly from 1870 to 1914, there was a high capital mobility, mainly from Britain, France, and Germany (about 3–9 per cent of the GDP) to Australia, Canada, New Zealand, and Sweden. Such capital flows were used primarily for investment but also as official reserves (gold and foreign exchange), mainly by the United States, Russia, India, Belgium, and Sweden. A similar phenomenon can be observed in our day with the capital flow in emerging nations, which is used primarily for reserve holdings. In all these cases, the role of investment banks in 1870–1914 was important in stimulating global capital flows, as it is now.

Monetary Systems in the Americas

In the Western Hemisphere, the Incas, covering most of the coast and Highlands of western South America, had no monetary system of any kind, whereas in the American colonies, coins brought over by European immigrants and Indian wampums (ornamental cloth) were initially used as money. Corn was mainly used as a medium of exchange (1631) in Massachusetts, whereas tobacco and rice were used in the south.

In order to facilitate trade with the Spanish colonies, the Spanish silver dollars, or fractions of them, were also used in the Americas. After George Washington's inauguration (1789) as the first president of the United States, gold and silver full-bodied coins were used.

In the United States, for practical purposes, silver was used from 1792 to 1834 and primarily gold from 1834 on, although the Coinage Act of 1792 provided for a mint and stipulated that the principal coin would be the $10 Eagle (weighing 270 grains and containing 247.5 grains of pure gold out of 480 grains in a troy ounce). In 1837, the price of an ounce of gold was fixed by the U.S. Congress at $20.67.

In 1832 and later, Robert Owen of England introduced a paper money in "the Owenite communities in America," mainly in Cincinnati, Tennessee, and Ohio, with nominal values in labour hours. These labour notes entitled "National Equitable Labour Exchanges," based on the utopian teachings of Charles Fourier of France, were short-lived, primarily because of the difficulties in exchanges.

Nevertheless, bank notes and U.S. Treasury notes were mostly used because they were less costly and more convenient than gold. But, as David Ricardo mentioned, "In issuing paper money...it is only necessary that its quantity should be regulated." Moreover, international payments were made in bills of exchange, comparable to postdated checks. Thus, a U.S. exporter would receive gold or more usually bills of exchange from the importers of other countries and sell them for U.S. dollars in New York or other cities.

Because of the Civil War and the increase in prices, payments in gold in the United States were suspended in December 1861. The convertibility of gold for the dollar was restored at $20.67 in January 1879 and remained so until 1933. The pure gold standard system was introduced in 1900 in order to avoid relative price fluctuations in the prevailing bimetalic system of gold and silver. The United States managed to hang onto gold during World War I, but prices increased by more than double from 1914 to 1920, and then by 1932 they fell more than they had risen.

However, new discoveries of gold led to changes in prices and economic instability. Also, when a country had a deficit in the balance of payments, a net outflow of gold would take place, and under a gold standard system, money supply and eventually prices would be reduced, with the possibility of a recession or depression and unemployment. Ceteris paribus, lower prices would lead to more exports and less imports, thereby restoring the balance-of-payments equilibrium. The opposite is expected in countries with surplus in the balance of payments, which would lead to a net inflow of gold, an increase in money supply and prices, less exports and more imports until the balance-of-payments equilibrium is restored.

As mentioned earlier, metals, primarily gold and silver, were used as money mainly in international transactions by different societies. Metals are generally accepted as money because they are homogeneous commodities, easily portable, divisible, storable, and relatively scarce and have a cost to produce and a value in industrial use.

In 1933, the United States abandoned the pure gold standard system, in which anybody could get gold. In its place, the gold reserve system was introduced, in which a certain percentage of the money supply was kept in gold. The price of gold was determined at $35 per ounce in January 1934, but in practice, it was used only for the settlement of international transactions. In March 1973 the price of gold was left to the free market of supply and demand.

The Bank of North America, established by the Continental Congress in 1781, and the Bank of the United States, established by Alexander Hamilton in 1791, were the first U.S. banks. In order to manage money and credit more effectively, the Federal Reserve Bank ("Fed"), as an institution independent of the federal government.

INTERNATIONAL MONETARY FUND

The most effective international organizations, formed by agreements among a large number of nations, are the International Monetary Fund (IMF), the International Bank for Reconstruction and Development or World Bank, and the General Agreement on Tariffs and Trade (GATT), recently named the World Trade Organization (WTO). The IMF and the World Bank were established by forty-four countries at Bretton Woods, New Hampshire (United States), in July 1944, whereas the GATT was negotiated in Havana, Cuba, and established in Geneva in 1948. The International Monetary Fund (IMF), which is a pool of central-bank reserves and national currencies, was established at Bretton Woods in 1944 under the auspices of the United Nations, but it actually started operations on March 1, 1947. In order to facilitate international finance and help correct fundamental balance-of-payments disequilibriums, it tied all currencies to gold and hence to each other.

The IMF, with headquarters in Washington, D.C., was created to help finance balance-of-payments deficits and to reform the international monetary system towards mutual cooperation and freely convertible currencies among the member nations. The waves of devaluations in the currencies of a number of countries before World War II, mainly in 1931–1936, as a way to increase exports and reduce imports at the expense of their trading partners (beggar-thy-neighbour policies) was the rationale of the creation of the IMF. These policies resulted in frequent changes in exchange parities, economic instability, and high unemployment.

The IMF makes its own stock of currencies available (gives loans) to the members. It functions as a pool of currencies or an international clearing institution, using the assigned quotas of the member countries to arrange international payments. Also, it provides short-term loans and advice to member countries, primarily emerging nations, with balance-of-payments difficulties. Member nations were committed to keep their currencies within plus or minus 1 per cent of parity, although further changes in exchange rates were permitted if needed. From that standpoint, the system can be characterized as an "adjustable peg" exchange rate system. Moreover, because the dollar, being the key currency, was convertible into gold (1/35 ounce of gold), every currency had a gold value related to the dollar, which may be considered as a yardstick of value. The Bretton Woods system then may also be characterized as a gold exchange standard system.

Each member nation was responsible to subscribe to the capital of the IMF, paying one fourth in gold and three fourths in its currency (in demand notes), depending mainly on its share of world trade. The member countries were responsible to sell their currencies to the IMF, which could also borrow currencies from its members above their subscribed quotas. Initially the IMF had a total quota of $8.8 billion, but that was increased gradually to about $260 billion (198 billion Special Drawing Rights or SDRs) and 182 members presently.

Immediately after World War II, the United States had about 33 per cent of the voting power in the IMF and 35 per cent in the World Bank, because of its dominant economic position. Thereafter, the U.S. voting power steadily declined to the current levels of less than 20 per cent in the IMF and around 17 per cent in the World Bank. As we enter a new millennium, international institutions, mainly the IMF, are expected to play a more important role in regulating financial cooperation and reducing tensions among member nations, particularly between rich and poor nations, which have heavy debts.

Nevertheless, gold is an expensive reserve asset, as human resources are used to dig it in distant areas and bury it in heavily guarded places in central banks or in the IMF in Washington. That is why Professor Robert Triffin of Yale University suggested that central bank deposits with the IMF be denominated in a new international unit of account or a form of paper gold.

A similar system was proposed by John M. Keynes, as an alternative to the U.S. plan for the IMF at Bretton Woods in 1944. Moreover, the use of gold for the determination of money supply may lead to excessive liquidity and global inflationary pressures, when excessive amounts of gold are available, as well as to inadequate liquidity, when not enough gold is available, resulting in recessions or even depressions, as happened with the severe recession of 1907 (rich man's panic) and the Great Depression of the 1930s.

Although the Bretton Woods system performed well in the 1950s, the fact that the United States had large deficits in its balance of payments in the 1960s increased the dollar reserves of other countries and consequently the demand for gold, forcing the United States to apply first voluntary controls and then mandatory controls to capital outflows. At the same time, Japan, West Germany, and other European countries with surpluses refused to revalue their currencies, suggesting that the United States eliminate its balance-of-payments deficits.

In an attempt to further discourage European companies from raising capital in the United States, the interest-equalization tax was imposed in the mid-1960s to equalize the cost of raising funds in the United States, where interest rates were lower. Moreover, the U.S. Treasury issued medium-term bonds with an exchange-rate guarantee, known as Roosa bonds, to discourage foreign central banks from cashing their excess dollars for gold. Also, U.S. short-term interest rates were raised to attract foreign funds, but long-term interest rates remained low to encourage domestic investments, a policy known as "operation twist." Nevertheless, the "dollar glut" continued in the 1960s, mainly because of the U.S. trade deficits, in contrast to the "dollar shortage" in the 1950s.

In 1969, a special quota (of $10 billion) was created by the IMF to be used for automatic drawings. They are Special Drawing Rights (SDRs), which are gradually replacing gold as a reserve asset. The acceptance of SDRs is an obligation for members, subject to some limitations. Each member can buy currencies directly from other countries up to the amount allocated by the IMF, without going through the regular Fund operations. In the case of SDRs the IMF acts as an intermediary or guarantor. Although large amounts of SDRs are allocated to developed countries, a growing number of emerging nations receive SDR allocations lately.

The IMF carries on its books $5 billion gold, but at market prices the gold the fund owns is worth more than $30 billion. Therefore, the fund can write off some $8 billion that forty poor countries owe it, but under conditions that would not give them incentives for further borrowing with the expectation of not paying back future loans.

Each member paid one fourth of its quota in gold or in dollars and the rest in its own currency. This pool may be considered as an extension of the central-bank reserves and aimed at stable exchange rates. It was accepted that drawings of member countries could be made on permission, as Harry D. White, the U.S. representative, insisted, and not automatically, as John M. Keynes, the British representative, suggested.

The quotas, which are revised every five years to reflect economic changes of members, determine the number of votes and the borrowing limits of the member countries. As mentioned previously, the United States has almost 20 per cent of the total voting power, followed by Germany and Japan with 5.7 per cent each, and then Britain and France with 5.1 per cent each. These five developed countries with more than 40 per cent voting power dominate the IMF, which operates as a central bank for central banks. Member governments select governors, who constitute the highest governing body of the Fund and meet every September in Washington, whereas power is vested in the Board of

Executive Directors (some twenty persons). A member of the Fund can borrow 25 per cent of its quota without restrictions (gold tranche) and higher amounts with restrictions (credit tranches), but repayments are normally to be made within three to five years.

Approximately, the quotas (in billions of Special Drawing Rights or SDRs) (one SDR is equal to about $1.3) are: 27 for the United States; 8 each for Germany and Japan; 7 each for Britain and France; 5 for Saudi Arabia; 4 each for Canada, Italy, and Russia; 3 each for Belgium, China, India, and Netherlands; 2 each for Australia and Brazil; and close to 2 each for Mexico, Spain, and Venezuela, and so on. The U.S. official reserve assets in March 1998 were $69.35 billion, $30.22 billion of which were foreign currencies, $11.05 billion gold, $10.11 billion holdings of IMF SDRs, and $17.98 billion was the reserve position, that is, the U.S. ability to draw foreign currencies from the IMF.

As the cure for sick economies, the IMF usually prescribes tough austerity measures, which lead to deep cuts in public spending, tight credit, high unemployment, sharp currency depreciation, severe stock market decline, and even social unrest. Some of these symptoms occurred in Mexico and the Southeast Asian countries. Some countries blame Washington and other Western capitals for their strong influence on the IMF. Such austerity measures may result in high unemployment, and many people blame IMF for worsening their misery and for losing their jobs (arguing that IMF stands for I'M Fired?). Moreover, the loans from the IMF are relatively small compared to about $2 trillion traded daily in the international currency market. Although it provided more than $150 billion for the Asian and Mexican bailouts lately, as a lender of last resort, it is criticized that in its effort to save weak economies, it discourages the private sector and the related governments to take the necessary painful fiscal and monetary measures to correct the problems of crony capitalism. That is why the U.S. Congress is skeptical on providing additional financing for the IMF.

THE WORLD BANK AND ITS AFFILIATES

Together with the IMF, the International Bank for Reconstruction and Development (World Bank) was created at Bretton Woods in 1944. The member nations must pay 10 per cent of the subscription (1 per cent in gold), and the rest is subject to call any time the bank needs it. Its main source of money, though, is borrowing from the free money market.

The World Bank and its affiliates—the International Finance Corporation (IFC), created in 1956, and the International Development Association (IDA), created in 1960—provide development assistance by extending loans to emerging nations. The IFC specializes mainly in promoting private enterprises through investment in indigenous and foreign sources, whereas the IDA makes long-term loans for housing, sanitation, irrigation, and other projects in poor member nations at subsidized rates. Moreover, within the World Bank Group is a globally operating intergovernmental organization providing investment insurance against political risks, and the International Centre for Settlement of Investment

Disputes (ICSID), which provides facilities for arbitration of disputes between foreign investors and governments.

The authorized capital of the World Bank accounts for $171.4 billion, that of IFC for $1.3 billion, and that of MIGA for $1.1 billion. Also, the capital received by IDA in the form of pledged contributions totals $68.6 billion. Borrowing from the World Bank stands at about $12 billion per year and is expected to increase, as external financing remains essential for many emerging nations.

The World Bank, which lends money to emerging nations, issued $4 billion in dollar-denominated global bonds, the largest ever. It was priced to yield 5.703 per cent for maturity in 2003, that is, 14 basis points above a similar Treasury security. A basis point is one one-hundredth of a percentage point (0.0001). For this issue, which was the largest of the 14 dollar-denominated bond issues by the World Bank, Europe subscribed for 45 per cent, the United States for 35 per cent, and Asia for 20 per cent.

Some other regional development banks, with limited effectiveness, are the Inter-American Development Bank (IDB) created in 1959 mainly to promote the Alliance for Progress programme; the African Development Bank (AFDB), organized in 1964; and the Asian Development Bank (ADB), established in 1966.

GOVERNMENT FINANCIAL INSTITUTIONS

Other institutions dealing with international trade and investment financing, mainly through low-interest loans, are those created by the U.S. federal government to help exporters and investors. They include the Export-Import Bank (EXIMBANK), which was created in 1945 as an independent government institution to aid U.S. exporters and foreign importers through loans, guarantees, counseling, and training. When commercial banks hesitate to give loans to high-risk countries, the EXIMBANK may guarantee such loans, thereby helping poor nations and U.S. exporters to be able to compete with foreign receiving subsidies. Moreover, the Commodity

Credit Corporation (CCC) was created to support U.S. exports of agricultural products through long-term loans, mainly to poor nations, in competition with other countries providing similar loans.

Finally, the Overseas Private Investment Corporation (OPIC) was created to support U.S. investment in other countries, mainly friendly emerging nations. Other industrial countries provide export subsidies, mainly Japan and Europe, in many cases disguised, although this is unfair in international economics. For that reason, the United States raises, from time to time, serious complaints against other nations providing such concealed subsidies, which are financed by the governments involved.

BANKING OPERATIONS

Central banks control and regulate commercial banks, primarily through discount rates, reserve requirements, open market operations, and other monetary policy tools. In their efforts to manage money and credit, they influence trade financing, inflation, and exchange rates. They are lenders of the last resort. Also, they intervene in the financial markets in order to reduce volatility or influence exchange rate levels.

Commercial banks are middle-persons or agents of the public. They accept deposits from the entrusting public and lend them back to the public, charging a higher interest rate than they pay to depositors, who are the ultimate lenders. The amount of borrowers' demand for credit depends on the banks' propensity to lend and the rates they charge.

Although they do not create legal-tender money, they create money (or credit) in the form of bank notes. As it is usually said, "Money talks and banks command."

The creation of money depends on the reserve requirement and the money-supply multiplier. For example, if the reserve requirement (RR) on demand deposits (checking accounts) is 10 per cent, the money-supply multiplier is 10 (or 1/RR = 1/0.10 = 10). This means that, assuming no leakage in loans and redeposits, a $100 demand deposit would create $1,000. From that standpoint, bankers are not only middle-persons but also "manufacturers" of money and may affect business cycles. This was the case with the policies of John Law in France in 1720 (the Mississippi Bubble), who was mistaking money for wealth or credit for capital, as well as in other inflationary policies in history that led to serious international financial crises. In addition to commercial banks, credit unions are engaged in a wide range of banking activities. Thus, in the United States about 70 million people are members of credit unions, which maintain their cooperative structure and their tax-exempt status.

Banks are crucial to domestic and international economies, as they gather savings, make loans, and coordinate financial transactions. In the industrial countries they are the prime providers of financial services, and in the emerging nations they are the heart of the financial markets. However, over the past twenty years, about three fourths of the member countries of the International Monetary Fund have faced problems with bank failures, and many of them considered or adopted measures to protect their financial systems. Thus, in its effort to reform the banking system, the government of Brazil decided to rescue the Banco de Brazil, the largest bank of Latin America, by buying risky bonds worth $3.4 billion. The same policy was used earlier with another bank, run by the federal government, Bovespa. However, sooner or later, both banks would follow the path of privatization implemented currently by Brazil.

Offshore Banking

The volatility of financial markets around the world makes it nearly impossible to discipline them without some form of coordination and regulation. National banking regulations are unable to keep pace with the rapid development of global financial markets. There is no international institution to initiate changes and play the role of an international regulator. Even the International Monetary Fund (IMF) finds it difficult to convince member countries to take measures of exchange rate stabilization and other policies to avoid economic crises. Although more than 100 countries signed an agreement in December 1997 to dismantle national barriers and open their markets to foreign banks, insurance companies, and investment firms, such measures were largely ignored, and the financial turmoil in Asia, Latin America, and other parts of the world continues.

Bermuda is an attractive place for offshore banks and mutual funds. It is considered by affluent international investors as a lightly regulated tax sanctuary. There are around 1,000 funds on the island, with more than $20 billion net assets, about 30 per cent more than from last year. A recent law deals with money laundering and the formalization of mutual funds regulation. It requires approval for any money received, whereas the administrators must prove an acceptable source. Other Caribbean islands are also used for offshore banks and mutual funds as in Bermuda.

On the Cayman islands, which are a British dependency, there are 575 banks with about $500 billion deposits. More than 20,000 huge and small corporations, including hedge funds, are chartered on the Caymans, where there are financial secrecy laws and no income tax, no inheritance tax, no capital gains tax, no sales or other consumption taxes, and no tax treaties.

Other offshore sanctuaries, in addition to Bahamas and the Cayman islands, include the British Virgin Islands, Antigua, the Isle of Jersey, Panama, Liechtenstein, the Netherlands Antilles, Luxembourg, and Switzerland. Although the Group of Seven industrialized nations said that disclosure rules should prevail, it is difficult to implement such rules in practice.

Extensive controls on a global scale may be impossible or ineffective to slow the rapid growth of financial markets and the movement of capital and other banking services from one place to another. Such controls may be difficult to implement in today's advanced technology and may have negative effects on the economies involved, as they may lead to recessions or depressions. Probably the strengthening of the banking system in weak emerging and other economies will promote financial stability and global economic growth. Also, a specialized international institution, possibly under the IMF, may solve the problem.

Intervention by Central Banks and Governments

If a country, say the United States, wants to defend its currency (the dollar) and keep a constant exchange rate with another currency, say the Japanese yen, and the value of the first currency (the dollar) is declining because of higher inflation or other reasons, then the central bank (the Federal Reserve Bank or Fed) would buy some of its currency in order to avoid a reduction in the market value and an expected depreciation. This is what happened in a number of cases when the value of the dollar gradually declined from more than 250 yen to less than 100 yen per dollar.

The demand for dollars is declining and the demand curve shifts from D to D1, then the Fed, which wants to defend the dollar, would buy ac dollars at a price (say 100 yen per dollar) determined by the equilibrium of supply (S) and demand (D), instead of letting it to drop to a lower price (say 80 yen). The opposite would occur when the price of the dollar is going up and the Fed wants to keep it down to the equilibrium point, in which case the Fed would sell dollars for yen.

In many cases, if commercial banks are in trouble, the government can spend money from the budget to bail them out, thereby avoiding a depreciation in its currency and possible decline in the stock market. Thus, in order to bring stability to its volatile financial system, the Japanese government decided to spend more than $500 billion to bail out banks.

Such an action is expected to help dispel pessimism, calm the stock market, and support the currency. As a result, the Nikkei index, which was fluctuating around 17,000 at the beginning of 1999, and the yen, which was quoted at around 120 yen to the dollar at the same time, began to improve. The hope was to help out banks, which had about $620 billion in bad loans, and avoid further credit squeeze and corporate bankruptcies.

Other measures were enacted to guarantee bank deposits and strengthen the Deposit Insurance Corporation (DIC), an institution similar to the U.S. Federal Deposit Insurance Corporation (FDIC). Also, the Japanese government decided to buy preferred shares in banks, as the U.S. government did in the 1930s to pull the country out of the Depression. However, it would be better to allow ailing banks to close down or be merged in order to avoid similar problems in the future. Japanese banks with bad loans include the big banks Daiwa Bank Ltd. and Sumitomo Bank Ltd., as well as Dai-Ichi Kangyo Bank Ltd., Industrial Bank of Japan Ltd., Sakura Bank Ltd., Sanwa Bank Ltd., and Tokai Bank Ltd. After foreign exchange controls were lifted in Japan in April 1998, large amounts of capital are flowing out of the country. Now, more and more Japanese retail and corporate clients are willing to take on foreign exchange risk to enjoy higher returns in stock exchanges. Moreover, the 10-year government bonds in Japan yield only 1.7 per cent currently, which is far lower than in other countries.

Hoping to help restore worldwide confidence in the financial system and make it competitive internationally, the Japanese government, which decided to bail out weak banks, tries to imitate the American policy of bailing out banks by the Reconstruction Finance Corporation of the 1930s. However, this is not well accepted by several Japanese banks, which are issuing preferred shares in New York to raise money on their own. In its effort to make the financial system more attractive, the Japanese government is also adopting international accounting standards, relaxing regulations on disclosure, and making the financial system free, fair, and global. Also, it is privatizing the huge Post Deposits with $2 trillion in deposits, which is offering better interest rates than the private sector and better services, as the mailman collects deposits from households every morning.

The once-mighty economy of Japan has been stalled in recent years, and severe fiscal measures are needed to reverse its economic decline and spur the economy, mainly through public works and tax cuts. However, the Organization of

Economic Cooperation and Development, a group of twenty-nine industrial countries based in Paris, and other nations in Asia and elsewhere criticized these measures as insufficient to uplift the Japanese economy as well as the other ailing trading partners in Asia. Moreover, the feeling in the United States, which has been urging Japan for years to open its economy to more imports, is that Japan should spend more and save less than some 28 per cent of its national income, thereby reducing its huge foreign trade surpluses. In order to shore up its four gigantic state-owned commercial banks, with some $200 billion in bad loans, China floated a $32 billion bond issue in April 1998 and speeded up economic reforms through streamlining, downsizing, and privatizing public enterprises. This is in addition to the $32 billion the Chinese government pumped into these banks recently, including the Guangdong International Trust and Investment Company, also known as Gitic, for which the government assumed a large part of its $2.4 billion foreign debt after its recent closing.

Although China does not have a convertible currency and it is not immediately affected by the financial turmoil in other countries, it is expected to do that in the near future after privatizing state banks. The Chinese government is in the process of closing many debt-ridden trust and investment companies. Beijing plans to close some 200, out of a total 240, such companies with about $10 billion in foreign debt.

An important measure to counteract an economic downturn as a result of the Asian financial crisis is the plan of the Chinese government to spend $1 trillion in public works projects, thereby hoping to keep the 8 per cent growth rate of the $900 billion GDP and avoid high unemployment. The financing of these projects would include domestic and foreign bonds and loans as well as allocations from central and provincial governments. With a relatively small foreign debt of $120 billion and about $140 billion in foreign exchange reserves, China is not expected to face serious problems to find international lenders.

Furthermore, in order to avoid the faltering of private banks, some nations resort to the nationalization of banks, a measure that might create more problems in the future. Thus, the Thai government, which shuttered fifty-six of fifty-eight nonbank finance companies and speculative lenders in the early 1990s, nationalized three large private banks (First Bangkok City Bank, Siam City Bank, and Bangkok Bank of Commerce) in February 1998.

This happened after the Thais failed to attract Western banks, such as Citibank (a unit of Citicorp of the United States) and the ING Bank of the Netherlands, to create alliances and bail them out. Neverthe-less, purging the financial system is a condition of the IMF's $17 billion bailout of the country. Although Thailand relaxed some strict regulations for foreign ownership, foreign banks cannot hold more than 50.1 per cent stake and cannot increase shareholding in Thai banks, many of which are owned by powerful Thai and Thai-Chinese business families.

Another tool the government can use, through the central bank, is to raise interest rates so that private investors would be induced to increase their demand for its currency. The use of the interest rate as a tool of exchange rate stability is extensively used in our day. Recently, it was used by many emerging nations to avoid currency depreciation (devaluation) due to the Asian turmoil.

CONSOLIDATION OF BANKS AND OTHER FINANCIAL INSTITUTIONS

Cross-Atlantic Banking Mergers

Merger mania, which can be observed domestically, is gradually becoming an international phenomenon. The open and competitive world markets require large companies with global reach. Megamergers, such as the Travellers Group, which recently bought Salomon Brothers, intertwined with nine other firms around the world and merging with Citicorp later, are globalizing the financial markets. In competition with other global heavyweights such as Merrill Lynch and Company and Morgan Stanley, Dean Witter, Discover and Company, Salomon also acquired other firms around the world, including most of County NatWest brokerage businesses in Sydney, London, Tokyo, and other cities.

Such acquisitions can exaggerate the volatility in world stock markets and currencies and create economic havoc. Nevertheless, such Goliaths usually introduce new technology, reduce cost, and facilitate capital investment worldwide.

The recent financial deregulations all over the world are allowing banks and other firms to operate internationally and to underwrite securities and distribute stock offerings. However, there are serious concerns regarding the public interest. The ferocious competition of American, European, Japanese, and other financial giants may lead them to speculative trading in risky options and futures contracts. Although powerful financial firms would not be allowed to fall, as governments would shore them up, extensive risky operations may result in international crises. Perhaps this may invite commercial banks and other firms to merge and operate on a global scale.

The cross-border financial services of money management firms, including banks, mutual funds, brokerage firms, and other investment companies, are rapidly growing. Such companies manage huge amounts of savings for pension funds, insurance firms, and ordinary investors in a global scale. Big American financial firms, such as Fidelity Investments, Merrill Lynch and Company, J. P. Morgan and Company, and Citigroup, are accelerating their movements in other countries to become international money managers. Other big money firms eager to expand internationally include Deutsche Bank, the largest German bank, which acquired Bankers Trust, a big U.S. bank; AXA-UAP of France; the Swiss Bank Corporation; and the Zurich Group of Switzerland, which agreed to buy Scudder Stevens and Clark, the American mutual fund company.

Merrill Lynch, based in New York, agreed to acquire Mercury Asset Management Group P.L.C., based in London. Merrill, with $272 billion of funds under management, 5,200 employees, and $22 billion market capitalization plans to finance the acquisition with preferred stock and long-term debt. The Bank of New York Company agreed to buy trust businesses from the British bank Coutts and Company, a unit of National Westminster Bank P.L.C., for an undisclosed amount. This will add some $15 billion to the about $400 billion business of the bank outside the United States.

Mercury, with assets of $177 billion under management and nineteen offices around the world, announced that there would be no layoffs among its 1,500 managers and employees. With $4 billion capitalization, it was spun off from S.G. Warburg and Company, a company that was acquired by the Swiss Bank Corporation in 1995. Mercury manages money for about half the companies in the Financial Times–Stock Exchange 100 index and handles funds for half of the largest fifty company pension funds in Japan.

In order for the countries of the world to trade, international financial institutions must exist to facilitate exchanges of different currencies and other transactions. The growing use of the flexible-exchange-rate system, compared to the old gold standard or the fixed-exchange-rate mechanism and the intermediate managed-exchange rate-regime, necessitates the development of sophisticated international banking.

As long as there are barriers to cross-border investment, international financial intermediary institutions are needed to deal with different national jurisdictions and investment diversification. From that standpoint, commercial banks play a vital role in dealing with direct and portfolio investment, private debt, different-country risks, and the associated cross-border fees or penalties.

Financial liberalization, diffusion of technology, competition, and trade and capital flows undermine political autonomy and reduce national divergence. Controls over allocation of credit, guided liberalization, and state financing gradually change towards private financing and self-financing on a global scale, as almost all countries try to attract foreign capital.

An important international banking market is the Eurocurrency market. In addition to the European countries,

Eurocurrency banking centres include the Bahamas and other Caribbean islands, Canada, Japan, Singapore, Hong Kong, and the United States. The Eurocurrency market, which appeared in the 1950s, grew drastically thereafter to account now for about $4 trillion.

Deutsche Bank A.G., the biggest bank of Germany, agreed to acquire Bankers Trust Corporation, the eighth-largest American bank, for some $9 billion. Deutsche Bank had also acquired Morgan Grenfell of Britain in the early 1990s and lately 10 per cent of the Eurobank of the Latsis group, which agreed to acquire the Bank of Athens. Recently, in order to focus more on international banking, Deutsche decided to spin off its industrial assets, worth $24 billion, in such companies as DaimlerChrysler, a car industry, and Allianz, the biggest insurer of Germany, where it holds large stakes.

Through banks and other financial institutions, large amounts of money from pension funds move to international stock markets. Thus, the U.S. Teachers Insurance and Annuity Association and College Retirement Equities Fund (TIAA-CREF), available to over 6,100 educational and research institutions with 1.8 million participants and more than $250 billion in assets, is moving aggressively to profitable European, emerging, and other well-established world stock markets.

On both sides of the Atlantic, merger fever continues. Recently, the U.S. Federal Reserve Bank approved the merger of the Swiss Bank Corporation, with operations in the United States, and the Union Bank of Switzerland. The new bank, named United Bank of Switzerland, is the biggest bank in the world, after the Bank of Tokyo-Mitsubishi, with some $706 billion assets.

United States Banking Mergers

Recently, many banks follow the general trend of mergers and acquisitions in order to reduce operational costs and be more efficient in the global financial markets. Also, severe competition from brokerage firms, mutual funds, and credit card firms forces them into the creation of mammoth banks with national and international aspirations.

The merger of Citicorp and the Travellers Group in 1998, worth $77.6 billion, formed Citigroup Inc., with a market capitalization of $153.9 billion. This merger created the largest financial service company in the world and deals with banking, securities (stocks and bonds), and insurance activities worldwide. The Citigroup is in fierce competition with Merrill Lynch, American Express, Goldman Sachs, American International Group, and Morgan Stanley, Dean Witter in the field of global investment banking. The Nationsbank Corporation and the BankAmerica Corporation agreed to merge to create the largest U.S. bank in terms of total branches and deposits and the second bank in total assets. The deal involves a stock-to-stock transaction worth more than $61.6 billion. Furthermore, the Bank One Corporation merged with the First Chicago NBD Corporation, creating the fifth-largest banking company by assets worth $30 billion.

Their combined deposits are more than $340 billion, compared to about $200 billion each for Citicorp and Chase Manhattan and around $170 billion each for BankAmerica and Nationsbank.

Mainly because of the stock market exchange, the Corestates Financial Corporation accepted the merger deal with the First Union Corporation, which it had rejected some time before when the market prices were not favourable. First Union of Charlotte, North Carolina, and Corestates of Philadelphia (the first U.S. banking capital) have combined assets of about $204 billion and plan to reduce cost primarily by laying off a large number of the 11,000 employees of Corestates.

Wells Fargo and Company agreed with Norwest Corporation in a $31.4 billion merger to create a banking group with $191 billion assets, smaller than Citigroup (with $697 billion assets) and BankAmerica (with $571 billion assets), but bigger than Washington Mutual Inc. (with $144 billion assets). The new group, based in San Francisco, is named Wells Fargo Bank.

Other megamergers in the banking sector, in addition to the First Union's deal with Corestates for $17.1 billion, include the purchase of Barnett Banks by Nationalbank for $15.5 billion and that of the Washington Mutual Inc., a large savings and loans association in Seattle, and the H.F. Ahmanson and Company in Los Angeles, which agreed to merge in a $9.9 billion stock swap and create a new company with $149.2 billion assets, trailing the BankAmerica Corporation but surpassing Wells Fargo and Company.

Merrill Lynch, with some 18,000 retail brokers, is under consideration to be taken over by American International General for $30 billion. Also, Chase Manhattan and Bank of America are in negotiations to buy Merrill Lynch.

The Bank of New York (BoNY) agreed to a friendly takeover of Mellon Bank Corporation for $24 billion, creating a large banking institution. Mellon, which recently acquired a $7.9 billion serving portfolio from the Bankers Trust New York Corporation, expects to sell its commercial mortgage business, including $17 billion of servicing rights, and concentrate on residential mortgages. Moreover, Mellon, parent of the Dreyfus Corporation, agreed recently to buy the Denver-based Founders Funds.

Fleet Financial Group agreed to buy Bank Boston for $16 billion. The new Fleet Boston Corporation, based in Boston, has some $178 billion assets and is about half the size of Citigroup. Moreover, Fidelity Investments and Lehman Brothers, both big investment companies, announced a broad alliance for distribution channels, research, and other activities.

It is expected that such deals would put pressure on other banks, mutual funds, and financial firms in general to merge so that they can compete internationally. More consolidations are expected after the United States changed, on November 12, 1999, the Glass–Steagel Act of 1993 and the Bank Holding Company Act of 1956, which did not permit banks to get into securities and insurance operations. Other goverments are expected to enact similar banking and other antitrust laws to encourage global competition.

Banking Mergers in Europe

Merger mania in the United States affected Europe as well. Thus, UBS merged with Swiss Banking Corporation, and

Dresder Bank of Germany formed alliances with Commerzbank in other European countries.

Moreover, Banque Nationale de Paris increased its hostile takeover offer for Societe Generale and Paribas to $40 billion.

In order to gain approval by the European Union of a $16.6 billion government bailout of Credit Lyonnais, a state-owned bank with heavy losses, France decided to sell a large amount of assets, as well as half of the bank's "commercial presence" in other European countries. Such an action would increase competition in the banking sector of France, as well as among other members of the European Union.

In competition with Fortis, the Belgo-Dutch financial group, ABN Amro, the largest bank of the Netherlands, offered $12.3 billion for Generale de Banque of Belgium so that it can increase its international operations, mainly in Europe, which is expected to achieve a monetary union soon. Such a merger was necessary as other big banks in Belgium and other countries are involved in similar mergers and takeovers. At the same time, Fortis sold 624,000 shares it owns in Munich Re, a large reinsurance company, to Lehman Brothers, which then sold them to European and U.S. investors. Also, Fortis agreed to buy the American Bankers Insurance of Miami for $2.6 billion in cash.

Lloyds TSB P.L.C. acquired Scottish Widows for $11.1 billion to create Britain's biggest bank and insurance group. Expecting growth in the stock price of Assurances Generales de France S.A. on the Paris Stock Exchange, the Allianz A.G. of Germany agreed to buy 100 per cent of the shares of the company, as the French law requires, with $10.4 billion, higher than the $9.5 billion offer by Assicurazioni Generali S.p.A. of Italy. As a result, Allianz shares rose in Frankfurt and Assicurazioni Generali fell in Milan.

The Lend Lease Corporation, with shares in the Sydney and London stock markets, in competition with the Latsis Group and a Portuguese firm, is interested in buying some 350 acres of land in Attica for construction development from the Mesogea A.E. Moreover, Lend Lease recently acquired the Equitable insurance company of the United States. The government of Poland, which is easing restrictions on foreign banks, sold a 37 per cent stake in Bank Przemyslowo-Handlowy S.A. to Bayrische Hypo-und Vereinsbank A.G. of Germany, which is publicly traded for $607 million (1 billion DMs).

Unicredo Italiano, a large bank in Italy, agreed to buy Banca Commerciale Italiana (B.C.I.) for $16 billion, offering eight of its own shares for every five in B.C.I. The Deutsche Bank owns shares in both banks. Also, Unicredito agreed to be acquired by Credito Italiano S.p.A, the largest bank of Italy, for $10.7 billion, thereby creating a financial group with $168 billion in assets and about 3,000 branches. It is expected that the new banking group would be able to compete with other European banks, not only in Italy but in other neighbouring countries as well.

Furthermore, the Instituto San Paolo di Torino, the largest commercial bank of Italy, and IMI, a banking group in Rome, plan to merge to create one of the largest EU banks.

The Bankgesellschaft Berlin A.G., which was formed through the merger of three state-owned banks in 1994, agreed to buy the Norddeutsche Landesbank Girozentrale for $3.54 billion in cash and stock. As the EU adopted a common currency, the euro, German states, which operated their own banks for two centuries, plan to keep 60 per cent ownership of Bankgesellschaft and trade publicly the rest. As a result of this consolidation, the new bank moved to fourth place behind Dresdner Bank A.G. Moreover, the Deutsche Bank A.G., with global investment banking business in North America and other places, plans to concentrate in Europe in order to be able to face the expected stiff competition into the European Union.

Expecting that the monetary union of Europe will shake out the banking sector, Banco Bilbao Vizcaya (BBZ) and Banco Santander, both in Spain, plan to cooperate and eventually to merge because banking concentration became inevitable in a wider Europe. Already, the group has cemented a partnership with the Royal Bank of Scotland, raised to 100 per cent its stake in CC Bank of Germany, and is moving aggressively into Latin America, mainly Brazil and Chile. To make the banking sector more competitive with other international banks, mergers are sometimes encouraged. Thus, Spain approved the merging of Banco Espanol de Credito and Banco Central to create the biggest commercial bank in Spain and the twentieth in the world in capital and reserves. The combined profits of the two banks are more than 60 billion pesetas (120 pesetas to the U.S. dollar) per year. Their total assets are more than 7 trillion pesetas, deposits about 5.5 trillion, and equity 530 billion pesetas. In competition with the Piraeus Bank S.A., the European Financial Group (EFG) owned by the Latsis family, which owns already a 15.6 per cent stake in Ergo plus 5 per cent owned by its parent Deutsche Bank, agreed to buy Ergo Bank S.A. for $5.2 billion. The new bank, with its subsidiaries, Hiosbank A.E. and Macedonia-Thrace Bank A.E., would have more than 250 branches. Such mergers are needed so that the Greek banks would be able to survive strong competition from EU banks before the adoption of the euro in 2001.

In the process of privatization and reorganization of state enterprises, the National Bank of Greece announced its merger with the National Mortgage Bank of Greece through the exchange of 1.9 shares of National Mortgage Bank for each share of the National Bank. The new financial institution, with more than 12.5 trillion drachmas assets and some 10 trillion drachmas deposits, has 605 branches in Greece and more than 100 branches abroad. Moreover, the Bank of Piraeus acquired 37 per cent of the Bank of Macedonea-Thrace and 51 per cent of the Marathon Bank, which is based in New York and has a number of branches. Other banks privatized or under privatization include Ionian Bank, Cretabank, Central Bank of Greece, and Commercial Bank of Greece.

UBS merged with Swiss Banking Corporation, and Dresdner Bank of Germany formed alliances with Commerzbank in other European Countries.

Other Banking Mergers

Consolidation and restructuring eliminate banks in almost all countries through acquisitions, mergers, and joint ventures. The rapid consolidation of banks became a worldwide phenomenon. In Canada, the Royal Bank of Canada and the Bank of Montreal announced their merger in early 1998 to create the largest bank of Canada with some $333 billion assets. About three months later, the Canadian Imperial Bank of Commerce and the Toronto-Dominion Bank announced their merger to create the second-largest bank in Canada and the tenth in North America with assets of about $320 billion (United States) and 2,300 branches all over Canada. The market capitalization of the new bank, named ICBC, is estimated at $30 billion. Moreover, there are expectations that the two remaining large banks that is, the Bank of Nova Scotia and the National Bank of Canada, with a market capitalization of about $18 billion, may merge in the near future.

In contrast to the U.S. unit-banking system, Canada has the branch-banking system, which is highly concentrated in four large banks, after these mergers, creating problems for government regulators and consumers regarding competition stifling. Such deals would also affect financial services in the United States, where Toronto-Dominion owns Waterhouse Securities and Waterhouse Bank, whereas Canadian Imperial owns CIBC Openheimer, a securities firm.

Under the $58 billion IMF rescue programme, Korea decided to sell two large banks to foreign investors. Thus, Newbridge Capital of the United States agreed to acquire Korea First Bank. Also, HSBC Holding, a British financial group, agreed to buy SeoulBank.

Barclays, an international bank, and Standard Chartered, which covers Africa, Asia, and the Middle East, are discussing the creation of a $60 billion international banking group.

Salomon Smith Barney, which is an investment banking arm of the Travellers group of the United States, agreed to buy the National Westminster's Australian and New Zealand banking firm, which makes sizable profits from flotation and privatization. This is the first international acquisition of Solomon since its merger with the Travellers group in November 1997, worth $9 billion, whereas plans exist for expansion in the Asian Pacific area. As a result of the relaxation of Australia's resistance to takeovers by foreign investment banks, other investment firms, such as Morgan Stanley, Goldman Sachs, and Credit Suisse First Boston, plan to move into Australia.

Garantia S.A., a big investment bank in Brazil, was purchased by Credit Suisse First Boston, a Swiss-American investment banking group, for $675 million in cash and stock. In competition with Merrill Lynch, which won a mandate to underwrite the $6 billion privatization of Petrobras, Brazil's national oil company, Credit Suisse Group, which paid $10 billion to buy the Winterthur Insurance Company of Switzerland in 1997, is making serious efforts to expand in Asia, Europe, and other areas.

Citibank, a unit of Citigroup, agreed to take over the Banca Confia SA of Mexico, after the government pays $1 billion for the bailout of the bank. Banco Bilbao Vizcaya S.A. reached an agreement to acquire, for $450 million, a 55 per cent stake in Banco Excel Economico, which is based in São Paulo.

9

International Financial Integration

RELATIONS BETWEEN INTEREST RATES AND EXCHANGE RATES

Conventional wisdom holds that international capital mobility is close to perfect. It is sometimes thought that perfect capital mobility implies that arbitrage equalizes interest rates across countries, on either a nominal or a real basis. The equalization of interest rates, if valid, would have powerful implications. It would mean, for example, that the domestic interest rate would no longer be free to reflect expansionary monetary policy: in the Mundell-Fleming theory, the high degree of international financial integration would imply that the exchange rate had displaced the interest rate as the primary indicator of the easing or tightening of monetary policy.

Perfect capital mobility, in the sense of low barriers to the movement of capital across national boundaries, does not imply the international equalization of nominal or real interest rates, however. The reason is high exchange rate variability under floating exchange rates (which may itself be in part a result of high capital mobility). Countries' interest rates are expressed in their own currencies and thus may differ because of factors associated with the currencies in question rather than the national boundaries.

UK and Japan in 1979 removed capital controls to join the club of countries integrated into world financial markets and how liberalization has spread to more countries in the 1980s. It argues the possibility that covered interest differentials did not vary enough in the 1980s to be important sources of variation in international short-term interest differentials. I then consider how liberalization affected the correlations of exchange rates with short- and long-term interest rates in the 1980s. Even if perfect capital mobility does not eliminate interest differentials completely, so that the domestic interest rate continues to be affected by monetary policy, one might think that the exchange rate would nevertheless be a very good indicator of the stance of monetary policy. But the exchange rate sometimes fluctuates sharply for reasons that are apparently unrelated to macroeconomic fundamentals. I discuss an alternative possible indicator for monetary policy: the term structure of interest rates.

I make the obvious point that the monetary authorities would be well advised to look at many available indicators simultaneously. However, I emphasize the advantages of announcing a single *intermediate target* as opposed to relying on a single indicator to attain the target. It is concluded that, of the alternative intermediate nominal targets that have been proposed, nominal GNP may be the best. This is all the more true in the international context, where I have called the proposal international nominal targeting.

RECENT LIBERALIZATIONS

A number of different criteria for measuring the degree of international capital mobility have been proposed and have been reviewed elsewhere. If the aim is to measure the extent of 'country barriers'-capital controls, transaction costs and other barriers to the integration of national financial markets across political boundaries-then the best measure is the covered or 'closed' interest differential, i.e. the difference between offshore and onshore interest rates, hedged so as to eliminate exchange risk. The virtues of this measure are well illustrated by three major liberalization episodes of the 1970s: Germany in 1973-4, the UK in 1979 and Japan in 1979-80.

In the early 1970s, Germany had stringent capital controls in place, designed to discourage the acquisition of German assets by foreign residents. The government essentially prohibited the payment of interest to non-residents on large bank deposits, taxed any new credits by non-residents to German banks and prohibited non-residents from buying German bonds. Most of these controls were removed in late 1973 and 1974. The lower two lines are the Euro-mark interest rate and the covered Euro-dollar interest rate in London, which are always virtually identical because covered interest parity always holds within the London Euromarket. During most of 1973, these Euro-rates lay far below the German interbank rate, indicating that the controls were indeed effectively preventing foreign residents from obtaining assets within Germany. The gap narrowed at the end of 1973 and disappeared in the course of 1974, confirming the removal of controls.

Japan maintained stringent controls on capital inflows through most of the decade. Foreign residents were prohibited outright from holding many kinds of assets in Japan. The Ministry of Finance removed the prohibition against foreign investment in April 1979 and formalized the liberalization in December 1980. Further liberalization measures followed, relaxing controls against both inflows and outflows, notably the yen-dollar agreement between the Ministry of Finance and the US Treasury in May 1984.

During the period January 1975 to April 1979, the differential between the Gensaki interest rate (a three-month rate) in Tokyo and the Euro-yen interest rate in London averaged 1.84 per cent, showing the efficacy of the controls on capital inflow. During the period May 1979 to November 1983, the differential fell sharply to "0.26 per cent. The fact that the differential was actually somewhat negative during this period is evidence that the controls that remained were working to discourage outflow more than inflow. In the period 1985-8, the differential was essentially zero, showing evidence of complete liberalization.

A third liberalization took place in Britain in 1979. The incoming Thatcher government removed the restrictions requiring British banks to keep their 'offshore' accounts separate from their domestic accounts. The three-month Euro-pound interest rate averaged 1.43 per cent per annum higher than the UK interbank interest rate, indicating effective controls against capital outflow. The differential fell to 0.29 per cent per annum in 1979 and to zero soon thereafter.

The liberalization trend spread more widely in the 1980s. Australia began to liberalize early in the decade and New Zealand followed suit. France, which strengthened controls on outflow when the Socialists came to power in 1981, began to remove the controls in the late 1980s.

France and Italy are both expected to meet a mid-1990 deadline for full liberalization among the twelve members of the EC. In the enlarged EC, only Spain, Portugal, Greece and Ireland are expected to need later deadlines. Most tests of covered interest parity have somewhat artificially tested the hypothesis of 'perfect' capital mobility; these tests, however, generally provide little indication about the degree of capital mobility because the covered interest differential is never *exactly* zero.

Furthermore, most tests have been confined to small subsets of the G10 countries, as theirs are the only currencies that have well-developed Euromarkets. However, it has recently become possible to obtain London forward rate quotes for more countries for the period since September 1982. These data used together with local interest rates are ideal for studying the extent of integration in the 1980s. Frankel examined the magnitude and variability of the covered interest differentials over the *average* of the period. Here we examine the *trend* for each of twenty-three countries in order to look for evidence of liberalization taking place within the sample period 1982-8.

Twelve countries show statistically significant downward trends (at the 95 per cent level). The seven with the most rapid estimated trend, listed in descending order, are as follows: Portugal, Spain, France, New Zealand, Denmark, Australia and Italy.

This is precisely the list that one would have expected for countries liberalizing in the 1980s. The other five countries with significant downward trends are as follows: Germany, Switzerland, the Netherlands, Sweden and Japan. This groups already had small differentials at the beginning of the sample period anyway. The same is true of six of the ten countries with statistically insignificant: Austria, Belgium, Canada, Hong Kong, Norway and Singapore. Only one country appears to have a statistically significant *upward* trend in the magnitude of its covered interest differentials during the sample period, namely the UK, which was starting from the third lowest position of any of the twenty-three countries. The implication is that there are only four countries in the sample that by 1988 had still made little effort towards liberalization: Greece, Bahrain, Malaysia and South Africa.

The dollar is the currency relative to which the forward rates of the other currencies are measured. But for the USA as well, the differential between the offshore interest rate and the domestic rate has fallen over time, perhaps as the result of innovation in the Euromarkets. Reinhart and Weiller find that the Euro-dollar-US CD differential had a statistically significant downward trend over the period 1971-87 and that 'the initial gap is all but eliminated by the end of the period'. In particular, the differential was smaller after 1983 than during the period 1978-82. All the preceding results, and most of the tests of closed interest parity that others have done in the past, apply only to international arbitrage among short-term deposits. Feldstein and Horioka (1980) surmised that international arbitrage does not work as well for long-term bonds. As Akhtar and Weiller (1987) point out, there is a need to test closed interest parity at the longer end of the maturity spectrum. Recently, a few studies have attempted to extend the tests to long-term bonds.

The differential between long-term interest rates in the USA and in the Euro-dollar bond market can be seen to have declined in the course of the 1980s. Popper (1990), using currency swap data, finds that the differential between swapped Japanese and US government bonds by 1986 was as small as the differential between short-term assets. The (tentative) conclusion is that bonds issued by different major industrialized countries, when otherwise similar in nature, have in fact become relatively close substitutes in the course of the 1980s.

CURRENCY BARRIERS

Decomposition of the forward discount into the exchange risk premium and expected depreciation. It is well known that the elimination of barriers to the movement of capital across national boundaries as reflected in covered interest differentials is not enough to equalize interest rates across countries. Let i be the US interest rate and i^* be the foreign interest rate. The first term, the covered interest differential, is associated with the country or political jurisdiction in which an asset is issued, not with the currency in which it is denominated. We have already seen that liberalization sharply reduced the differential in 1979 in the cases of Japan and the UK and gradually reduced it in the 1980s in the cases of France and other countries. The second and third terms, which are the exchange risk premium and expected depreciation respectively, are associated with the currency of denomination, not with the political jurisdiction. Given the high volatility of floating exchange rates, it is quite possible that the latter terms have increased in size and variability in the 1980s rather than decreased.

The conventional wisdom among economists is that the expected depreciation term is small in magnitude and variability, and the risk premium term larger in both magnitude and variability. This conventional wisdom emerges from the rational expectations methodology. The rational expectations methodology infers what investors must have expected *ex ante* from what actually happened *ex post*. The common application in international finance is the interpretation of findings of bias in the forward discount. The null hypothesis of unbiasedness is represented by all the variation in the forward discount would be explained as variation in expected depreciation rather than as variation in the risk premium

The standard finding is that the coefficient b is in fact significantly less than unity. Often it is close to zero. Under the rational expectations methodology, this rejection of the null hypothesis is interpreted as evidence of an exchange risk premium that varies over time with the forward discount.

When results show an estimate of *b* that is insignificantly different from zero-an instance of the popular random walk findings-the rational expectations methodology interprets it as evidence that there is no variation in expected depreciation and that all the variation in the forward discount represents variation in the exchange risk premium.

The alternative interpretation argues that one cannot reliably infer *ex ante* expectations from movements that are observed *ex post*, even when the systematic component of the movement appears statistically significant by standard criteria. The rational expectations methodology could fail either because agents do not act rationally or because distributional difficulties associated with the 'peso problem' invalidate the test statistics in conventional sample sizes. The proposition that observed patterns of movement in the exchange rate reflect investors' expectations is a proposition that one would like to be able to test rather than impose *a priori*.

In recent years, a number of researchers have begun to use survey data as an alternative method of measuring investors' expectations.

A measure of expected depreciation based on survey data is exempt from some of the problems that plague conventional measures and can be used to test propositions such as a constant risk premium and the validity of the rational expectations methodology itself. Of course, the survey data undoubtedly have problems of their own; their measurement of market participants' expectations may be subject to error. Nevertheless, even allowing for the possibility of measurement error, one can learn much from this approach.

Most of these papers so far have used data that only went up to 1985. One might wonder whether the results changed in any way in the late 1980s, as a result of either the continued process of financial integration documented in the first section, a new era in the history of the dollar or new forecasting techniques used by participants in the foreign exchange market. Furthermore, because these data sets are so new, three additional years of data are of interest in that they can increase the sample size by one-half.

The earlier tests to include data through 1988. It is a regression of the expected depreciation of the currency against the forward discount. For two out of the three terms studied, the coefficients are even closer to unity than they were in the 1981-5 results. The results support the view that the variation in expected depreciation is large and the variation in the risk premium is small-precisely the reverse of the conventional wisdom-even more strongly than did the earlier results.

Three null hypotheses are relevant: and The first null hypothesis would represent the view that none of the variation in the forward discount represents variation in expected depreciation; it is easily rejected at the 99 per cent level of significance. The second represents the middle-of-the-road case where the variance of expected depreciation is equal to the variance of the exchange risk premium; it is also rejected at conventional significance levels in favour of the hypothesis that expected depreciation is more variable than the risk premium. The third hypothesis represents the view that *all* the variation in the forward discount represents variation in expected depreciation and *none* represents variation in the risk premium; the results by a wide margin do not reject this hypothesis.

These findings do not imply that the risk premium is zero. A majority of the *t* ratios, when computed for the five individual currencies, show statistically significant constant terms, part of which could be due to constant risk premiums (as opposed to the convexity term). Moreover, the results do not even imply that the risk premium is necessarily constant. However, the finding does suggest that variation in the forward discount does not reflect variation in the exchange risk premium as conventionally thought.

The sum of the covered interest differential, and the exchange risk premium, is the uncovered interest differential, or the expected difference in rates of return across countries:

In view of the evidence that the magnitude and variability of the first term have been small in the 1980s and that the magnitude and variability of the second have also been small (relative at least to what is conventionally inferred on the basis of the rational expectations methodology), one might expect that the same is true of the uncovered interest differential. The survey data to measure expected depreciation, find that this is indeed the case: for the sample period October 1984 to June 1986, the average uncovered interest differential between Japan and the USA is opposite in sign to, and less than one-twentieth the size in absolute magnitude of, the differential inferred by the rational expectations methodology on the basis of the difference in *ex post* rates of return, even though this differential appears statistically significant at the 99 per cent level.

HOW RETURN CORRELATIONS ACROSS GERMANY, JAPAN, THE USA AND THE UK CHANGED IN THE 1980S

In this section, we look at how correlations across the four countries that are the most important financially changed in the 1980s. We start the sample in March 1973, with the beginning of generalized floating, and go up to February 1989. We divide the sample at 1979, the year of the initial Japanese and British liberalizations. We choose October 1979 as the precise breaking point because we shall need to take account of the fact that US interest rate and exchange rate volatility increased in the 1980s, and the increase can be dated from the October change in operating procedures on the part of the Federal Reserve.

The short-term interest rates did indeed become more volatile in the 1980s in the UK and the USA, and long-term interest rates did so in all four countries. The variability of the dollar-pound, dollar-mark and dollar-yen exchange rates also increased in the 1980s. In the case of the pound, the increase in variability only occurred in the early 1980s; during the four-year period beginning March 1985, the variance was not much higher than in the 1970s. Stock markets also became more volatile in all four countries in the 1980s.

How would we expect the correlation of interest rates across countries to have changed in the 1980s? On the one hand, the results of the first section show that the covered interest differential, virtually disappeared in the course of the 1980s. Thus one might guess that the variability of the interest differentials fell and the correlation of interest rates across countries increased in the 1980s. On the other hand, the evidence from the second section suggests that although the variance of the exchange risk premium, may have been small in the 1980s, the variance of expected depreciation, the third term, was large. This suggests that the correlation of interest rates across countries may have fallen rather than risen. Indeed, the association among major countries' nominal interest rates became looser in the 1980s than it had been in the 1960s or 1970s.

Specifically, they find a decline in the correlation between US short-term interest rates and those of Germany, Japan the UK and Canada (though the correlations of long term) and increased somewhat further after dispersion across the five countries' interest rates also increased sharply after 1972 (mean absolute deviation of countries' rates, whether short term or long-term interest ratess increased sharply). The 1979 when German and Japanese interest rates failed to rise as much as the rates of the other countries, German, Japanese and US money market interest rates. All six correlations have increased in the period since October 1979.

All six cross-correlations among these countries' long-term interest rates also increased, as did the correlations among the changes in interest rates. Evidently, the high variability of expected depreciation in the 1980s was not enough to overcome the low variability in covered interest differentials and exchange risk premiums. The correlations among the four long-term interest rates increase both in the October 1979 to June 1984 and July 1984 to April 1989 subperiods. The same is true of the correlations of the stock markets, except that the three correlations with the German stock market decline in the period from July 1984 to February 1989. The pattern among the money market rates is more varied. To sum up the overall evidence on return correlations, it is consistent with the view that the degree of international capital mobility increased in the 1980s.

Indicators for Monetary Policy

The October 1979 change in Federal Reserve operating procedures represented an acknowledgement that nominal interest rates were not a useful indicator of whether monetary policy was tight or loose, in part because of the difficulty of distinguishing changes in the nominal interest rate from changes in the real interest rate. Since 1982, however, it has become widely acknowledged that M1 and other monetary aggregates are also not reliable indicators, because of large and lasting shifts in velocity. Thus there has been a search for new indicators.

One indicator/guide for monetary policy that has been suggested is the exchange rate. Theory tells us that when exchange rates are fixed and capital mobility is low, monetary policy is primarily reflected in interest rates, but that, under modern conditions of floating exchange rates and high capital mobility, changes in monetary policy should be reflected primarily in exchange rates.

There is evidence that exchange rates do indeed contain useful information about market expectations regarding future monetary policy. One example comes from the period in the late 1970s and early 1980s when unexpectedly high weekly money announcements would regularly cause nominal interest rates to jump significantly upward. Clearly, during this period, market participants were using the news in the announcements to revise their expectations regarding the ease of future monetary policy. The question was whether an observed increase in the nominal interest rate was an increase in the real interest rate, signifying the expectation of tighter monetary policy in the future, or an increase in the expected inflation rate.

The foreign exchange market contains the answer. In the late 1970s, positive money surprises were associated with increases in the price of foreign exchange, indicating that the increases in the nominal interest rate were increases in expected inflation. In the period July 1980 to November 1982, the reverse was true. Positive money surprises were associated with decreases in the price of foreign exchange, indicating that the increases in the nominal interest rate were increases in the real interest rate (in the expectation that the Federal Reserve would act to bring the money supply back towards its intended path).

Another indicator/guide for monetary policy that has been suggested is the price of gold and other basic mineral and agricultural commodities. There is similar evidence that such prices contain useful information about market expectations regarding future monetary policy. In the period July 1980 to November 1982, positive money surprises were associated with decreases in the prices of commodities, indicating again that the increases in the nominal interest rate were increases in the real interest rate and were signs of a tighter, rather than looser, expected future monetary policy.

Note, however, that the usefulness of the exchange rate or commodity prices as immediate indicators of the perceived stance of monetary policy does not mean that it would be wise for the authorities to pre-commit to targets for these prices, any more than to M1. There are large disturbances in the demand for foreign exchange, the demand for gold and the demand for M1. Committing to a fixed number or target range for any of these three magnitudes would mean that the disturbances would be more fully transmitted to the level of real GNP and the general price level.

Yet another possible indicator of the expected future ease of monetary policy, which has received increased attention since it was cited in a speech by Federal Reserve Vice Chairman Manuel Johnson (1988), lies in the term structure of interest rates. The idea is that, when the yield curve becomes steeper, this is a sign that the market expects inflation to increase in the future, and when its slope falls, a sign that the market expects inflation to decrease. A simplistic interpretation of this idea would assume that the real interest rate is constant, from which it follows that the term spread is equal to the difference between the inflation rate expected in the long term and the inflation rate expected in the short term.

A more realistic model would allow for the fact that the short-term real interest rate is not constant in the short run, but would assume that there is a tendency for it to approach a constant gradually over time (as would be true in a model with goods prices that are sticky in the short run). Let us assume further the expectations hypothesis of the term structure: that the long-term interest rate is the average of the expected short-term interest rates over the relevant maturity, up to a possible (but constant) term premium. Then it is easy to show that the expected inflation rate can be expressed (up to a constant term) as a linear combination of the long-term and short-term interest rates (with weight greater than unity on the former and negative weight on the latter, so that the linear combination is extrapolating out along the yield curve).

It then follows that the difference between any expected long-term inflation rate and any expected short-term inflation rate is proportional to the spread between any long-term interest rate and any short-term interest rate. But the constant of proportionality is not unity, as in the case of a constant real interest rate, and investigators need not use interest rate maturities that correspond to the horizon over which they wish to forecast inflation.

The first column shows regressions in which the terms of the interest rates used in the forecast match the terms of the inflation rates to be forecast, as would be required under the theoretical framework that assumes that real interest rates are constant. The estimate for the coefficient on the interest rate spread is greater than zero and less than unity. This finding suggests that, on the one hand, there may indeed be forecasting power in the term structure, but that, on the other hand, the real interest rate does not appear to be constant. Thus far, the results match those obtained by Mishkin (1988, 1989).

But the practical advantage of the alternative theoretical framework allowing for short-term variation in the real interest rate is that it allows one to use a more reliable estimate of the slope of the yield curve, rather than being restricted to a narrow term spread that matches the inflation rates to be forecast. As indicated by either *R* or significance levels, the ability to predict changes in the inflation rate is greater than when the one-year/three-month term spread was used. The conclusion is that the alternative framework may be more useful for forecasting the future movement of inflation, reinforcing the theoretical desirability of allowing for variation in the real interest rate.

CHARTISTS, FUNDAMENTALISTS AND TRADING IN THE FOREIGN EXCHANGE MARKET

The conclusion from the preceding section is that even though the standard macroeconomic theories of exchange rate determination draw some empirical support from observed reactions to news (such as the money announcements discussed in the fourth section), and even though real interest differentials appear to have explanatory power for exchange rates on *levels,* the ability to predict *changes* in the exchange rate is close to nil.

During most of the period since 1973, the real value of the dollar has been highly correlated with the differential in real interest rates between the USA and trading partners. At times, however, the dollar departs from the path dictated by macroeconomic fundamentals. The most notable episode is the period from mid-1984 to February 1985, when the dollar continued to appreciate at an accelerated speed despite the fact that the real interest differential-and virtually all other measures of macroeconomic fundamentals as well-was moving in the opposite direction. Some have suggested that the appreciation of the dollar in 1988-9 may have been of a similar nature. Ken Froot and I have suggested that such episodes may be examples of speculative bubbles, and that they are best described by models in which market participants are *not* necessarily assumed to agree on the correct model for forecasting the exchange rate.

Let us begin with the tremendous volume of foreign exchange trading. The Federal Reserve Bank of New York (1989) has just released its triennial count of transactions in the US foreign exchange market. It showed that in April 1989 foreign exchange trading (adjusted for double counting) totalled $110.5 billion among banks (an increase of 121 per cent from March 1986) and $18.4 billion among non-bank financial institutions (an increase of 116 per cent). What is the importance of trading volume? There are three possible hypotheses. First, the higher the liquidity of the markets, the more efficiently is news regarding economic fundamentals processed and the smaller is 'unnecessary volatility' in the exchange rate. Second, the foreign exchange market is already perfectly efficient, so trading volume is irrelevant and uninteresting. Third, much trading is based on 'noise' rather than 'news', and leads to excessive volatility. Choosing convincingly among these three hypotheses is far too large a task to accomplish here.

There is evidence that trading volume, exchange rate volatility and the dispersion of forecasters' expectations (as reflected in the survey data) are all positively correlated. The direction of causality has not yet been definitively established. But Granger-causality tests show that the degree of dispersion has strong effects on the market. Dispersion Granger-causes volume at the 90 per cent level in three currencies out of four. Dispersion also Granger-causes volatility. The contempo raneous correlation between volume and volatility is high. One interpretation of these results is that the existence of conflicting forecasts leads to noise-trading-the causation runs from dispersion in expectations to the volume of trading, and then from trading to volatility-though there probably exist other interpretations as well.

In a study of minute-by-minute foreign exchange market data, 'no signs at all of sudden major jumps on the receipt of "news"'. For the most part, foreign exchange markets in a given country are open during exactly the same hours that news is released, so that it is difficult to do a study of noise trading and volatility such as that carried out for the stock market. However, some evidence in hourly data that could be interpreted as supporting the view that spot rate movements occur in response to trading volume and not just to news. The variance of changes over the weekend is small, even though a lot of news relevant to the foreign exchange market comes out over the weekend.

Moreover, each Monday morning the volatility for each European currency is high in the first hour of trading in the geographical market where that particular currency has the highest trading volume, even when other markets open earlier in the day and could in theory have been just as able to process any weekend news. Finally, trading volume in London and volatility both reach daily low points during the lunch hour, even though news is still coming out then.

Interestingly, the banks in the 1989 New York survey reported that only 4.9 per cent of their trading was with a non-financial firm; the non-banks was only 4.4 per cent. In other words, more than 95 per cent of the trading takes place among the banks and other financial firms, rather than with customers such as importers and exporters. If the 1986 data are a guide, similar proportions apply in London (still the world's largest foreign exchange market). Clearly, trading among themselves is a major economic activity for banks.

Goodhart has surveyed banks that specialize in the London foreign exchange market: 'Traders, so it is claimed, consistently make profits from their position-taking (and those who do not get fired), over and above their return from straight dealing, owing to the bid/ask spread'. Apparently they consider the taking of long-term positions based on fundamentals, or of any sort of position in the forward exchange market, as too 'speculative' and risky.

Bankers recall the Franklin National crisis and other bank failures caused by open foreign positions that were held too long. But the banks are willing to trust their spot exchange traders to take large open positions, provided the traders close most of them out by the end of the day, because these operations are profitable in the aggregate. According to Goodhart and others, a typical spot trader bases decisions to buy and sell not on any fundamentals model but on the knowledge of what deals other traders are offering at a given time and a feel for what their behaviour is likely to be later in the day.

The theory of speculative bubbles developed says that over the period 1981-5 the market shifted weight away from the fundamentalists and towards the technical analysts or 'chartists', this shift being a natural response to the inferior forecasting record of the former group; the shift in the weighted-average forecast of future changes in the value of the dollar in turn shifted the demand for dollars and therefore its price in the foreign exchange market.

Is there any sort of evidence for such a theory? *Euromoney* magazine runs a yearly August review of between ten and twenty-seven foreign exchange forecasting services. The trend is very clear. In 1978, eighteen forecasting firms described themselves as relying exclusively on economic fundamentals, and only two on technical analysis. By 1985, the positions had been reversed: only one firm reported relying exclusively on fundamentals, and twelve on technical analysis.

A number of firms combine the two approaches or offer a separate service of each kind. In this case, technical analysis is typically used for short-term forecasting and fundamentals for long-term forecasting. This pattern matches up well with the results from surveys of market participants' exchange rate expectations, at horizons of one week and one month, respondents tend to forecast by extrapolating recent trends, while at horizons of three, six and twelve months they tend to forecast a return to a long-run equilibrium such as PPP.

In short, it may indeed be the case that shifts over time in the weight given to different forecasting techniques are a source of change in the demand for dollars and that large exchange rate movements may take place with little basis in macroeconomic fundamentals.

ASIAN CAPITAL MARKETS

The countries in the Asian Pacific region, as a group, have been enjoying the highest economic growth rate in the world. The combined market value of the region's common equities accounts for approximately one-third of the world's total capital market volume. The strategic importance of capital markets in this region for international investment decisions is well demonstrated by the increasing number of mutual funds specializing in Asian equities. It is also demonstrated by the phenomenal success of many closed-end investment companies including the Asia Pacific Fund (1986), the Korea Fund (1986), the Korea-Europe Fund (1987), the Malaysia Fund (1987), the Taiwan Fund (1984) and the Thai Fund (1986) in the US and London capital markets.

One of the most significant international financial developments of the 1980s has been the gradual opening of the capital markets of Asian Pacific countries to the outside world. In September 1987, the Securities Exchange of Thailand set up an Alien Board to facilitate trading of Thai securities among foreign investors as part of its effort to open the Thai market. Starting in August 1989, foreign investors are allowed to exchange their Korean convertible bonds into stocks, which will open the door for direct foreign ownership of Korean blue-chip firms such as Samsung Electronics Co., Daewoo Heavy Industries Co., Yukong Ltd and Gold Star Co. From 1991, foreign brokerage houses are allowed to join the Korea Stock Exchange as members through establishing joint ventures with Korean firms. At the time of writing (1990), twenty-five foreign securities firms are active members of the Tokyo Stock Exchange (TSE) while trading by foreign investors of Japanese shares amounted to 17 per cent of total trading value in 1989. Beginning in 1991, foreign investors are allowed to invest directly in the Taiwan Stock Exchange but the trading volume for foreign investors is limited to $5 million per day.

In spite of their economic growth and their important role in world trade, it has only been in recent years that the Asian capital markets have received any attention from academic researchers. Most of these, however, have concentrated on Japan. The topics studied include the small-firm effect, the P/E ratio effect, the January effect and the day-of-the-week pattern of daily stock returns. More recent papers move beyond addressing stock market anomalies to examine fundamental issues such as the normality of return distribution, the return and volume variance effect, rights offering cross-market initial public offerings volatility. This new set of studies broadens the range of research topics and is an encouraging development in the research on Asian markets. The studies stimulate further research not only in Japan but also in other countries in the region.

The microstructure of the Asian equity markets. It is intended to enhance an understanding of each of the major exchanges in Asia by presenting their profile current status.

MARKET SIZE

At the end of 1989, a total of 3,836 firms were listed on the major stock exchanges of nine Asian Pacific countries: Hong Kong, Indonesia, Japan, Korea, Malaysia, the Philippines, Singapore, the Republic of China (Taiwan) and Thailand. Total market capitalization amounted to $4,829.7 billion. This amount is 2.58 times as large as the NYSE's market capitalization. The market capitalization of the TSE was $4,260.4 billion, accounting for 88.21 per cent of the entire Asian equity markets. Next in order are Taiwan with 4.88 per cent, Korea with 2.91 per cent and Hong Kong with 1.61 per cent.

Of the 3,836 firms listed on the Asian exchanges, 3,450 firms were domestic and the remaining 386 firms were foreign firms. The number of firms reported for Japan includes the TSE-listed firms only. There are seven other independent exchanges in Japan located in Osaka, Nagoya, Kyoto, Hiroshima, Fukuoka, Niigata and Sapporo. The TSE, the largest among the seven, has 79 per cent of all listed companies in Japan and 97 per cent of the market value.

Of the 1,597 firms, 945 domestic firms were cross-listed between the TSE and the remaining seven exchanges, while 652 firms were listed only on the TSE. However, 422 firms were listed not on the TSE but on the remaining seven exchanges. Indonesia and the Philippines are the other two countries in the region which have multiple exchanges. There are two stock exchanges in Indonesia: the Jakarta Stock Exchange and the Surabaya Stock Exchange. In the Philippines there are the Manila Stock Exchange and the Makati Stock Exchange. In both countries, the securities are required to be cross-listed. The reported market capitalization for Indonesia and the Philippines represent those of the Jakarta Stock Exchange and the Manila Stock Exchange, respectively.

TRADING VALUE AND TURNOVER RATIO

In 1989, the total annual trading value of the nine Asian Pacific countries was $3,618.0 billion, which is 2.36 times that of the NYSE. The TSE accounted for 67.20 per cent of the total trading value, followed by Taiwan with 26.98 per cent and Korea with 3.34 per cent. In terms of turnover ratio, Taiwan has the highest turnover ratio of 537.50 per cent, followed by Korea with 106.87 per cent and Thailand with 85.90 per cent. It is amazing that even though the Taiwan Stock Exchange accounted for only 4.88 per cent of the combined market capitalization in the region, it had 27 per cent of the combined trading value, making the Taiwan Stock Exchange one of the busiest stock exchanges in the world.

Stock Market Indices

Stock market indices computed by the stock exchanges of nine countries. The base index and base date vary from one exchange to another. Comparable indices in the USA are the Standard and Poor's Composite Indices and NYSE Common Stock Indices.

For the purpose of maintaining the continuity of the reported index numbers, the base AMV must be adjusted for:

- New listings;
- Delistings;
- Rights offerings;
- Public offerings;
- Private placements;
- Mergers;
- Exercises of warrants; and
- Conversions of convertible securities into common stock.

The major composite index is supplemented by subindices as well as other composite indices. For example, in addition to the Tokyo Stock Price Index (TOPIX), which covers 1,136 stocks listed in the First Section, the TSE computes a composite index called the Second Section Stock Price Index covering 446 stocks listed on its Second Section. The TSE's First Section comprises the larger listed shares which meet the listing criteria while the Second Section shares are relatively new on the exchange and are those issued by smaller firms. Additionally, the TOPIX subindices for twenty-eight industry groups and three indices for large, medium and small firms are also computed and published (TSE 1990b). Another popular index in Japan is the Nikkei-Dow Average Share Price Index, which is computed on a formula similar to the Dow-Jones Industrial. The computation method of stock market indices of Korea, Taiwan and Thailand is identical to that of the TOPIX indices.

The Stock Exchange of Hong Kong Ltd adopted a new composite index called the Hong Kong Index (HKI) on 2 April 1986 after consolidating the Far East Stock Exchange Ltd, the Hong Kong Stock Exchange, the Kam Ngan Stock Exchange Ltd and the Kowloon Stock Exchange. The HKI is computed using forty-nine constituent blue-chip stocks selected from six representative industries in Hong Kong. Another popular index, the Hang Seng Index, is computed by the Hang Seng Bank Ltd. It is composed of thirty-three constituent stocks which include four finance stocks, six utilities, nine properties and fourteen commerce and industrials. Of the thirty-three stocks in the Hang Seng Index, thirty-one are included in the HKI.

MARKET PERFORMANCE

The performance of Asian equity markets has far exceeded that of the US market as measured by the Standard and Poor's 500 Composite Index. For example, the US stock market registered an average monthly return of 0.99 per cent during the ten-year study period. Over the same period, the nine Asian equity markets yielded a market-capitalization-weighted average local currency return of 1.55 per cent per month.

The average return in US dollars of the Asian markets amounted to 1.93 per cent. Of this amount, monthly foreign exchange gain was 0.32 per cent. In terms of local currency return, the performance of the Taiwan market portfolio is the best with an average return of 2.39 per cent, followed by Korea with 1.84 per cent, Japan with 1.53 per cent and Thailand with 1.48 per cent. When measured in returns of US dollars, Taiwan, Japan and Korea are the top three performers, with respective monthly returns of 2.66 per cent, 1.97 per cent and 1.56 per cent. The returns on Taiwan and Japanese market portfolios were augmented by respective foreign exchange gains of 0.25 per cent and 0.37 per cent per month. In contrast, Korean won depreciated against US dollars by 0.30 per cent per month and Thai baht depreciated by 0.21 per cent per month.

These phenomenally high returns have not been achieved without risk. The total risk of investments in Asian equity markets, as measured by the standard deviation of local currency returns, is on average 1.5 times greater than that of the US market.

The market portfolios of Hong Kong, Malaysia, the Philippines and Taiwan have standard deviations at least twice as large as the US market portfolio. During the study period, Japan was the only country with a smaller standard deviation than the USA, 0.0413 versus 0.0480. The total risk of Asian market portfolio returns in US dollars is larger than the total risk measured using the local currency returns. For example, the total risk rises from 0.0413 to 0.0585 as the yen-denominated returns are converted into US-dollar-denominated returns.

The difference between the two, 0.0172, is the contribution of currency risk. However, note from the last column that the exchange risk as measured by the standard deviation of the rate of change in spot rates is greater than this difference. The exchange risk of Japanese yen is 0.0357. This indicates that more than half of the exchange risk is eliminated by the diversification effect.

This would be true when portfolio returns in local currency have low correlations with the rates of change in spot exchange rates. Usually, the observed correlations between the two are very low, and sometimes even negative. For example, the estimated correlation between returns on the market portfolio in Japanese yen and the rates of change in the yen value is only 0.18.

They are estimated using a market model in which monthly local currency returns, as well as US dollar returns, on each country's market portfolio are regressed on the US market portfolio's returns. The estimated âs when local currency returns are used range from Korea's 0.20 to Malaysia's 0.93. All the â estimates except for Korea and the Philippines are significant at the per cent level. The estimated âs increase slightly when the US dollar returns are used for the regressions. The results strongly indicate that the correlation between each of the Asian markets and the US market is fairly low.

PRICE-EARNINGS RATIOS AND DIVIDEND YIELDS

In 1989, the TSE reported the highest P/E ratio of 70.60, followed by Indonesia with 63.80, Taiwan with 55.91 and Malaysia with 36.22. The P/E ratio of the NYSE-listed shares was 15.00. The lowest P/E ratio of 10.76 was reported from Hong Kong. P/E ratios of Korea and the Philippines were also relatively low. In terms of dividend yields, Hong Kong and Thailand reported high dividend yields of 6.05 per cent and 5.30 per cent respectively. The average dividend yield of the NYSE stocks was 3.20 per cent. In contrast, low dividend yields were observed for Japan with 0.45 per cent and Taiwan with 1.58 per cent.

Two reasons may be cited for this trend:

1. Many Asian firms maintain a dividend policy under which a fixed percentage of the par value is paid as dividend; and
2. Stock prices had been steadily going up in the past few years.

Brokerage Fees and other Transaction Costa

The brokerage fee varies depending upon the price per share in Kuala Lumpur. For the convenience of illustration, it is assumed that the share is priced at M$ 1.00 or above. Whenever relevant information is available, other transaction costs including stamp taxes, exchange taxes, registration fees etc. are included. For an investment of $10,000, transaction costs range from $15 in Taiwan to $221 in Australia. For a larger investment of $100,000, Malaysia is the most costly while Taiwan is the least costly. Low transaction costs in Taiwan explain why the Taiwan Stock Exchange is one of the busiest in the world. Investors in Thailand and Korea also enjoy relatively low transaction costs.

Trading Hours and Trading Days

At 7 p.m. eastern standard time (EST) in the USA, the TSE begins trading, followed by the Korea Stock Exchange at 7.40 p.m., the Taiwan Stock Exchange at 8 p.m. and the Manila Stock Exchange at 8.30 p.m. At 9 p.m., stock exchanges in Hong Kong, Kuala Lumpur and Singapore will be open. The Stock Exchange of Thailand and the Jakarta Stock Exchange will be the last to open at 9.30 p.m. and 10 p.m. respectively. The first ones to close are stock exchanges in Kuala Lumpur and Singapore at 3 a.m., EST. All exchanges in Asia have short trading hours, ranging from 2 hours to 3¾ hours, in contrast to 6½ hours of trading at the NYSE. As of December 1989, the Korea Stock Exchange and the Taiwan Stock Exchange are the only two exchanges in Asia which conduct business on Saturdays. The trading days for Asian exchanges range from 289 days for Korea to 244 days in Malaysia.

FOREIGN EXCHANGE CONTROL AND FOREIGN OWNERSHIP

The accessibility of US investors to the Asian equity markets is determined by two major factors:

1. Foreign exchange control and
2. Limitation on foreign ownership.

The nine Asian countries can be classified into four categories depending upon the degree of government control over foreign exchange and foreign ownership.

These categories are as follows:

- *Category 1:*The *laissez-faire* economy, where neither exchange control nor any limitations regarding ownership of domestic firms by foreign investor's exists. Hong Kong is the only market in this category.

- *Category 2*: The capital markets are fully liberalized except for restrictions on selec tive industries and/or firms in 'national interest'. Japan and Singapore may be classified in this category. Neither country has foreign exchange control and, in general, there is no limitation on the acquisition of domestic firms by foreigners except those firms/industries so designated by the government.
- *Category 3*: The capital markets are substantially open but not completely liberalized. Australia, Indonesia, Malaysia, New Zealand, the Philippines and Thailand belong to this category. Usually, foreign exchange controls do not exist or they are minimal for normal investment portfolio activities. However, foreign ownership of domestic firms is limited to a fixed percentage of the shares outstanding or of voting rights.
- *Category 4*: The capital markets are in the process of being opened. Foreign exchange controls exist and foreign investors do not have direct access to local equity markets. Korea and Taiwan are in this category. Some foreigners do have stakes in domestic firms through joint ventures or direct foreign investment approved by the government.

Korea and Taiwan are expected to allow foreigners to invest in domestic securities in 1991. Currently, foreign investors can have indirect access to local markets only through purchase of shares issued by authorized mutual funds or closed-end investment companies.

Since October 1981 the Korean government has allowed five mutual funds and two closed-end investment companies to be launched for portfolio investment in Korean securities by non-residents. Under similar arrangements, four investment companies had been introduced for foreign investors who wanted to have access to the Taiwan market. Although foreign investors have direct access to the Thai capital market, there are eight investment companies participating in the Thai market and a few more waiting for approval from government authorities.

WITHHOLDING TAX RATES FOR FOREIGN INVESTORS

Withholding tax rates on dividends, interest and capital gains in the nine Asian countries. Three countries have bilateral tax treaties with the USA. As a result, low withholding tax rates are applicable for US investors in Japan, Korea and the Philippines. Hong Kong,

Malaysia and Singapore do not impose dividend income taxes although no bilateral tax treaties exist. Most of the Asian nations do not penalize investors, foreign as well as domestic, on capital gains from normal portfolio investment operations, except for Thailand. Among the non-tax-treaty countries, the withholding tax rate on interest is highest in Singapore at 33 per cent. Thailand comes next with a 25 per cent tax rate on interest. Indonesia and Malaysia impose a 20 per cent withholding tax.

10

International Debt Facility

A common proposal designed to deal with the developing countries' debt problem is that there be set up an 'international debt facility' that would buy debt at a discount and then mark down its contractual value, hence providing debt relief. This facility could be envisaged either as a major scheme that, over a period, would deal with most or all outstanding commercial debt owed or guaranteed by governments, or as a more modest arrangement dealing with only small portions of debt, possibly only that which is owed by the governments of particular countries. Many such proposals have been advanced. They vary in their details and there are many difficulties, some major. Nevertheless, the frequency with which such proposals are made makes it worth examining them carefully in their many permutations.

MAIN ISSUES

There are three principal parties to the proposed transaction-the debtor governments, the creditor banks and the 'owners' of the facility. The central question is how the costs and benefits would accrue to various parties. Is there an element of 'foreign aid' or of a 'bank bail-out'? Alternatively, would the banks give up something? Could all three parties gain or, at least, could some gain without the others losing significantly, if at all? In other words, is there some systemic benefit? The proximate redistributive effects-and possibly also the systemic effects-will depend crucially on three prices: the price at which the debt is bought, the price or value to which it is marked down and the price or perceived value to which remaining debt that is retained in the private sector moves as a result of the whole operation. The full economic effects will depend, of course, on how the various parties react to or deal with the proximate gains or losses. In considering the details of such a scheme there are many choices to be made.

- The debt might be bought by the facility at the minimum price required for the banks to part with it voluntarily; it might be bought at current market prices; it might be bought at the market prices that existed at some earlier 'cut-off' date; or it might be bought at some other set of prices representing discounts on the contractual value. Conceivably it might even be bought at its contractual value.
- Purchased debt might be marked down to the cost at which the facility bought it, or to a higher or lower value than cost.
- The debt that is not sold by banks might maintain its present contractual status; it might be subordinated to the debt that the debtor countries will now incur to the facility; or it might be marked down by the debtors to an extent that would force the banks to sell all their debt to the facility.

A crucial question is how the facility would be financed. Here, also, there are differences among the various proposals, and the possibilities will be discussed shortly.

A SIMPLE SCHEME

Let us suppose that the scheme applies to any one debtor country. The facility goes into the market and offers to buy given amounts of debt. In the detailed example spelled out below, it will be assumed that the facility offers to buy half the stock of debt. Of course debt is not homogeneous, so that various decisions would have to be made on which debt to buy. It is quite likely that the facility would have to pay more than the initial market price, but one can assume that the facility would buy debt at a discount from the contractual value. The important question of what would determine the price, and in which direction it would move, will be taken up later.

The facility pays for the purchased debt with new bonds guaranteed by its owners. The banks are thus able to dispose of debt with the original contractual value that is subject to default risk in exchange for debt of a lower contractual value that is subject to much lower, possibly zero, default risk. One's first thought is that those that sell could not be worse off as a result. After all, selling is voluntary; there is no compulsion in this scheme.

This conclusion is not necessarily true, and will have to be looked at again in the fourth section. The facility would then mark down the contractual value of the debtor country's debt that it has acquired. It marks the debt down to the cost price to it-i.e. the contractual value of the new bonds it has issued to the banks.

No funds are thus required from the owners of the facility-i.e. the governments that have underwritten the facility. But, of course, the facility's new assets are somewhat risky and, because of the guarantees on the bonds it has issued, this risk has been taken over by the facility's owners.

Given this risk, there will be a potential need for funds from the owners, who may actually wish to finance contingency reserves specifically to allow for the risk. A major, and possibly overwhelming, obstacle to the establishment of a facility is the reluctance of governments to assume such risks.

A question to be discussed below is whether this risk can be reduced or eliminated. The debtor country apparently benefits because the contractual value of its debt has been reduced. But the gain to it will not necessarily be as great as it might seem at first. One possible view is that the market's perception of default risk, which led to the initial discount, was justified in the sense that this represented the true probability of default.

In other words, there was a good chance in any case that the country would not repay the full contractual value of its debt. Reducing the contractual value as a result of the operation of the facility would not necessarily reduce actual payments (or the probability of actual payments expected to be made) to the same extent. Indeed, one might ask whether there is likely to be any gain to the debtor country at all.

HOW DEBTOR AND BANKS MAY GAIN

This matter of the possible gain to the debtor, and also to the banks, can be analysed more precisely if the concept of the debtor's 'capacity to pay' is introduced. This is defined as the ability to make resource transfers abroad to cover interest payments and repayment of principal. It depends on the country's output over a period of time, on its minimum consumption level and on its ability to transform output into tradeables (exports and import-competing products) required to generate the transfer. It also depends on the terms of trade.

It will be supposed at this stage that capacity to pay can vary as the result of various exogenous, uncertain events-such as terms-of-trade developments-but does not vary because of changes in the policies of the debtor country itself, which are simply taken as given. This is the assumption of 'exogeneity'. It will also be assumed for the moment that expectations about capacity to pay are the same among market participants, debtor countries and the decision-makers of the facility. This is the assumption of 'uniformity of expectations'. These two simplifying assumptions are important for the analysis of gains and losses from the establishment of a facility and therefore will be reconsidered in the seventh section.

There are two steps in the analysis. First I show why the banks might gain at the expense of the facility, and then I show why the debtor might gain. The second effect depends crucially on uncertainty.

Gain to the Banks

To begin with, there is the 'market price effect'. It can be shown that the banks will gain at the expense of the facility provided that the debt that they retain is not subordinated to the marked-down debt that the facility now holds. The reason is that the market price of the debt will rise (the discount will fall). The argument is quite simple when there is complete certainty about the capacity to pay (or repay).

Let us suppose that the contractual debt is $1,000 and the capacity to pay is $600. Assume at this stage that the latter is fixed. Hence the debtor country will neither gain nor lose; whatever happens, it pays $600. This is thought of as a single sum paid in a single future period, the sum consisting of principal and interested combined. Given the initial contractual debt, default or debt relief is then inevitable. The 'default ratio' would be 40 per cent.

The facility then offers to buy a proportion of the $1,000 in contractual debt from the banks at a discounted price. Here it will be assumed that it buys half the debt ($500) and that the price it pays is 80 cents to the dollar. Hence the facility pays $400 and marks the debt it has acquired down to its cost price. The contractual value of the total debt owed by the debtor country is thus reduced to $900. With the same capacity to pay as before, the default ratio becomes 33.3 per cent. The facility will finally get 66.7 per cent repayment of the debt it holds, thus making a loss of $133. The banks will get $333 for the debt they have retained (with a contractual value of $500), and when this is combined with the $400 they received from the facility they end up with $733, which is an improvement of $133 on what they would have received if the facility had not bought and marked down some of the debt. The discount on debt held by the banks has fallen from 40 per cent to 33.3 per cent.

In this example the facility's purchase price is 80 cents but the market price has risen only from 60 cents to 67 cents. The purchase price could therefore be reduced, leading to a bigger decline in the contractual value and hence to a further rise in the market price. The equilibrium price (where purchase and market prices are equal) would actually be 70 1/2 cents when the facility buys half the debt. If it bought a greater proportion, the price would be higher. There has been a pure transfer from the facility to the banks. All this will be reflected in the market price rising (discount falling) when the facility enters the market. It has to pay a higher price than the initial price to induce the banks to sell any debt to it. The banks will foresee that debt not sold will rise in value when some marking down takes place, and hence they will only sell at a sufficiently higher price. The price would not necessarily rise to its equilibrium value immediately, and could also overshoot, since banks and others in the market would not be able to predict this equilibrium in advance. The account given here, with its impression of precision, merely indicates likely tendencies.

The essential point can be restated as follows. When the contractual value of the total debt is reduced while total capacity to pay stays constant, each dollar's worth of contractual debt must be worth more in the market than before, provided that all dollars of contractual debt would be treated equally if there were some default.

Gain to the Debtor

Uncertainty about capacity to pay and the 'ceiling effect' can now be introduced. The mean expected repayment might be $600, but it could also be greater, up to a ceiling of complete repayment of $1,000, and it could be less, with a floor of zero. There is thus both upside and downside risk, and this will be taken into account in the market price. If the contractual value of the debt is reduced, say to $900, the ceiling will be lowered to $900. If the terms of trade, for example, turn out to be quite favourable, so that capacity to pay is actually $950, the actual payment will be $50 less than if the contractual value had stayed at its initial level. Thus the debtor gains at the expense of creditors from a markdown of the contractual value because the downside risk remains as before, whereas the offsetting upside risk (or gain) becomes less.

SUBORDINATION: CAN A GAIN TO THE BANKS BE AVOIDED?

An interesting question is whether a gain to the banks at the expense of the facility-i.e. a 'bank bail-out'-can be avoided. The key here is subordination of the debt retained by the banks relative to the debt now owned by the facility.

When one talks about a gain to the banks, one means a gain relative to the initial situation when there was already a discount in the market. Earlier, of course, the banks incurred a loss once the probability of some default or forced debt relief was perceived by them or the market. Presumably, as long as the bank gets less then $1,000 they will have incurred some loss as normally defined, even though the margin above the LIBOR that they charged originally must have taken into account the possibility of some default or of heavy pressure to provide some relief.

Suppose that, again, the facility buys half the debt and marks it down to cost. It buys it at 80 cents per dollar and so pays $400, total contractual debt being thus marked down to $900 as before. One now proceeds in two stages. First, let us assume that there is no doubt at all that the capacity to pay will be at least $400.

If it could be firmly established that, whatever is the capacity-to-pay outcome above $400, the debt held by the facility would always be paid first-i.e. would be 'senior' debt-then the facility would not make a loss and its owners would run no risk. But the banks would lose potentially, and the debtors gain, because the 'ceiling payment' has been reduced. Previously the maximum payment the banks could have received was $1,000, whereas now it is $500 for the debt they have retained plus the $400 they have already received from the facility. If capacity to pay turned out to be $950, previously the banks would have received $950, but now they can only receive $900. In contrast, the minimum they can receive remains $400. Subordinating debt retained by the banks to facility-held debt thus ensures that the facility neither loses nor gains, taking on no risk, while the debtor countries gain potentially at the expense of the banks because of the ceiling effect. The expected loss to the banks would be reflected in a decline in the market price.

If it were desired for some of the loss to the banks to be shared with the facility, the latter could mark down the debt by more than the discounted purchase price, hence making a clear loss now. Alternatively, only part of its debt might be given seniority. Here there is scope for many variations in the details of such a scheme, and these may have significant effects on the gains or losses for the banks and the facility. The key point is that the banks and the facility combined must make a potential loss-i.e. forgo the benefits of a very favourable capacity-to-pay outcome. The risk of an unfavourable outcome has not been eliminated, but the possibility of a very favourable return (above $900) has.

The second stage of the analysis is to assume that capacity to pay could be less than $400. In that case there would be some possibility that even debt given senior status would not be fully repaid. Hence risk for the facility would not be completely eliminated. The conclusion that subordination of debt retained by the banks to the debt owned by the facility would eliminate all risk for the facility hinges completely on the assumption that some minimum total payment-equal to the value of the debt that the facility has bought ($400 in the example)-is utterly assured. But the larger the proportion of the initial total debt that the facility takes over and marks down, the less likely it is that all risk for the facility would be eliminated by giving the debt it holds senior status. If the facility had bought up all the debt, no one but the facility could assume the risk.

There can never be utter certainty about prospective capacity to pay, so that some risk for the facility is inherent in the scheme. This implicit risk is particularly relevant for proposals that would have the facility take over a large part of the foreign debt of a country. The inevitable risk helps to explain the reluctance of governments of creditor countries to support proposals for such a facility.

REDUCTION OF UNCERTAINTY

Another possibility, worth exploring carefully because it is implicit in some proposals, can now be considered. The suggestion is that the Fund or World Bank may be able to increase or ensure certainty of payment at the new, marked-down value of the debt. The assumption maintained so far-that the actual repayment outcome depends only on exogenously determined capacity to pay, subject to the 'ceiling' imposed by the contractual value-is relaxed. Repayment can also depend on policies.

Suppose that initially the mean expected capacity to pay was $600, with a probability of creditors getting more or less. If the total debt were marked down to $600, there would then be a $600 ceiling to the repayment. In addition, suppose that the Fund or World Bank were able to ensure that $600 also became the minimum repayment. This assurance might have been obtained with the aid of conditionality. Given this arrangement, there is no longer a necessary loss to the banks and the facility combined from the imposition of a reduced ceiling because that ceiling is associated with the imposition of a raised floor. Upside and downside risk have both been eliminated. Certainty has been obtained-or at least uncertainty has been reduced. Certainty represents a net gain for the banks and the facility combined, given that they are risk averse. With subordination, the whole of this gain from certainty would go to the banks in the first case just discussed, in which a minimum repayment sufficient to cover the debt held by the facility was in any case ensured. But in the more general case, in which the facility has carried some of the risk previously (whether because no minimum was ensured or because there was no subordination), the gain would go partially to the facility.

It is often implied in debt relief proposals that the marked-down value of debt would have no more risk attached to it (or very little risk) because it would be close to the expected capacity to pay. It is doubtful whether this assumption is realistic. The implication is that willingness to repay-and the resolve to make the necessary adjustments-is not exogenous but rather can be made more 'certain' in return for debt relief. Perhaps a commitment that would successfully reduce perceived default risk could be obtained from the debtor country in some way or other. Debtor governments could make certain policy commitments. No doubt the Fund's conditionality procedures can play a role here. Conditionality can conceivably reduce uncertainty and default risk, although it can surely not eliminate them.

A reduction in uncertainty of repayment without necessarily any net change in the mean expected repayment is clearly a gain to the banks and the facility. But it is not necessarily a gain for the system as a whole. If uncertainty in the capacity to pay-for example, uncertainty in terms of trade movements-could be reduced, that would be a net gain. But if uncertainty in capacity to pay continues while repayment becomes more certain owing to conditionality, there has simply been a transfer in the burden of uncertainty towards the debtor country. For example, if the terms of trade turned out to be particularly adverse, the country would have to bear the whole burden instead of sharing it with the banks or the facility through some degree of default or debt relief.

This approach assumes that the mean expected capacity or willingness to pay stays unchanged but that the floor is raised and the ceiling lowered. There are also two other possibilities.

The first is rather similar to the one just discussed. Conditionality may raise the mean without raising the floor: it may raise expected capacity to pay through bringing about an improvement in policies. Although the banks lose through the ceiling effect, they may then nevertheless gain.

The other quite contrary possibility is that the probability of repayment is actually reduced when the facility takes over debt. As just noted, it is usually argued that, through associating conditionality with the establishment of a facility, the certainty of repayment can be improved. But a contrary view is that a facility that is subject to political pressure and that has no strong penalties available to it may be a less effective debt collector than private banks, which can threaten the withdrawal of trade credit as a potential penalty.

INTERESTS OF THE DEBTOR COUNTRIES AND MORAL HAZARD

There are several ways in which the debtor country might gain from the arrangement. Some have already been referred to, but they will now be brought together.

Reducing the Default Ratio

A gain that seems obvious at first sight but turns out to

be primarily cosmetic is the reduction in the default ratio. The default ratio *D* equals 1"*R/C*, where *R* is the actual debt repayment made-i.e. the resource transfer-and *C* is the contractual value of the debt. *D* is reduced when the contractual value is marked down, even though the actual payment (which has been assumed to be exogenous so far) does not change. Does it really matter if this default ratio falls, possibly to zero, when the resource transfer remains unchanged? One might say that the effect is purely cosmetic. If an emperor has few clothes, is it really necessary to proclaim the fact? Against this it can be argued convincingly that debt relief voluntarily provided by the creditors is always better than default. There would clearly be a preference on the part of the debtor country for debt relief over default if penalties were associated with default. Even in the absence of current penalties, reputation-and hence future creditworthiness-may be influenced by whether there has been formal default rather than debt relief. Note that it has been assumed here that default depends purely on exogenous capacity to pay; hence penalties related to the default ratio would seem less likely or reasonable. Because capacity to pay completely determines actual repayments, there would be no point in the creditors imposing penalties.

Lowering the Ceiling

The debtor country gains owing to the 'ceiling effect'. As has been pointed out, if capacity to pay turns out to be particularly favourable-above the new contractual value-the gain would go to the debtor rather than to the creditors because the ceiling for potential repayments has been lowered. This benefit to the debtor might disappear (and could even turn into a loss) if conditionality manages also to raise the floor for the repayment, shifting more of the risk towards the debtor country.

Marking Debt Down Below cost

The facility might mark the debt down by more than the cost price to it-possibly by much more-and the contractual value might then fall below the capacity to pay, even when the capacity to pay turns out to be quite low. At the limit, the debt might be marked down to zero. This would represent a straightforward transfer from the owners of the facility to the debtor countries-a case of foreign assistance. It is equivalent to the owner countries donating funds to the debtor country to buy back its debt.

Asymmetric Expectations

A fourth kind of gain has not been referred to so far but is implicit in much advocacy of debt relief and could be important. The markets, specifically the banks, may be pessimistic and believe that there is some probability of default. Hence there is a market discount on the debt. But the government of the debtor country may have no intention of defaulting. There are 'asymmetric expectations'. Capacity to pay, after all, is not something clear cut. The government foresees difficulties and adjustment problems and seeks debt relief but-possibly for fear of penalties-does not intend ever to default, even though it has not succeeded in convincing the market of this. The issue of asymmetric expectations will be discussed further below. Here it can be noted that, if the government of the debtor country has no intention at all of defaulting, the whole of the fall in the contractual value of the debt brought about by debt relief through the operation of the facility or in some other way would represent a clear-cut gain to the debtor country in reduced prospective resource transfers.

The creditors, however, having different expectations, do not perceive this reduction in the contractual value-or all of it-as a loss to them. They may expect to lose through the ceiling effect but also see some virtue in an explicit recognition of what they believe to be realities-that the country has limited capacity or willingness to pay, that the emperor has fewer clothes than the initial contract specified.

Moral Hazard

For three of the four reasons given here (other than the

third, marking debt down below cost), the debtor country would want the price at which the facility buys debt from the banks to be as low as possible. The lower the price, the greater is the decline in the contractual value; hence, the lower the default ratio, the lower is the ceiling applying when events turn out favourably, and the lower are actual repayments if default is never intended.

If this purchase price is equal to or closely related to the market price, the debtor country therefore has an incentive to get the market price down. This can be done by making 'default noises'-just a hint here, a threat there-and the banks will be glad to sell at a low price, in the extreme case at any price above zero. This is the familiar 'moral hazard' problem.

A possible solution from the point of view of creditors seems to be for the facility's purchase price not to be determined by the market price, or at least by the market price ruling once the likelihood of such a facility being established has become serious. Market prices at some earlier 'cut-off date might be taken. If the banks are to sell voluntarily, the purchase price will have to be no lower than the current market price. But it could be higher.

The problem is to fix a price that does not give a gain, or an undue gain, to the banks; otherwise there would be a bail-out. But what is a gain? Given the expectations created by their anticipation of the debtor country's capacity to pay, combined with the default noises made by the debtor government or others in that country, a sale of the debt to the facility at a very low price may still seem to be a gain to the banks. This is true even though the price is likely to represent a loss relative to the expectations at the time the loans were originally made. Presumably the facility should aim to avoid either gain or loss to the banks relative to the situation at some 'pre-discussion-of- facility' date-i.e. an appropriately early cut-off date.

Most proposals for a facility do not pursue in detail the critical question of how the price at which debt is to be purchased is to be determined, given that there is a moral hazard problem and that there must presumably be a separate price (discount) for each country. It is at this point that the greatest practical problems arise. Sometimes elaborate calculations, which are essentially estimates of capacity to pay, are proposed, but the political difficulties that such estimates would involve cannot be ignored. Given the thinness of existing markets, actual market prices, whether current or at some earlier cut-off date, may not be adequate guides.

TWO ASSUMPTIONS RECONSIDERED

At the beginning two crucial assumptions were made: that the debtor's capacity to pay was exogenously determined-for example, by the terms of trade-and that expectations about the capacity to pay were the same among all the relevant parties. Given these assumptions, a fairly straightforward analysis followed that showed that a facility would yield a gain to the banks because of the market price effect and a gain to the debtor because of the ceiling effect. These gains would be at the expense of the facility, which would be taking over a risk. It was further assumed that debt owed to the facility would not be given seniority over debt retained by the banks. If the latter were subordinated, a gain to the banks and loss to the facility might be avoided.

Subsequently, the two initial assumptions have been removed in particular ways. In the fifth section the possibility was explored that the facility (or the World Bank or Fund acting on its behalf) could actually affect the debtor's policies so that capacity to pay would be improved to ensure certainty of repayment of the marked-down value of the debt. In other words, capacity to pay might no longer be exogenous. In the last section, one case of asymmetric expectations was noted. The debtor government may have no intention of defaulting, but the market may not be convinced of this. In addition, moral hazard was introduced. Prospective repayment may depend not only on capacity to pay but also on willingness to pay (for given capacity), and threats of reduced willingness would affect the market price. These complications to the initial approach are really special cases, but there are further cases that analysts of these issues sometimes have in mind. A more systematic approach is therefore needed.

First, the concept of expected capacity to pay determined by exogenous factors could be redefined as 'expected total repayment' determined both by expected capacity to pay and by expected willingness to pay. Both would be influenced, or even determined, by policies. When the original concept of capacity to pay is broadened in this way, it becomes more plausible. If the redefined concept is to apply to the initial analysis it has to be assumed that expected policies are exogenous in the sense of not being expected to change as a result of the establishment of the facility or its activities.

The next step is to allow for endogenous policies affecting capacity and willingness to pay. The endogeneity of policies is central to many debt-strategy proposals. As noted in the fifth section, the basic idea is that the benefit to the debtor from debt relief provided through the intermediation of the facility would be reciprocated by improvements in the debtor's policies, and that some kind of assurance about these policies can be obtained, perhaps with the help of conditionality. In this way more certainty of repayment can be ensured.

With regard to endogenous willingness to pay, two points are usually made. The first, as noted above, is the moral hazard problem: threats of reduced willingness to pay can bring the market price down. A second idea not mentioned so far is that, when the contractual value of the debt is partially forgiven so that it is brought down to a more realistic level, the debtor government may have a greater willingness to repay the remainder. If the contractual debt was $1,000 and capacity to pay was $600, some default would be inevitable. It has then been argued that a large default is as bad as-and incurs similar penalties to-a more modest default, so that willingness to pay in that case might fall to zero. But if the contractual debt were marked down to $600, there would be a good chance that default could be avoided, and willingness to pay might become 100 per cent.

As regards asymmetric expectations about the capacity and willingness to pay, there are several possibilities worth noting. First, as already mentioned, the debtor may not intend, and hence not expect, to default while the market contrarily believes that there is a positive probability of default, thus explaining the market discount. In that case the debtor government will believe it would gain from any debt relief, whereas the creditors-selling their debt voluntarily on the market (and assuming no subordination)-will not expect to lose. If the facility paid the banks a price above the initial market price-still with a discount-the banks may believe that they would actually gain, even though, if the debtor government's expectations were correct, the banks would actually have lost by selling.

A scheme could conceivably be worked out whereby the facility pays, for example, $400 for debt with a contractual value of $500 and marks that debt down to only $450, with the margin of $50 adequately compensating the facility for the risk it incurs so that it neither gains nor loses. In this case the creditors believe that they gain through the market price effect, the debtor government believes that it gains because there is some reduction in the contractual price, and the facility neither gains nor loses.

This scheme leads into the second possibility, whereby the facility actually makes a profit or at least is expected to do so by its owners or managers. The market may have an unduly pessimistic view of the debtor's prospects, and hence there may be a large market discount. But the facility only marks the debt down by a little, so that the contractual value of the marked-down debt it holds stays well above the cost price and there is a high degree of certainty that there will be low or zero default. All this depends on confidence in the ability to get the debtor's policies improved sufficiently to disprove the market's pessimistic expectations.

Finally, it has been argued in the main analysis here that the market price effect represents a benefit for the banks, at least relative to the situation after the debt crisis and the discount developed. But there may be some holders of debt who do not sell to the facility because-contrary to the expectations of marginal holders-they do not believe that the probability of default is high at all. They may value the debt they hold at the contractual value, not near the market price.

They may have made a more optimistic assessment of capacity or willingness to pay. If they feel assured that there will be full repayment in any case, it would make no difference to them if the total contractual claims are reduced through the operation of the facility. But if they really believed that the debt is worth more than its market price, the question then arises why they did not buy up the debt held by others and so bring the price up to their optimistic expectations. The argument assumes that the market is, in some sense, imperfect.

WOULD NEW INVESTMENT INCREASE AS A RESULT OF THE FACILITY?

There are three parts to the answer to this question. If the debt of the facility is given senior rights the answer is not clear; it is possible that new investment would actually be discouraged.

First, the analysis has shown that for various reasons there may be an actual reduction in resource transfer from the debtor country as a result of the facility-i.e. the debtor country may actually gain something. Indeed, in the view of some this is the primary objective of the exercise. An expectation of such a gain would lead also to an expectation of lower taxation than otherwise-including taxation of profits and capital-and this may well encourage new investment.

Second, if the debt held by the facility does not acquire senior rights, so that the discount in the market falls as described earlier, there should indeed be a tendency for investment inflows to resume or to increase. The facility will have assumed some of the burden of potential default on the existing debt, and new investors will have a lesser burden to bear than before.

Finally, the matter is not so simple if the existing debt is subordinated to the facility's debt. The question then is whether new debt incurred in the market would also be subordinated, or whether it would acquire seniority over the facility's debt. The reasonable assumption is that the facility would enjoy complete seniority. As noted above, in the absence of increased certainty, subordination would actually reduce the market price (raise the discount) owing to the 'ceiling effect'; hence new investment would be further discouraged. If all old debt had been sold to the facility, in effect new debt would then be completely subordinated to old debt.

IS THERE REALLY NEED FOR AN INTERNATIONAL FACILITY?

A central question remains. One might grant the desirability of a reduction in the contractual value of the debt but still wonder why an intermediary in the form of a facility along the lines proposed would be needed.

Although banks can sell the developing countries' debts in the market at a discount, bank managements may not feel free to grant outright relief in the form of reduction of the contractual value, possibly because of legal obstacles. In practice, however, relief in the form of long-term debt rescheduling and various debt transformations can be and has been granted-although such arrangements are different from reducing contractual value. One could also argue that there is no incentive for any private holder to grant relief because of the ceiling effect. There is always the possibility that the full contractual value will be repaid, so why forgo this possibility? Incentive for relief may be created, however, by the threat of more severe default.

One can think of three arguments in favour of the establishment of a facility from the points of view of the banks and the debtor countries involved.

A Channel for Resource Transfer

The most obvious argument from the point of view of both parties is that the facility could act as a channel for the transfer of current resources (i.e. aid) from the countries that underwrite it, or for the possible transfer of future resources if some default risk is perceived. This, of course, is also an argument *against* a facility from the point of view of its potential owners if they are not interested in providing aid either in general or specifically to the debtor countries. This point will be taken up again below.

If foreign aid to the debtor countries is indeed intended, one alternative could be for the parties to negotiate debt relief contracts bilaterally and then for some or all of the industrial countries to guarantee the marked-down debts in part or in full. This arrangement would give particular industrial countries an opportunity to help those debtors that are of special interest to them. The familiar difficulty here is that the banks are not a single 'party', as the problems of organizing concerted lending have shown.

For the debtor countries the other alternative is to receive direct bilateral aid. The aid could be used by the debtor country to buy back some of its own debt. Again, there would be an opportunity for industrial countries to discriminate in favour of particular debtor countries. But the fundamental question is highlighted in that case: are funds received in aid best spent in buying back debt? They could perhaps be better used to finance extra investment.

A More Orderly Process

It could be argued that, if world economic conditions turned adverse, the alternative to the operation of such a facility would be a decentralized process of debt restructuring with relief. In that situation numerous bilateral arrangements-with the banks represented by committees that have difficulty in getting support from sufficient banks-could get rather disorderly. The facility could be an intermediary that would bring more orderliness to the process. An element of automaticity and consistency across countries and kinds of debt in the choice of purchase prices, the extent of relief and so on could smooth the restructuring and debt relief process. The facility might thus avoid default crises that could lead to political difficulties and disruption of trade flows.

Greater Realism And Certainty

A key feature of such proposals is that very uncertain obligations, with contractual values well above what is expected to be paid on a probability basis, would be replaced by more realistically valued debt that (in the view of proponents) would be more certain to be repaid and, ideally, would be free of serious default risk.

It might be argued that the increase in certainty (if it could be obtained) is in general desirable even though, to an extent at least, it does shift the burden of exogenous uncertainty (for example, in the terms of trade) back towards the debtor countries. This is possibly a gain because some uncertainty is believed to be endogenous-a result of the lack of firm political will by debtor governments rather than capacity-to-pay uncertainty. Then there is a role for conditionality and, hence, for the Fund or the World Bank. This does not necessarily mean that the two institutions or their owners should, through the facility, take on the remaining risks.

One negative point is also important. It refers not to the actual operation of a facility but to the effects of expectations that it might come into operation. It concerns a moral hazard problem. If the banks and the debtor countries believe that there is some chance that an institution such as the.facility might be established to take over some of the risks, they will have less incentive to arrive at debt relief agreements directly or without disruption. The threat of disruption, particularly of trade flows, could be an inducement leadig the international community to establish such a facility. But if such an institution were never seen as being even a possibility, the parties directly involved would have an incentive to arrive at agreements. They would try to avoid prolonged uncertainty and disruption because it is damaging to them all.

IS ANY COMPULSION INVOLVED?

To what extent would such a scheme be voluntary? I first consider the debtor country and then the creditors.

On the Debtor

On the one hand, if conditionality were not involved, a debtor country would have nothing to lose in the short run from debt relief through the medium of the facility. But in the long run it might lose some creditworthiness, since future creditors may well think that what has happened once can happen again. Therefore a debtor government, confident that it will be able to repay the full contractual value of its debt and wanting to take a long view, may benefit from staying out of the scheme.

This is true even though there may be a market discount on its debt that suggests that, so far, the debtor country has not been able to convey its confidence to the market.

On the other hand, if conditionality were part of the scheme, then each debtor country could decide whether it preferred to accept the burdens of conditionality and get debt relief through the facility or whether it preferred to stay out. There would not need to be any compulsion.

On the Creditor

Each bank could be free to sell or to keep as much as it liked of the debt it holds at present. Sales of debt need not be compulsory. As described here, the facility would operate in the market, even though this is not a feature of all proposals. But this freedom of the banks to sell or not to sell could be somewhat illusory. The willingness to sell will be influenced by the debtors' actions. A decision by the debtor government to subordinate debt that is not sold would lower the market price-as would threats of, or actual, default. Furthermore, changes in bank regulations in creditor countries that reduced the attractiveness to banks of holding on to debt could also increase the willingness to sell to the facility.

Index

A

B

C

D

E

G

H

I

K

L

M

N

P

Q

R